W9-AWS-870

REAL CITY

London

REAL CITY

London

www.realcity.dk.com

Previously published as the popular eGuide series

LONDON, NEW YORK,
MELBOURNE, MUNICH AND DELHI
www.dk.com

Contributors
Jonathan Cox, Michael Ellis, Andrew Humphreys, Lisa Ritchie

Photographer
Max Alexander

Reproduced in Singapore by Colourscan
Printed and bound in China by Hung Hing Offset Printing Company Limited

First American Edition, 2007
07 08 09 10 9 8 7 6 5 4 3 2 1

Published in the United States by
DK Publishing, Inc.,
375 Hudson Street, New York, New York 10014

ISSN: 1933-4567
ISBN: 978-0-75662-686-0

The information in this Real City guide is checked annually.

This guide is supported by a dedicated website which provides the very latest information for visitors to London; please see page 7 for the web address and password. Some information, however, is liable to change, and the publishers cannot accept responsibility for any consequences arising from the use of this book, nor for any material on third party websites, and cannot guarantee that any website address in this book will be a suitable source of travel information.
We value the views and suggestions of our readers very highly. Please write to:
Publisher, DK Eyewitness Travel Guides,
Dorling Kindersley, 80 Strand, London WC2R 0RL, Great Britain.

Contents

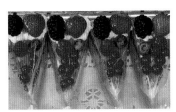

The Guide

Real City London

Stay ahead of the crowd with **Real City London**, and find the best places to eat, shop, drink and chill out at a glance.

The guide is divided into four main sections:

Introducing London – essential background information on the city, including an overview by one of the authors, the top tourist attractions, festivals and seasonal events, and useful travel and practical information.

Listings – eight themed chapters packed with incisive reviews of the best the city has to offer, in every price band and chosen by local experts.

Street Finder – map references in the listings lead you to this section, where you can plan your route and find your way around.

Indexes – the By Area and By Type indexes offer shortcuts to what you are looking for, whether it is a pub in Islington or a Japanese restaurant.

The Website

www.realcity.dk.com

By purchasing this book you have been granted free access to up-to-the-minute online content about London for at least 12 months. Click onto **www.realcity.dk.com** for updates, and sign up for a free weekly email with the latest information on what to see and do in London.

On the website you can:

- **Find the latest news** about London, including exhibitions, restaurant openings and music events

- Check what other readers have to say and **add your own comments** and reviews

- **Plan your visit** with a customizable calendar

- See at a glance **what's in and what's not**

- Look up listings by name, by type and by area, and check the **latest reviews**

- **Link directly** to all the websites in the book, and many more

How to register

⟩ Click on the London icon on the home page of the website to register or log in.

⟩ Enter the city code given on this page, and follow the instructions given.

⟩ The city code will be valid for a minimum of 12 months from the date you purchased this guide.

city code: **london71953**

introducing london

London is one of the world's most cosmopolitan cities, boasting superb modern architecture, bold street fashion, a vibrant arts scene, and restaurants and nightlife for every taste. This guide leads you to the city's latest and best, kicking off with a run down of the top attractions and a selection of our favourite festivals and events.

INTRODUCING LONDON

The great 18th-century literary figure Dr Samuel Johnson declared that London contained "all that life can afford", and that familiar quote has never seemed more apt than it does today. Having lived here for 20 years myself, I haven't tired yet of this beautiful, messy, maddening, fascinating city. The Tube can be a drag, people are sometimes brusque and roads are forever being dug up, but this city is alive with a magnificent cross-fertilization of cultures, fashions, cuisines and languages – a marketplace for ideas and styles.

Lisa Ritchie

A Tale of Many Cities

It is the city's eclecticism and ability to surprise that gives London its unique charm. It feels like several cities in one, its sprawling mass divided into numerous neighbourhoods or villages, each with its own character. Contrast the affluent boho enclaves of Primrose Hill or Westbourne Park – with their bijou cafés, celebrity-frequented boutiques and gastropubs – with East London's Bethnal Green and Spitalfields, their streets lined with cheap cafés and markets, their nightlife scenes both edgier and more cutting-edge than anywhere else in the city. Even in central London, areas retain their distinct identity: slip behind the frenetic retail thoroughfare of Oxford Street to Marylebone, for example, and you may think you've been transported to a stylish provincial town with an elegant array of shops and eateries. No matter how often you return to this multi-layered city, you will discover new territories and hidden corners – the maze of lanes around the gastronome's paradise Borough Market, for example, or the peaceful squares and alleyways of Clerkenwell.

Complementing the city's streetlife are London's parks. The formality of Regent's Park, the open vistas of Hyde Park, the lake overhung with willows in St James's and the bleached fields of Hampstead Heath in summer are soothing counterpoints to the beat of the city.

Cultural Assets

The range and quality of London's cultural riches is staggering. Although visitors and residents alike complain of the high cost of living, the arts are accessible to all. The capital's peerless national museums – the British Museum, the National Gallery and the two Tates, to name a few – are free of charge. And beyond the glut of obvious cultural treasures are quirky, lesser-known attractions such as the idiosyncratic Dennis Severs' House *(see p110)* and Sir John Soane's Museum *(see p103)*. Despite the unparalleled prestige and quality of West End theatre, seeing a show here is positively cheap compared to New York's Broadway. And the South Bank Centre's programme of live performance, film and art is superb. You'll need to go beyond the centre of town,

a city primer

however, to see the most experimental performances, in theatres such as the Tricycle (*see p135*) and the Almeida (*p132*), and at dance venues such as Laban (*p136*).

A Cosmopolitan Cocktail

London is at once a bastion of tradition and a centre of cutting-edge style, utterly civilized and outrageously irreverent. Although the iconic Routemaster buses have sadly passed into the city's history (you can still catch one on special 'heritage routes', numbers 9 and 15), this ever-changing city nevertheless preserves plenty of wonderful anachronisms. You can still browse the specialist shops of St James's for soft-bristle shaving brushes and bespoke shoes, but you can also check out the latest creations by some of the world's most innovative designers. Even on once-stuffy Savile Row, traditional gents' tailors now rub shoulders with avant-garde fashion emporia. Then there is the ethnic mix. Always cosmopolitan, London is less a melting pot than a lightly cooked melange, in which individual flavours are preserved more or less intact. Nowhere is this more apparent than at street markets, such as Brixton's, where British apples and carrots are sold alongside Caribbean produce and African textiles. Brick Lane in the East End has become a colourful conglomeration of funky boutiques, galleries, spice shops and curry houses since a young, arty crowd infiltrated the large Bangladeshi community there. And generations of Londoners born of immigrant families are bringing their dual heritage to the art, design and food scenes, with exciting results. Ethnic influences have helped transform what was once the meat-and-two-veg culinary joke of Europe into the most exciting place to eat in the world. All of these disparate elements converge to create the thrilling, vibrant jumble that is contemporary London.

✅ The Good Value Mark

Cities can be expensive, but if you know where to go you can always discover excellent-value places. We've picked out the best of these in the Restaurants, Shopping and Hotels chapters and indicated them with the pink Good Value mark.

INTRODUCING LONDON

If you have time to take in only a dozen London sights, consult our must-do list. The following have been selected for their historical and/or cultural pre-eminence as well as their enduring popular appeal. Get an overview of the city from the heights of the London Eye, then gain a more detailed perspective through its architectural monuments and unrivalled museums. Loved by Londoners and visitors alike, these are places to return to time and time again.

St Paul's Cathedral

10 B3

Ludgate Hill, EC4 • 020 7236 4128 • ⊖ St Paul's
>> www.stpauls.co.uk Open 8:30am–4pm Mon–Sat

Wren's masterpiece has been restored to its former glory to celebrate the building's tercentenary in 2008 – revealing in the process paintings previously hidden above the Whispering Gallery. Mount the 530 steps to the top of the massive dome for sweeping views. **Adm**

Houses of Parliament

15 G1

Old Palace Yard, SW1 • 020 7219 3000 • ⊖ Westminster
>> www.parliament.uk See website for access times to the visitors' galleries

The seat of British government since medieval times, the Palace of Westminster was rebuilt in Neo-Gothic style following a fire in 1834. Tours in the summer recess (Aug–Sep) incur an admission fee, but it's free to watch parliamentary debate from the visitors' galleries.

Westminster Abbey

15 F1

Broad Sanctuary, SW1 • 020 7222 5152 • ⊖ Westminster
>> www.westminster-abbey.org Open 9:30am–3:45pm daily (to 6 Wed, 1:45 Sat)

Both a starting point and a final resting place for monarchs, the mainly Gothic abbey has been a setting for coronations since 1066. The 16th-century Lady Chapel with its intricate fan-vaulted ceiling, the octagonal Chapter House dating from the 13th century, and the literary memorials in Poet's Corner are among the highlights. **Adm**

For the very latest on London go to >> **www.realcity.dk.com**

top attractions

National Gallery 9 F4
Trafalgar Square, WC2 • 020 7747 2885 • ⊖ Charing Cross
>> www.nationalgallery.org.uk Open 10am–6pm daily (to 9pm Wed)

The national collection of European art has grown to more than 2,300
paintings dating from 1250 to 1900. The earliest works are housed in
the Sainsbury Wing, while the original building, presiding over
Trafalgar Square, contains those from 1500 onwards *(see p101)*.

London Eye 9 H5
Jubilee Gardens, SE1 • 0870 5000 600 • ⊖ Waterloo
>> www.ba-londoneye.com Open 10am–9pm daily (to 8pm Oct–May)

A glass capsule on the world's largest observation wheel, revolving
at a gentle 26 cm (about 10 inches) per second, affords a breath-
taking panorama. The rotation, or "flight", takes 30 minutes and from
the top the view stretches 25 miles (40 km) in every direction. **Adm**

Tower of London 11 F4
Tower Hill, EC3 • 0870 756 6060 • ⊖ Tower Hill
>> www.hrp.org.uk Open 9am–6pm Tue–Sat, 10am–6pm Sun & Mon

The infamous fortress – home to the Crown Jewels, the Chapel of
St John and the recently restored Medieval Palace – contains a
historical legacy dating back more than 900 years. Yeoman Warders
(Beefeaters) conduct tours, enthusiastically recounting tales of such
lurid events as the execution of Anne Boleyn on Tower Green. **Adm**

>> *Pre-book a "scheduled flight" on the Eye to save time queueing for tickets*

INTRODUCING LONDON

British Museum 9 F2

Great Russell St, WC1 • 020 7323 8000 • ☺ Russell Square
>> www.thebritishmuseum.ac.uk Open 10am–5:30pm daily (to 8:30pm Thu & Fri)

Founded in 1753, the world's oldest museum has a collection of
seven million objects spanning the globe and two million years.
Luckily, as admission is free, you can dip in at your leisure, entering
the galleries via Norman Foster's redesigned Great Court *(see p104)*.

Shakespeare's Globe 10 C4

New Globe Walk, SE1 • 020 7902 1400 • ☺ London Bridge
>> www.shakespeares-globe.org Exhibition: 9am–5pm daily

This faithful facsimile of the Elizabethan theatre that premiered
many of the Bard's plays stages a season of his works from May to
October. A year-round exhibition and tour provide a lively exploration of Shakespeare's London and the city's theatres *(see p136)*.

Buckingham Palace & the Queen's Gallery 14 D1

Buckingham Gate, SW1 • 020 7766 7300 • ☺ Green Park
>> www.royalcollection.org.uk State rooms open Aug–Sep 9:30am–5:30pm
daily; Queen's Gallery open 10am–5:30pm daily

The 19 state rooms – furnished with exquisite antiques and paintings
by Rembrandt and Rubens among others – are open to the public while
the Queen summers at Balmoral. Treasures from her excellent painting
collection can be seen year round at the Queen's Gallery. **Adm**

top attractions

Tate Modern `10 B4`
Bankside, SE1 • 020 7887 8000 • ⊖ Southwark
>> www.tate.org.uk Open 10am–6pm Sun–Thu, 10am–10pm Fri & Sat

Tate Modern recently had its first rehang since opening in 2000, and the permanent collection (1900–present) is now divided into four wings reflecting key artistic movements: Cubism, Futurism and Vorticism; Surrealism; Abstract Expressionism; and Minimalism *(see p117).*

Natural History Museum `13 H2`
Cromwell Rd, SW7 • 020 7942 5000 • ⊖ South Kensington
>> www.nhm.ac.uk Open 10am–5:50pm Mon–Sat, 11am–5:50pm Sun

Alfred Waterhouse's glorious building is a fitting home for the largest natural history collection in the world – more than 70 million specimens. The cathedral-like Central Hall accommodates such massive items as a diplodocus skeleton and a 1,300-year-old giant sequoia.

Science Museum `13 H2`
Exhibition Rd, SW7 • 0870 870 4868 • ⊖ South Kensington
>> www.sciencemuseum.org.uk Open 10am–6pm daily

From the hands-on exhibits of the Launch Pad gallery to George III's collection of 18th-century scientific apparatus, the Science Museum appeals to all ages. Glass cases housing huge 19th-century machinery contrast with displays that focus on cutting-edge science in the Wellcome Wing – where you'll also find an IMAX cinema.

>> *The carvings on the Natural History Museum depict living species on the west side, extinct species on the east*

INTRODUCING LONDON

While the majority of us are still wrapped in our winter cocoons, London's diary of events kicks off with vibrant festivities in Trafalgar Square to bring in the Chinese New Year. Runners on the streets help energize the city in April with the marathon, and the Chelsea Flower Show is a perennial marker, ushering in summer. Once the season is in full swing, it's party time, whether you favour garden concerts in Hampstead, the family fun of the Coin Street events, the pink power of Pride, the Caribbean culture at Notting Hill or the bonhomie of the Proms.

Chinese New Year
www.chinatownchinese.com

The main celebration has outgrown Chinatown and moved to Trafalgar Square, which is decorated with lanterns and flowers. The entertainment includes lion and dragon dances, and fireworks in Leicester Square. Food stalls spring up all along Gerrard Street. **Jan/Feb**

London Marathon
www.london-marathon.co.uk

More than 45,000 runners set off from Greenwich Park, and follow the Thames through Docklands and along Victoria Embankment to The Mall. You can join the party atmosphere in one of over 50 participating pubs, which open in readiness for the 9am start. **Apr**

Chelsea Flower Show
Royal Hospital, Chelsea (Map 14 C4), www.rhs.org.uk

The Royal Horticultural Society's Chelsea Flower Show has become an amazingly popular occasion, with crowds packing the Royal Hospital Gardens for a chance to see the show gardens, which range from restrained, contemporary spaces to mystical landscapes. You'll also find dazzling floral arrangements and have the chance to buy rare plants, seeds and bulbs. **May**

Outdoor Concerts
Kenwood House (see pp114 & 178), www.picnicconcerts.com
Somerset House (see p100), www.somerset-house.org.uk
Holland Park (see p176), www.operahollandpark.com

What could be more magical than listening to music outdoors in a beautiful setting? On a balmy summer's evening, pack a picnic and throw down a blanket in the grounds of Kenwood House. Concerts feature big names in jazz, pop and classical music, and end with a fireworks display over the lake. In central London, the magnificent courtyard of Somerset House hosts concerts each summer. Recent acts include Goldfrapp, Jose Gonzalez and Lambchop. For something more classical, Opera Holland Park performs amid flowerbeds – a canopy ensures the show goes on whatever the weather. Check schedules on the websites. **Jun, Jul & Aug**

spring and summer

Open Garden Squares Weekend
www.opensquares.org

A rare, fleeting opportunity to slip into some of London's secret gardens. More than 80 private squares – usually the preserve of privileged key-holding residents – open their gates to the public. Refreshments, live music and other entertainments are offered in some. Maps and full details are on the website. **Jun**

Coin Street Festival
Bernie Spain Gardens (Map 10 A4), www.coinstreetfestival.org

Ethnic diversity is celebrated with live world music, dance and art workshops at this free, community-based festival. Events take place over a series of theme days and weekends throughout the summer. **Jun–Aug**

Pride London
www.pridelondon.org

The gay and lesbian festival is one of London's largest, with flamboyant floats, dancers and, of course, drag queens. It begins in the morning with a parade through central London. In the afternoon, a massive party kicks off in central London, with live music and high campery, and continues into nightclubs across town. **Jul**

The Proms
Royal Albert Hall (Map 13 G1), www.bbc.co.uk/proms

Launched over 100 years ago to promote classical music appreciation among the masses, the Proms offer very cheap "promenade" (standing) tickets on the night, as well as prebooked seats for over 70 concerts. Securing a ticket for the famously high-spirited Last Night is tricky, but there is a big-screen link-up in Hyde Park. **Jul–Sep**

Notting Hill Carnival
1 Notting Hill Gate or Latimer Road (Map 7 E4),
08700 591111, www.nottinghillcarnival.org.uk

The famous Carnival still has a heavy Caribbean accent. Exotic floats and costumed dancers parade the streets, while revellers strut their stuff to calypso, salsa, R&B and hip-hop. Food stalls dish up rice'n'peas, jerk chicken and salt-fish patties. **Aug Bank Holiday Weekend**

INTRODUCING LONDON

Ever optimistic for early autumn sunshine, London hosts several outdoor events in September and October. Both the Brick Lane and Thames festivals are relatively new, and each year they attract greater numbers and offer more entertainment. Once winter begins to bite and the nights draw in, it's time to head for the warmth of the cinema for the London Film Festival, and over the Christmas period take a spin round a skating rink in a memorable setting.

Brick Lane Festival

Brick Lane & Allen Gardens (Map 11 F1),
www.bricklanefestival.com

The streets around Brick Lane are thronged on the second Sunday in September for this local festival that celebrates the diverse cultures and traditions of the neighbourhood, principally through food and music. Expect live performances by Bhangra musicians, as well as R&B singers and DJ sets too. Most – but by no means all – of the food has an Asian flavour. The area's many curry houses put out street stalls, which fill the air with pungent, tantalizing aromas. **Sep**

Open House Weekend

www.londonopenhouse.org

Over 500 London buildings, most of which are not usually accessible to the public, throw open their doors for just one weekend. The list of participating buildings changes annually, but each year's event includes a fabulous selection of grand mansions and contemporary houses; public housing schemes by renowned architects; lavish government departments such as the Foreign Office; industrial buildings; theatres; church crypts and more. You have to book for some, and there are always queues for well-known towers such as the "Gherkin" (30 St Mary Axe) and the Lloyds Building. Check the website for all details. **Mid-Sep**

Thames Festival

www.thamesfestival.org

Launched 10 years ago, the Thames Festival is a burgeoning weekend showcase for public art, street theatre, musical performances, dance and all round spectacular fun. Events take place on and along the river (mostly on the South Bank) between Westminster Bridge and London Bridge, with stalls in the River Market (food and crafts) running from the London Eye to City Hall. The festival weekend culminates in a Night Carnival, in which exotic costumes are worn by performers processing with lantern-lit floats from Victoria Embankment (on the north bank) across Blackfriars Bridge to the South Bank. **Mid-Sep**

autumn and winter

Frieze Art Fair

Pavilion in Regent's Park (Map 2 C5), www.friezeartfair.com

London's newest and best contemporary art fair draws work from 150 galleries around the world, including big hitters Marian Goodman and Leo Koenig in New York, Jablonka Gallerie in Cologne and Galerie Yvon Lambert in Paris. The gathering is organized by international art magazine *Frieze* and lasts for four days. Aside from getting the chance to peruse the world's galleries in one convenient location, you can also see new work specially commissioned by *Frieze*. The pieces are exhibited in and around the main pavilion, and in a temporary sculpture park set up for the duration of the fair. **Mid-Oct**

London Film Festival

www.lff.org.uk

More than 300 films are screened during this two-week festival, at selected cinemas in central London. A diverse programme includes gala previews of big-budget movies, international and art-house features, and appearances by filmmakers, writers and actors. **Late Oct/Nov**

Seasonal Ice Rinks

Somerset House *(see p100)*; Natural History Museum *(see p15)*; Tower of London *(see p13)*; Royal Botanical Gardens, Kew *(see p181)*

There's no more cheery winter activity in London than gliding around an ice rink in one of these four beautiful settings, especially in the evening, when they are illuminated with flaming torches. Choose from the courtyard setting of Somerset House; the turrets of the Tower of London; the beautifully carved sandstone backdrop at the Natural History Museum; or the largest rink of all, by the glasshouses of Kew. Next to each rink you'll find a temporary café, serving hot chocolate and possibly mulled wine. **Nov–Jan**

New Year's Day Parade

www.londonparade.co.uk

American-style razzmatazz is brought to London on the first day of the new year, with marching bands and dressed-up revellers wending from Parliament Square to Piccadilly via Trafalgar Square. **1 Jan**

London's Underground train (the "Tube") and bus networks are extensive and easy to navigate, though frequently crowded and subject to delays. A weekday Congestion Charge for drivers operates in the centre of town, and it has recently been extended westwards as far as Notting Hill and Kensington. Traffic now flows a little better, with bus and taxi journeys noticeably quicker. Numerous guided tours are available, and riverboats offer a fantastic way to see the city.

Arrival

There are five international airports near London, of which Heathrow is the busiest. Waterloo is the terminal for trains coming from mainland Europe. From these international points of entry there are various ways to travel into central London.

Heathrow Airport

The **Heathrow Express** train is the fastest and most comfortable way to travel into central London. Trains depart every 15 minutes and take 15–20 minutes to travel non-stop to Paddington Station. The cheapest option for time-rich travellers is a Tube train (Piccadilly Line), which takes about an hour into central London. You can also catch the A2 bus. A taxi into central London is the most expensive option (about £45), unless you are travelling in a group of five.

Gatwick Airport

Gatwick is about 30 miles south of central London. The **Gatwick Express** train usually runs every 15 minutes and takes about 30 minutes to travel non-stop to London's Victoria Station. There are also slightly cheaper, standard stopping services into Victoria and King's Cross Stations. A taxi into London will cost about £100.

Stansted Airport

Stansted Express trains depart from the airport every 15–30 minutes; the journey to Liverpool Street Station takes 45 minutes. There is also a standard stopping train once an hour. The A6 coach into central London is a bit cheaper but takes at least 90 minutes.

Luton Airport

The **Thameslink** train service runs from the airport to a number of central city stations, including Kings Cross, every 5–10 minutes. The journey takes 30–40 minutes.

London City Airport

A shuttle bus runs between this small airport and Liverpool Street Station, via Canary Wharf, every 10 minutes during peak hours. Otherwise, you can take a taxi into town.

Waterloo International Terminal

Waterloo Station, on the South Bank of the Thames, is served by the Underground's Bakerloo, Jubilee and Northern Lines. There are also taxi ranks and numerous bus stops outside.

Getting Around

Tube trains, buses and taxis are plentiful. Overland trains serve the suburbs and beyond.

Advance Booking Option for Overseas Visitors

Visitors planning to travel to London from Europe, the US, Australia and several other countries can purchase a Visitor Travelcard in advance through www.ticket-on-line.com. This covers unlimited travel on all trains, buses and the DLR, and there's an option for the Heathrow Express. The card is not available in the UK itself.

London Underground

The Underground network stretches to 275 stations across the city. Trains run from about 5:30am to 11:30pm or 1am, depending on the line. This is the oldest underground train network in the world and usually offers the quickest way to get around town. However, the ageing system is prone to delays and over-crowding. Tickets are expensive in comparison with the cost of subway travel in other major world cities.

Journeys are priced according to zones radiating out from the city centre (Zone 1) to the far reaches of Greater London (Zone 6). If you have missed buying a Visitor Travelcard *(see above)*, there are various options, including the basic Travelcard, which covers unlimited travel on the Tube, buses and DLR (Docklands Light Railway). There are daily (available after 9:30am), weekend or 7-day options. If you're travelling sporadically within Zone 1, buy a so-called "Carnet" of 10 discounted single tickets.

If you are travelling around London for more than a week, consider buying a rechargeable Oystercard (www.oystercard.com). Holders of Oystercards need only touch the card to the yellow pad on the turnstiles, and can recharge at the pad on the ticket machines.

Buses

Buses are cheaper than the Tube, but try to avoid rush hours (7:30–9:30am and 5–7pm). The flat fare is £1.50. In central London, you must buy a ticket before boarding – look for a ticket machine at the bus stop or buy a booklet of six discounted Saver tickets from Tube stations and some newsagents. Night buses operate 11pm–6am with a separate scale of fares. Oystercards *(see above)* are also valid on buses.

Car

Driving around and parking in London is frustrating and expensive. A **Congestion Charge** of £8 if you pay on the day, or £10 if you pay the next day, is levied on all cars travelling through the city centre between 7am and 6:30pm on weekdays. "C" signs mark the boundaries of the charging zone, and cameras record every car. You can pay online *(see directory)*, or at selected newsagents and garages. A hefty fine is issued if you fail to pay before midnight of the following day. Speeding, stopping in box junctions and using bus lanes also incur fines.

Parking is restricted almost every-where. Read street parking signs carefully or you'll probably return to a penalty notice or clamped wheel. It's best to use NCP car parks (www.ncp.co.uk) if in doubt.

Taxis

Classic black cabs are plentiful in central London, but tariffs are high, especially after 8pm and at weekends. Licensed minicabs (from offices) are usually cheaper.

Other Forms of Transport

Pedicabs (or rickshaws) congregate in Soho and some other areas, offering short hops. They are unregulated, though, and can be expensive.

There are several riverboat services along the Thames *(see pp102 & 106)* – Travelcard holders get one-third off the fare on some routes. Canalboats are operated by **The London Waterbus Company**. Trams are making a comeback in some suburban areas.

Tours

A qualified Blue Badge guide can be booked for either a general sightseeing tour or something tailor-made – see the **Association of Professional Tourist Guides'** website for individual profiles or book through their recommended agency, **Tour Guides Ltd**. Black Taxi Tours of London offers qualified tour guides too.

The **Original London Walks** is a good one to try for themed strolls – actors, experts and historians lead tours such as Ghosts, Gaslight and Guinness, or Jack the Ripper Haunts in the East End. Wellbeing centre **Kairos in Soho** offers a historical walking tour of Gay and Lesbian Soho. **London Open House** runs Saturday-morning tours led by architects and historians. Consult *Time Out* magazine for other unusual themed walks.

Directory

Airports
www.baa.co.uk
(Heathrow, Gatwick & Stansted)
www.londoncityairport.com

Association of Professional Tourist Guides
020 7939 7690
www.aptg.org.uk

Black Cabs
020 7432 1432
www.londonradiocars.com
www.dialacab.co.uk

Black Taxi Tours of London
020 7935 9363
www.blacktaxitours.co.uk

Congestion Charge
0845 900 1234 / cclondon.com

Kairos in Soho
020 7437 6063
www.kairosinsoho.org.uk

London Open House
www.londonopenhouse.org

The London Waterbus Company
020 7482 2660
www.londonwaterbus.com

The Original London Walks
020 7624 3978 / www.walks.com

Tour Guides Ltd
020 7495 5504

Trains
Heathrow Express *0845 600 1515*
www.heathrowexpress.com

Gatwick Express *0845 850 1530*
www.gatwickexpress.com

National Rail Enquiries
08457 484950
www.nationalrail.co.uk

Stansted Express *0845 600 7245*
www.stanstedexpress.co.uk

Thameslink www.thameslink.co.uk

Transport for London
The Tube, buses, DLR, taxis, riverboats & trams
020 7222 1234 / www.tfl.gov.uk

The information and tips here should help you have a stress-free visit to London. Some forward planning is often beneficial – start with the websites offering tourist information and listing events. Visitors with special needs, such as wheelchair users, are supported by a number of dedicated organizations, and gay and lesbian travellers are particularly well catered for in this city.

Disabled Travellers

Recent changes to the Disability Discrimination Act require anyone who provides a service to the public to make it accessible to disabled people, within reason. Equal-access campaigner **Artsline** has a constantly expanding online database listing over 400 arts and entertainment venues and their provisions for sensory-impaired people and wheelchair users. A factsheet from **Greater London Action on Disability** gives details of what to expect at well-known tourist attractions, and another lists accessible hotels. Improvements to the accessibility of the Tube are in progress, but at present only 40 stations can be reached without using stairs or escalators. For more information call 020 7222 1234. Buses are better – over 90% of the bus fleet has wheelchair access.

Emergencies & Health

In the event of a serious accident, medical emergency, fire or criminal incident requiring urgent assistance, call 999 and specify ambulance, fire service or police. Calls from any phone, including payphones, are free. Citizens of the European Economic Area and countries with a bilateral healthcare agreement with the UK are exempt from hospital A&E

charges. See the **Hospital Charges** website for full details of exemptions.

If you require an emergency prescription or less urgent medical attention, the private **Medicentre** chain offers walk-in clinics. Branches are located in train stations, central London and the City.

If you need advice outside clinic hours, call **Doctors Direct** to arrange a home visit or refer to the **NHS Direct** website's useful self-help guide.

Pharmacies are a good first stop for minor ailments. For late-night prescriptions, **Bliss Pharmacy** is open until midnight, while **Zafash** is London's only 24-hour pharmacy.

Gay & Lesbian Travellers

Soho is London's pink mecca, with the highest concentration of bars, clubs and gay-oriented shops. There is an established scene in Brixton, and nightspots have also sprung up in Vauxhall. Free pink paper **Boyz**, available in gay bars and businesses and online, features London listings. **The Gay Times** website has useful links to services from arts centres and bars to shops and support, while lesbian magazine **Diva** offers online area-by-area mini guides. The **London Lesbian and Gay Switchboard** has a 24-hour helpline. For recommended bars and clubs, *see p141*.

Listings/What's On

Time Out is London's hippest and most comprehensive weekly listings magazine, covering new shops and restaurants as well as arts and entertainment. It has an online guide, **www.timeout.com/london**.

Thursday's edition of the *Evening Standard* has good information for events and exhibitions in the city. It is affiliated to **www.thisislondon.com**. *The Knowledge*, in *The Times* on Saturday, rounds up London listings in a handy format.

Money

There's no shortage of bureaux de change in the city, but you may get a better exchange rate if you use your bank or credit card to obtain cash from ATMs. The practice of keying in your PIN rather than signing a credit card slip at point of purchase has been introduced in many businesses.

Opening Hours

London closes early in comparison with cities such as New York or Paris. Most **shops** are open from 10am–6pm Monday to Saturday, staying open an hour or two later on Wednesday or Thursday. Many open from noon to 5pm or 6pm on Sunday. Some major department stores, such as Harvey Nichols and Selfridges, stay open until 8pm every week night.

Restaurants tend to close at 11pm or midnight (last servings 10–10:30), and **pubs** call "time" at 11pm, 10:30pm on Sundays. The law changed in 2005, technically allowing longer hours, but the **Bars** with extended opening hours are usually only those offering some form of entertainment, such as live music or DJs. Most **nightclubs** close at 3am, though some stay open until 6am at weekends. **Banks** are open from 9:30am to 3:30pm or 4:30pm Monday to Friday, and **post offices** from 9am to 5:30pm on weekdays. Some banks and post offices are open on Saturday morning.

Phones & Communications

Public phones may be less plentiful than they once were because of the proliferation of mobile phones, but they have become more sophisticated. At BT Internet kiosks, you can surf the Internet, send and receive emails, or send a video text message as well as make a call. For long distance, it's worth buying an international phone card, available from newsagents, which gives you an access number and code for a cheaper rate.

Most mobile phones in the UK, Europe and Australia operate on GSM 900MHz or 1800MHz frequency bands. Visitors from the US and Canada will need a tri-band phone to connect with a UK network – check with your service provider before travelling.

The **easyInternetcafé** chain (www.easyeverything.com) dominates the drop-in web-surfing scene, but the city is dotted with numerous small Internet cafés.

Security

Crowded pubs, train stations and shops are prime spots for bag-snatchers and pickpockets, so keep your bag close to the front of your body and your wits about you. Also, particularly since the 2005 bombings, security is vigilant when it comes to left bags or packages, so don't leave your possessions unattended. Mobile phone theft is common, so be wary when using a phone, and also be alert when using ATMs. They have been the target of various scams, so protect your PIN and don't use a machine that looks like it's been fitted with extra attachments. Unlicensed minicabs also pose many dangers, especially to single women. Never accept a lift from a driver touting for fares on the street.

Tipping

As a guide, if service has been good, give 10–15 per cent to waiters (unless a service charge has already been added), hairdressers, beauty therapists and taxi drivers. It is not customary to tip in pubs, even if you order food, but tipping is common in cocktail bars. In hotels, £1–2 is a standard tip for luggage porters.

Tourist Information

London's official tourist organization is **Visit London**. Its excellent website contains a comprehensive directory, including bureaux de change, Internet cafés and hospitals. There are also sections for gay and lesbian, and disabled visitors. The official **Britain and London Visitor Centre** is near Piccadilly Circus. The privately run **London Information Centre** in Leicester Square operates in tandem with **www.londontown.com**.

Directory

Artsline
020 7388 2227
www.artslineonline.com

Bliss Pharmacy
5–6 Marble Arch, W1 (**Map** 8 B3)

Britain and London Visitor Centre
1 Regent Street, SW1 (**Map** 9 E4)
020 8846 9000 • www.visitbritain.com

Directory Enquiries
118 118 • 118 500 • 118 180 • 118 888

Doctors Direct
020 7751 9701
www.doctorsdirect.co.uk

Emergency Services
999

Gay & Lesbian Information
020 7837 7324 (24-hour helpline)
www.llgs.org.uk
www.gaytimes.co.uk
www.gaylondon.com
www.divamag.co.uk

Greater London Action on Disability
www.glad.org.uk

Hospital Charges
www.publications.doh.gov.uk/overseasvisitors/index.htm

London Information Centre
Leicester Square, W1 (**Map** 9 F4)
020 7292 2333
www.londoninformationcentre.com
www.londontown.com

Medicentre
0870 600 0870
www.medicentre.co.uk

NHS Direct
0845 4647
www.nhsdirect.nhs.uk

Visit London
www.visitlondon.com

Zafash Pharmacy
233–5 Old Brompton Rd, SW5 (**Map** 13 G3)

restaurants

London's gastronomic scene is booming. The range of places to eat and the diversity of cuisines on offer are rivalled only by New York. The quality of cooking is something to write home about, too, especially at top-end restaurants. Prices are high if you want to sample the work of famous chefs, but there are excellent choices in all price ranges if you know where to look and what to order.

RESTAURANTS

Over the past twenty years I have watched London's culinary map transform. Once a city of chips and tandoori, its restaurant scene now embraces the finest and most diverse of kitchens, from Japanese to North African. I love old stalwarts such as Rules and J Sheekey, but I am more excited by experimental chefs like Tom Aikens *(see p43)*. The kitchens in London's ethnic pockets are just as thrilling – and you can still get a fantastic curry.

Jonathan Cox

Best of British Cuisine

British food has undergone a revolution in the last decade, with better availability of excellent indigenous produce and an increased interest in British cooking. Try some of the fabulous new-wave restaurants such as **Roast** *(see p58)* and **The National Dining Rooms** *(see p35)*, or go to **St John** *(see p50)* for something trendsetting.

Small Plates

Grazing is a great way to taste lots of dishes and is increasingly popular. The ground-floor **Tapa Room at Providores** *(see p39)* is renowned for just such pick-and-mix dishes, while many Mediterranean restaurants are geared up to snacking with extensive tapas and meze menus; try **Tendido Cero** *(see p44)*, **Tas** *(see p57)* and **Noura** *(see p42)*.

World Kitchen

As one of the world's most cosmopolitan cities, London is a great place to try cuisines as diverse as South Indian *(see* **Rasa** *p32)*, Moroccan *(see* **Mômo** *p38)*, Vietnamese *(see* **Viet Hoa** *p52)* and Chinese *(see* **Hunan** *p42)*. And Indian restaurants such as **Red Fort** *(see p31)* arguably exceed the best that Delhi can offer.

choice eats

Gastropubs

A relatively recent innovation, gastropubs are similar to mainland Europe's *enotecas*, tapas bars and bistros. At leading venues such as **The Eagle** *(see p48)*, **Lots Road Pub** *(see p44)* and **The White Swan** *(see p49)*, you can expect a casual pub, where good quality dishes are served without fuss, and where you can eat a little or a lot.

Fast Food

London is a busy city, but fast food doesn't have to mean low-grade, mass-market fare. There are traditional favourites such as fish-and-chip shops *(see **Golden Hind** p38)*, great bakery shop/cafés such as **Paul** *(see p33)* and **Patisserie Valerie** *(see p30),* and a host of excellent new-wave burger bars and noodle and sushi joints *(see box on p47).*

Breakfast and Brunch

The fry-up is less of a breakfast tradition than it used to be, but you can still get an excellent Full English at places like **Smiths of Smithfield** *(see p49)* and the **S&M Café** *(see p46)*. For a greater variety of breakfast options, try **The Wolseley** *(see p36)*, and for something lighter and more continental, **Lisboa Patisserie** *(see p46)* or **Patisserie Valerie** *(see p30).*

Andrew Edmunds *modern European* `9 E3`
46 Lexington Street, W1 • 020 7437 5708
Open lunch & dinner daily

Dark and discreet, this long-time Soho stalwart is a seductive spot for contemporary cuisine. The crowd-pleasing food embraces the classics, such as a perfect lamb steak with flageolet beans. Seating is a bit cramped, and the room can be noisy, but the service is breezily relaxed. **Moderate**

Bodean's *North American barbecue* `9 E3`
10 Poland Street, W1 • 020 7287 0506
» www.bodeansbbq.com Restaurant open lunch & dinner Mon–Fri, noon–11pm Sat; diner open all day

Billing itself as "London's Original BBQ Smoke House", Bodean's is a classy US-style barbecue, featuring prime char-grilled steaks, racks of baby back ribs and smoked chicken. The ground floor is a casual eat-in/takeaway sports bar; the basement is more formal. **Moderate**

Donzoko *rare Japanese delights* `9 E3`

15 Kingly Street, W1 • 020 7734 1974
Open lunch & dinner Mon–Fri, dinner Sat

This modest Japanese eaterie is one of Soho's hidden gems. It's a friendly, bustling *izakaya*-style joint (an informal pub-restaurant), with a counter along one side and a long menu taking in all the greatest hits of Japanese cuisine. The aubergine fried with garlic and soybean paste is sublime. **Cheap**

Mar i Terra *superior Spanish* `9 E3`

17 Air Street, W1 • 020 7734 1992
» www.mariterra.co.uk
Open lunch & dinner Mon–Fri, noon–11pm Sat

Spanish food can move with the times. The decor here is clean and contemporary; the service cheery and unfussy. The menu lists Iberian classics alongside more unusual delights, such as stuffed peppers with crab, and Catalan grilled vegetable salad. **Cheap**

Wong Kei *legendary cheap Chinese* `9 E3`
41–3 Wardour Street, W1 • 020 7437 8408
Open noon–11pm daily (to 10:30pm Sun)

A capacious restaurant with oddly decorated rooms on many floors, Wong Kei revels in its reputation of having the rudest service in Chinatown. And yet it continues to pull in the punters thanks to a lively atmosphere, seriously low prices and unexpectedly fine roast meats. Great fun with a crowd. **Cheap**

Origin *Covent Garden sophistication* `9 G2`
The Hospital, Endell St, WC2 • 020 7170 9200
>> www.origin-restaurant.com
Open lunch & dinner Mon–Fri, dinner only Sat

The transformation of the highly acclaimed Thyme into Origin has resulted in a more sophisticated affair, with beautifully crafted dishes using well-sourced ingredients – poached organic chicken with English asparagus for example – and great service. **Expensive**

ECapital *Chinatown oasis* `9 F3`
8 Gerrard Street, W1 • 020 7434 3838
Open noon–11:30pm daily (to midnight Fri & Sat)

Few Chinatown restaurants offer distinctive cuisine, but ECapital is an exception: here you'll find a rare high-quality offering of rich-sweet-oily food from China's east coast. It's worth asking the staff to translate the Chinese menu to find the most interesting dishes, such as "lion's head meatball casserole". **Cheap**

Café Emm *hearty international fodder* `9 F3`
17 Frith Street, W1 • 020 7437 0723
>> www.cafeemm.com
Open lunch & dinner daily (to 11:30pm Fri & Sat)

It's hard to beat Café Emm for value, atmosphere and good, filling grub. Dishes include cajun potato skins, deep-fried brie, hearty lamb shanks, calamari, pecan pie and tiramisu, and all come in huge portions, served up by smiling staff in a fun environment. **Cheap**

Restaurants

Lindsay House *modern British* 9 F3
21 Romilly Street, W1 • 020 7439 0450
>> www.lindsayhouse.co.uk
Open lunch & dinner Mon–Fri, dinner only Sat

Irishman Richard Corrigan is a real chef's chef –
while many of his peers play the media game, he
sticks resolutely to fashioning imaginative dishes in
the kitchen. The results show just how good creative
British/Irish cuisine can be in the right hands.

The restaurant, set in a 1740s Georgian
townhouse, is as understated as the man himself.
Ring the bell to be let in, and you'll be shown to one
of various small dining spaces. The gracious staff
might be serving up globe artichoke, Cornish crab
and parsley dressing, followed perhaps by saddle of
rabbit, black pudding, polenta and confit garlic, and
then glazed apple turnover with caramel and prunes
to finish. If your wallet can bear the strain, consider
the seven-course tasting menu in order to sample
Corrigan's finest creations. **Expensive**

Patisserie Valerie *café for cakes* 9 F3
44 Old Compton Street, W1 • 020 7437 3466
>> www.patisserie-valerie.co.uk
Open 7:30am–8:30pm Mon–Fri, 8am–8:30pm Sat,
9am–6:30pm Sun

A Soho legend, the original Patisserie Valerie opened
in neighbouring Frith Street in 1926 and moved to Old
Compton Street after World War II. The cramped interior
is a 1950s Parisian time warp, with a cake-stuffed glass
counter at the front, a high ceiling, Formica tables and
Toulouse-Lautrec cartoons on the walls; there's also a
brighter, airier 50-seat first-floor café.

Light meals and a fine breakfast are served, but it's
the sweet stuff that's the main draw. Resistance is
useless against the likes of pear william franzipan
tart, mixed berry mousse, fresh fruit flan, and
chocolate, strawberry and banana gateaux. Such
indulgences and Valerie's unique atmosphere draw in
a mixed crowd of office workers, students, tourists
and the few remaining louche Soho habitués. **Cheap**

Red Fort *noble Indian* `9 F3`
77 Dean Street, W1 • 020 7437 2525
» www.redfort.co.uk Open lunch & dinner Mon–Fri, dinner Sat

For top-notch traditional northern Indian cooking in central London, you can't beat the Red Fort. The opulent setting (including a water feature) helps prepare you for the richness and depth of Mughal court cuisine. Chef Mohammed Rais' lamb biryani follows a 300-year-old family recipe. **Expensive**

Eagle Bar Diner *North American* `9 F2`
3–5 Rathbone Place, W1 • 020 7637 1418
» www.eaglebardiner.com Open noon–11pm
Mon–Sat (to 1am Thu–Sat), 11am–6pm Sun

A hip, all-day haven from the chaos of Oxford Street. The Eagle's remit stretches from breakfast to latenight cocktails, taking in first-rate burgers and grills, salads and sandwiches along the way. The look is New York chic, but the service is friendly. **Cheap**

Hakkasan *Chinese of the highest order* `9 F2`
8 Hanway Place, W1 • 020 7907 1888
Open lunch & dinner daily; bar noon–12:30am daily (to 1:30 Sat)

It's no exaggeration to say that Hakkasan has redefined Chinese dining in London – combining stunning design with exceptional high-quality Chinese cuisine. This airy basement restaurant and bar is the creation of Alan Yau, the man behind Wagamama *(see p47)*, but couldn't be more different from the noodle bar chain in terms of atmosphere (and prices).

The seductive interior is a cunning contemporary take on chinoiserie – all dark wood, lattice work and candle light. The Michelin-star-winning food shows off the full range and depth of China's varied cuisines. Savour beautifully balanced dishes such as roast pork with red rice, ginger and Shao Hsing wine, or roasted silver cod with champagne and Chinese honey. Even clichéd standards such as sesame prawn toast are exemplary. Prices are high, but for a splurge you can't beat Hakkasan. **Expensive**

Restaurants

Rasa Samudra *Keralan home cooking* `9 E1`
5 Charlotte Street, W1 • 020 7637 0222
➤➤ www.rasarestaurants.com
Open lunch & dinner Mon–Sat, dinner only Sun

Das Sreedharan has firmly placed the delicate cuisine of Kerala in southwest India on the London restaurant map. The first Rasa (55 Stoke Newington Church Street, N16) opened in 1994 and specializes in Keralan vegetarian cooking. Rasa W1 (6 Dering Street) offers a range of dishes, including meat, from northern Kerala; and the speciality at this branch is seafood.

In a maze of smart, pink-clad little rooms, you can experience such little-seen delights as *murukku* (crunchy rice-flour sticks) with home-made pickles and chutneys, Keralan shellfish soup, crab *thoran* (the chef's grandmother's recipe for crab stir-fried with coconut, mustard seeds and ginger) and *kappayum meenum* (spicy king fish and steamed cassava). If you can't make up your mind, order a set feast, either seafood or vegetarian. **Moderate**

Fino *modern tapas* `9 E2`
33 Charlotte St, W1 (entrance: Rathbone St) • 020 7813 8010
➤➤ www.finorestaurant.com
Open lunch & dinner Mon–Sat

Sleek, sassy and contemporary, Fino is a light, airy tapas restaurant and cocktail bar in which tortilla, Galician-style octopus and other classics are cooked with conviction and presented with flair. It has fine sherries and a globe-trotting wine list. **Moderate**

Navarro's *traditional Spanish* `9 E1`
67 Charlotte Street, W1 • 020 7637 7713
➤➤ www.navarros.co.uk
Open lunch & dinner Mon–Fri, dinner only Sat

The interior is a riot of Andalucian tiling and painted furniture, while the menu features some of the capital's most unusual Spanish dishes. Savour, for example, the velvety, piquant grilled chicken with prawns in an oloroso sherry and paprika sauce. **Cheap**

Sardo *pasta & other Italian classics* `9 E1`
45 Grafton Way, W1 • 020 7387 2521
>> www.sardo-restaurant.com
Open lunch & dinner Mon–Fri, dinner only Sat

No-nonsense, squeaky-fresh Sardinian specialities
are presented in a bright, simply decorated space. Try
the likes of *spaghetti bottariga* (with dried mullet roe)
or grilled steak topped with Sardinian blue cheese,
served by delightful, knowledgeable staff. **Moderate**

Matsuri *Japanese fun* `9 H2`
71 High Holborn, WC1 • 020 7430 1970
>> www.matsuri-restaurant.com Open lunch & dinner Mon–Sat

The team behind the acclaimed Matsuri in St James's
opened this more modern sister restaurant in 2002.
The *sashimi* (raw fish) and *teppanyaki* (grills) are as
authentically Japanese as you'll find in London. If
you're on a budget, try a lunchtime bento box;
otherwise, the set menus are excellent. **Expensive**

Rock and Sole Plaice *fish & chips* `9 G3`
47 Endell Street, WC2 • 020 7836 3785
Open 11am–11:30pm Mon–Sat, noon–11pm Sun

Founded in 1871, this Covent Garden fish-and-chip
shop has been run for the past 25 years by a Turkish
Cypriot, though the menu is traditional British.
Expect crisp, golden slabs of fish accompanied by
chunky chips and mugs of tea. You can eat in, sit at
pavement tables in summer or take away. **Moderate**

Paul *French-style café* `9 G3`
29 Bedford Street, WC2 • 020 7836 5321
>> www.paul.fr
Open 7:30am–9pm Mon–Fri, 9am–9pm Sat & Sun

You'll find no more agreeable lunch stop around
Covent Garden than this exemplary Gallic patisserie/
café. Take away tarts, cakes and breads or enjoy a
big salad, omelette or *tartine* (toasted bread with
toppings) from the elegant café at the rear. **Cheap**

>> *A great place to enjoy a snack from Paul's café is St Paul's Churchyard, just off Bedford Street*

Restaurants

Rules *British through & through*

9 G3

35 Maiden Lane, WC2 • 020 7836 5314
>> www.rules.co.uk
Open noon–11:30pm daily (to 10:30pm Sun)

Open continuously since 1798, and owned by just three families since then, Rules in Covent Garden is the capital's oldest restaurant and it positively drips with history. Venerable diners have included William Makepeace Thackeray, Evelyn Waugh, Graham Greene, Charlie Chaplin and Clark Gable.

The interior is a Victorian fantasy, with chandeliers and spectacular coloured-glass skylights illuminating walls lined with dark wood and crimson banquettes. Everywhere you look are portraits, pastoral scenes and animal trophies characteristic of the style of grand English country houses. The restaurant is particularly beautiful over Christmas, decked out in traditional ornaments. Altogether, there are three floors and several private dining rooms. One of the rooms is named after the best-known author of the Victorian era, Charles Dickens, who was himself a regular at this restaurant. However, what prevents Rules being a mere Dickensian pastiche are the slickness of its service and the supreme standard of its food. The menu is carnivore heaven, and one of the few places in London where you can sample superb game – especially wild duck and pheasant – much of which comes from Rules' own estate, Lartington Hall Park, in the High Pennines. (You can sign up for a shooting party or fishing at the estate, if you already have experience.)

Don't believe there's such a thing as high-quality traditional British cuisine? An indulgent meal here of, say, hare soup with armagnac, or Morecambe Bay potted shrimps, or roast young grouse with celeriac and damson sauce, or fillet of Highland venison with wild mushrooms and Chartreuse sauce is guaranteed to change your mind. Round off the experience with sticky toffee pudding oozing butterscotch and vanilla custard, or apple and blackberry crumble. **Expensive**

Hazuki *mid-range Japanese* `9 G4`
43 Chandos Place, WC2 • 0871 332 5606
Open lunch & dinner Mon–Sat,
dinner only Sun

Hazuki nimbly bridges the gap between pricey, formal Japanese restaurants and casual sushi bars. Its look is contemporary, its staff efficient, its food exemplary. Lunch dishes – such as grilled belly pork with rice and soup – are particularly good value. **Moderate**

J Sheekey *fish, pure & simple* `9 F3`
28–32 St Martin's Court, WC2 • 020 7240 2565
➤➤ www.caprice-holdings.co.uk
Open lunch & dinner daily (to midnight)

If you despair of ever getting a table at The Ivy *(see p38)*, fear not: its sister restaurant offers as seductive a setting, good food and lovely service. The emphasis is on fish, and the ethos is to keep it simple. You won't find a finer fish pie in London. **Expensive**

The National Dining Rooms `9 F4`
Sainsbury Wing, The National Gallery, WC2 • 020 7747 2525
Open 10am–5:30pm Mon & Tue, 10am–8:30pm Wed,
10am–5:30pm Thu–Sun

The revamped café inside the National Gallery is perfect for dabbling with British snacks from traditional baking to simple salads, while the restaurant offers an imaginative British menu in a dining room overlooking Trafalgar Square. **Moderate**

Le Caprice *classy comfort food* `9 E4`
Arlington House, Arlington Street, SW1 • 020 7629 2239
➤➤ www.caprice-holdings.co.uk
Open lunch & dinner daily

Le Caprice has been a famous name on the London dining scene for decades. There's a 1980s monochrome bistro look to the decor, but the slick service and modern European dishes never disappoint. Their fish and chips with mushy peas is heavenly. **Expensive**

The Wolseley *fashionable all-day haunt* `9 E4`

160 Piccadilly, W1 • 020 7499 6996
>> www.thewolseley.com
Open 7am–midnight Mon–Fri, 9am–midnight Sat,
9am–11pm Sun (breakfast to 11:30am)

Chris Corbin and Jeremy King are the talented double act behind the sustained success of the exclusive Ivy *(see p38)* and Le Caprice *(see p35)* over the past decade or so. Their involvement with these twin pillars of the fashionable London preening-and-dining scene may now be over, but their newest venture has become just as essential a stop on the celebrity circuit.

The Wolseley occupies the opulent 1920s former showroom of the eponymous car manufacturer. It has been made over to resemble a grand Mittel-European café, with a high vaulted ceiling, black-and-white tiled floor and lashings of gilt and black coating the walls. Highly professional staff serve up the type of reliable mix-and-match international dishes that will be familiar to anyone who's managed to bag a table at Le Caprice or The Ivy in the past, though there's an additional hearty Central European slant here to match the surroundings.

You could go for a spicy steak tartare, earthy cassoulet (meaty bean stew) or a superior hamburger, or head east for a wiener schnitzel, a Hungarian goulash or a German pancake-based dish called *Kaiserschmarren*. Perhaps the Wolseley's greatest strength, however, is that it's open all day, even offering breakfast and afternoon tea. **Moderate**

Kiku *exceptionally good Japanese* `8 D4`
17 Half Moon Street, W1 • 020 7499 4208
» www.kikurestaurant.co.uk
Open lunch & dinner Mon–Sat, dinner only Sun

Decked out in light wood and with artful flower arrangements, this smart restaurant is a utilitarian stage for virtuoso Japanese cuisine. The sushi is exemplary, as is *agedashi-dofu* (deep-fried tofu and dried fish in a broth with grated ginger and Japanese radish). **Expensive**

Tamarind *tandoori as it should be* `8 D4`
20 Queen Street, W1 • 020 7629 3561
» www.tamarindrestaurant.com
Open lunch & dinner Mon–Fri, dinner only Sat & Sun

This Michelin-starred restaurant shows just how varied and refined good Indian food can be. The menu's heart is the tandoor oven, stalwart of north-west India, from which emerge stunning meats, game, fish and breads. Service is impeccable. **Expensive**

Kaya *rare Korean* `8 D4`
42 Albemarle Street, W1 • 020 7499 0622
Open lunch & dinner Mon–Sat

The classiest of London's Korean restaurants is a serene spot in which to experience the subtleties of this under-appreciated cuisine. Grilling your own food on a tabletop griddle is fun, or you can rely on the traditionally dressed staff to recommend piquant dishes seldom encountered outside Korea. **Moderate**

Patara Thai *taste of Thailand* `8 D3`
3 & 7 Maddox Street, W1 • 020 7499 6008
Open lunch & dinner daily

The handful of London branches of this upmarket Thai restaurant group offer an impressively authentic overview of one of Asia's most versatile cuisines. Enjoy dishes such as black cod broth with ginger, or chicken and pork dumplings, against a restful backdrop of greenery and Thai antiques. **Moderate**

Restaurants

Al Sultan *Middle Eastern delicacies* `8 C5`
51–2 Hertford Street, W1 • 020 7408 1155/1166
>> www.alsultan.co.uk Open noon–midnight daily

For a taste of just how good high-class Lebanese cuisine can be, head for this discreet Mayfair restaurant near Hyde Park Corner. The chargrilled meats are superb, while the magnificent meze is thoroughly authentic, right down to the range of offal offered. *Beid ghanam* – lamb's testicles – anyone? **Moderate**

Mômo/Mô *Moroccan restaurant/tearoom* `9 E3`
23 Heddon Street, W1 • 020 7434 4040
>> www.momoresto.com Restaurant: lunch & dinner
Mon–Sat, dinner only Sun; tearoom: all day Mon–Sat

Mourad Mazouz's fabulously theatrical restaurant, Mômo, is an expensive treat, but you can also enjoy a similar ambience next door in a tearoom-cum-bazaar. Sip a mint tea or a fresh fruit juice while nibbling on excellent sandwiches and meze. **Expensive/Cheap**

Golden Hind *perfect fish & chips* `8 C2`
73 Marylebone Lane, W1 • 020 7486 3644
Open lunch & dinner Mon–Fri, dinner only Sat

The finest chippie in W1 has been serving up prime fish and chips since 1914. Bring your own booze (no corkage charge) and make an evening of it, with a big portion of moist, flaky haddock or cod, thinly coated in crisp batter, alongside perfect chips, mushy peas and home-made tartare sauce. Bliss. **Cheap**

The Hottest Tables in Towns

London's premier restaurants are world-class. The problem for ordinary mortals is securing a table. It's just possible that if you call on the day you might strike lucky; otherwise, you'll need to book months in advance. Among these hallowed temples of gastronomy are: **Locanda Locatelli**, the superlative Italian run by the ebullient Giorgio Locatelli; Jamie Oliver's much-publicised **Fifteen**; **The Ivy**, still the posh bistro of choice for most celebrities; even more fashionable **Nobu**, with its superb Japanese fusion menu; quite possibly London's finest restaurant, **Gordon Ramsay**; and certainly the capital's most expensive dining spot, gloriously over-the-top **Sketch**. For all restaurant contact details, *see pp224–5.*

Providores/Tapa Room *international* 8 C1

109 Marylebone High Street, W1 • 020 7935 6175
>> www.theprovidores.co.uk Open lunch & dinner daily (brunch Sat & Sun); Tapa Room 9am–10:30pm daily (from 10am Sat & Sun)

New Zealander Peter Gordon helped introduce the concept of "fusion" food to London when he opened the much-lauded Sugar Club in 1995. He remains one of the few chefs capable of consistently marrying diverse, pan-global ingredients harmoniously.

The good work continues at the Providores, a tiny, simple dining space with an agreeably relaxed vibe, and a regularly changing menu that might include pork cheek braised with five spice, cardamom and Turkish chilli on chorizo mash with pickled okra, or roast New Zealand venison on black bean and chocolate stew with roast celeriac, green beans and quince aïoli. The ground-floor Tapa Room is a combination of wine bar, breakfast bar and tapas bar. The "Tapa" in question, though, is a ceremonial cloth used for celebratory feasts throughout the Pacific. **Expensive**

The Orrery *modern European/French* 8 C1

55 Marylebone High Street, W1 • 020 7616 8000
>> www.orrery.co.uk Open lunch & dinner daily

Of all Sir Terence Conran's London restaurants, the Orrery is probably the classiest act (it is also very expensive). This is a long, light, elegant dining space with arched windows overlooking Marylebone Parish Church gardens. The largely Gallic waiting staff are extremely attentive and happy to talk you through the French-leaning menu.

An indulgent evening here might commence with seared sea scallops, pork belly and cauliflower, moving on to fillet of Scottish beef with slow-cooked oxtail, salsify (oyster plant) and red wine *jus*, before ending with a fondant of Amedei chocolate with milk ice cream. If you fancy something less than a full meal, head for the Orrery Epicerie (on the corner of Marylebone High Street and Beaumont Street), to find tasty breakfasts, light lunches and snacks, plus delicatessen products to take away. **Expensive**

Restaurants

Phoenix Palace *a Chinese treat*
8 B1
3–5 Glentworth Street, NW1 • 020 7486 3515
Open noon–11:30pm Mon–Sat, 11am–10pm Sun

You need to venture beyond Chinatown to find London's best Chinese food. This smart Marylebone restaurant is one of the finest – as the number of Cantonese clients here testifies. If you're feeling adventurous, try the monthly specials menu. The soup of the day is reliably tasty. **Cheap**

Original Tagines *North African*
8 B2
7A Dorset Street, W1 • 020 7935 1545
>> www.originaltagines.com
Open lunch & dinner Mon–Fri, dinner only Sat

If the scented, sweet-savoury allure of North African cuisine has passed you by, visit this restaurant. The eponymous tagines are excellent (and come in 11 versions – try the chicken with preserved lemon), as are the couscous dishes and grills. **Moderate**

Le Relais de Venise *steak & chips*
8 C2
120 Marylebone Lane, W1 • 020 7486 0878
>> www.relaisedevenise.com Open lunch & dinner daily

This is one restaurant where we can tell you exactly what's on the menu: a salad of green leaves and walnuts, then a main course of trimmed sirloin steak topped with a "secret sauce", and thin, crispy chips. The beef is always top quality, sourced from Donald Russell, supplier to the Queen. **Moderate**

Maroush Gardens *Middle Eastern*
8 A3
1–3 Connaught Street, W2 • 020 7262 0222
Branch: 21 Edgware Road • 020 7723 0773
>> www.maroush.com Open all day (noon–midnight) daily

This classy, sober spot is part of Marouf Abouzaki's Maroush chain, and specializes in fish – though the classic Lebanese meze and grills are equally fine. The atmosphere is a little more refined than at livelier sibling Maroush I. **Moderate**

Cinnamon Club *creative Indian* `15 F1`
Old Westminster Library Great Smith St, SW1 • 020 7222 2555
>> www.cinnamonclub.com
Open breakfast, lunch & dinner Mon–Fri, dinner only Sat

A spacious library has been sensitively transformed into one of London's finest Indian restaurants. The original parquet flooring remains, as do some of the bookshelves, but they've been augmented by marble and stone imported from Rajasthan to create a light-filled, spacious dining room. Vivek Singh's menu combines Indian flavours with European culinary techniques, as, for instance, in the French-inspired use of sauce reductions. This results in exquisite dishes such as clove-smoked tartare of Charolais beef with pickled beetroot, tandoori breast of pheasant with spiced mushroom sauce, and saffron-poached pear with cinnamon ice cream. The restaurant's proximity to the Houses of Parliament means that most of its clientele is curry-loving politicos and civil servants – but don't let that put you off. **Expensive**

Foliage *exquisite modern European* `8 B5`
Mandarin Oriental Hyde Park Hotel,
66 Knightsbridge, SW1 • 020 7201 3723
>> www.mandarinoriental.com Open lunch & dinner daily

Some tables enjoy wonderful views out over Hyde Park, and the food is beyond reproach. Dishes such as roast saddle of rabbit, pithivier of wild mushrooms, asparagus, Alsace bacon and vanilla cream will leave you stumbling for superlatives. **Expensive**

Patogh *superior kebabs* `8 A2`
8 Crawford Place, W1 • 020 7262 4015
Open noon–midnight daily

It's little more than a hole in the wall, but Patogh offers some of the most richly satisfying chargrilled meats in London. Choose from one of seven types of Iranian kebab dishes, grab a table if you can, then feast on a massive round of fresh flat bread, squeaky-fresh salads and your meat of choice. **Cheap**

Restaurants

14 D1
Noura *meze to astonish*
16 Hobart Place, SW1 • 020 7235 9444
>> www.noura.co.uk Open noon–11pm daily

The glamorous atmosphere at this Lebanese restaurant reflects its posh Belgravia location, but it's far from stuffy, and the quality of the food is superb. Grilled meats don't come any finer, while the range of hot and cold meze cannot help but impress, with around 50 choices on offer. **Moderate**

14 C3
Hunan *specialist Chinese*
51 Pimlico Road, SW1 • 020 7730 5712
Open lunch & dinner Mon–Sat

London's only restaurant specializing in the spicy cuisine of China's westernmost province is a pint-size treat. Leave your preconceptions about Chinese set meals at the door and let the staff put together a feast for you that you'll long remember. The stuffed baby squid with bitter melon is supreme. **Moderate**

14 A1
Zuma *high-class sushi & more*
5 Raphael Street, SW7 • 020 7584 1010
>> www.zumarestaurant.com Open lunch & dinner daily

Zuma aims to provide a sophisticated metropolitan take on traditional Japanese *izakaya*-style (informal pub) dining. This being Knightsbridge, the result is resolutely upmarket, though far from snobby. The large dining room is clad in soothing earth tones, with wood-slat screens dividing up the space. If you're popping in on a whim, you can sit at the sushi counter and watch expert chefs whip up a California maki roll or some choice *sashimi* for you. Or pick something like salt-grilled sea bass with burnt tomato ginger relish from the *robata* grill.

The full menu includes Zuma specials like baby chicken marinated in barley miso and oven-roasted in cedar wood. The freshness and quality of ingredients are exemplary. If you merely fancy a drink, there's a lounge and sake bar, which offers more than 20 types of sake as well as cocktails. **Expensive**

Zafferano *Italian greats*   14 B1
15 Lowndes Street, SW1 • 020 7235 5800
>> **www.zafferanorestaurant.com** Open lunch & dinner daily

Zafferano has long been recognized as one of the capital's premier Italian restaurants. It's a discreet place, where the emphasis is firmly on the food. Dishes such as risotto with white truffle and char-grilled lamb with aubergine allow the quality of the ingredients to shine through. **Expensive**

Racine *traditional French*   14 A2
239 Brompton Road, SW3 • 020 7584 4477
Open lunch & dinner daily

This hugely popular French restaurant has made a virtue out of simplicity. The decor is ascetically plain and the food is a glorious throwback to the days of classic Gallic cuisine. Expect succulent *daubes* (braised meat stews) and *marmites* (pot soups). For the quality of the food, prices are a steal. **Moderate**

Tom Aikens *modern European creativity*   14 A3
43 Elystan Street, SW3 • 020 7584 2003
>> **www.tomaikens.co.uk** Open lunch & dinner Mon–Fri

Michelin-starred Tom Aikens made his name in the 1990s and is now undoubtedly one of the most gifted chefs working in London. The sober, masculine tones of the almost brutally plain decor of his eponymous restaurant leave diners in no doubt that this is a serious restaurant for serious foodies. Even if you balk at over-complex food, it's hard not to admire the attention to detail and careful balancing of colour, texture and taste that distinguish his menu.

A typical meal might start with basil-marinated scallops, courgettes and almond mousse, followed by pigeon steamed with thyme, chestnut velouté, cannelloni and soft lettuce, and crowned with pineapple roasted with vanilla and rum. If you can stretch to a blow-out, you won't regret going for the tasting menu; those with smaller budgets can still eat like royalty with the set lunch. **Expensive**

Restaurants

Tendido Cero *well-chosen tapas* `13 G3`
174 Old Brompton Road, SW5 • 020 7370 3685
>> www.cambiodetercio.co.uk Open 11:30am–11pm daily

Much of the tapas in London tend to be lacklustre, but not so at Tendido Cero. This smart, sleek sibling of upmarket Iberian stalwart Cambio de Tercio (across the road) serves up the choicest Spanish cheeses, hams and charcuterie. There's no drinks licence, so you have to bring your own alcohol. **Moderate**

The Painted Heron *elegant indian* `13 H5`
112 Cheyne Walk, SW10 • 020 7351 5232
>> www.thepaintedheron.com
Open lunch & dinner Mon–Fri, dinner only Sat

Yogesh Datta's innovative, refined yet unfussy take on traditional Subcontinental cuisine is evident in dishes such as duck livers in tandoori spices, and spinach and partridge curry. The restaurant is as elegant and understated as the food. **Moderate**

Lots Road Pub *gastropub* `13 G5`
114 Lots Road, SW10 • 020 7352 6645
Open 11am–11pm daily (to 10:30pm Sun)

There may be a gastropub with airy, stripped-down decor on almost every corner these days, but this place remains one of the best. It's the friendliness of the staff and the quality of the food that mark it out; the ingredients are supremely fresh. You won't find a better burger in London. **Moderate**

Chutney Mary *intimate Indian* `13 G5`
535 King's Road, SW10 • 020 7351 3113
>> www.realindianfood.com
Open lunch & dinner Sat & Sun, dinner only Mon–Fri

A stylish makeover of restaurant and menu confirmed Chutney Mary as both a beacon of Indian culinary excellence and a chic, romantic spot. The pan-Indian menu exploits the depth and range of the country's cuisine, and service is impeccable. **Expensive**

The River Café *inspirational Italian* `12 A5`

Thames Wharf, Rainville Road, W6 • 020 7386 4200
≫ www.rivercafe.co.uk
Open lunch & dinner Mon–Sat, lunch only Sun

No London restaurant has had more influence on both restaurant food and (with the spawning of five books) home cooking than the River Café. When Rose Gray and Ruth Rogers opened up in 1987, most Italian eateries were stuck in a 1970s candle-in-a-chianti-bottle time warp. Their versions of simple Italian regional dishes, carefully sourced and immaculately prepared, were revelatory, and inspired a string of talented chefs who worked in their kitchen – Jamie Oliver among them

(see Fifteen on p38). The restaurant's appeal remains undimmed today. You do, though, pay heavily for the privilege, with few main courses under £25. The prices and ambience are not café-style.

A typical spring menu might include char-grilled marinated leg of lamb with fresh borlotti beans, Swiss and rainbow chard, and anchovy and rosemary sauce. The relatively stark, utilitarian dining space was designed by architect Richard Rogers (Ruth's husband) within converted 19th-century warehouses. Its floor-to-ceiling windows give access to a garden and the river beyond. To enjoy the restaurant to the full, try to book a table here in fine weather. **Expensive**

The Gate *top-notch vegetarian* `12 A3`

51 Queen Caroline Street, W6 • 020 8748 6932
≫ www.gateveg.co.uk Open lunch & dinner Mon–Fri, dinner Sat

For more than a decade, brothers Adrian and Michael Daniels have been running this classy, relaxed Hammersmith restaurant. The food they serve (aubergine schnitzel, Thai red curry) is so good that even devoted meat-eaters won't feel hard done by. Ask for a table in the leafy courtyard. **Moderate**

Lisboa Patisserie *Portuguese café*   `6 C2`
57 Golborne Road, W10 • 020 8968 5242
Open 8am–8pm Mon–Sat, 8am–7pm Sun

Today the heart of London's sizeable Portuguese community may be south of the river around Stockwell and Vauxhall, but Notting Hill's Golborne Road is home to one of the oldest and best-loved *pastelarias* in town. Such has been the success of Lisboa Patisserie that it has spawned a mini chain (currently numbering four branches) across the capital, but the original site is certainly the most fun to visit when the Portobello Road market *(see p165)* is in full swing.

Portuguese cakes and tarts are the speciality, and come in an impressive range and at low prices; you won't find better or more authentic cinnamon-topped *pasteis de nata* (custard tarts) in the city. Equally fabled are the *bolos de arroz* (rice cakes) and the *castanhas de ovo* (literally, "egg chestnut", a sweet, eggy nugget). Savouries are sold too – try the *pasteis de bacalhau* (salt cod and potato cakes). **Cheap**

S&M Café *bangers 'n' mash*   `6 D3`
268 Portobello Road, W10 • 020 8968 8898
» www.sandmcafe.co.uk
Open 11am–11pm Mon–Thu, 9am–11pm Fri–Sun

Simplicity is king at the S&M Café. Choose your type of sausage (including veggie options), mash and gravy, and feast on the likes of wild boar sausages with calvados and apples, or pork sausages with bubble-and-squeak, mash and red onion gravy. **Cheap**

E&O *Oriental in style*   `6 C3`
14 Blenheim Crescent, W11 • 020 7229 5454
» www.eando.co.uk Open lunch & dinner daily

This western sister to the Great Eastern Dining Room *(see p52)* is every bit as chic as its counterpart. It draws in the beautiful people of Notting Hill to preen, pout and gaze about while nibbling on the seriously tasty mix-and-match Oriental dishes. A great choice for vegetarians. **Moderate**

Al Waha *Middle Eastern*   `7 E3`
75 Westbourne Grove, W2 • 020 7229 0806
» www.alwaharestaurant.com Open noon–midnight daily

This gracious restaurant offers some of the best Lebanese food around town in modest, tranquil surroundings (the name means "the oasis"). Vegetarians are
well catered for in the list of almost 50 hot and cold
meze, and it's always worth trying the daily specials.
The set meals are particularly good value. **Moderate**

Magic Wok *cheap & cheerful Chinese*   `7 F3`
100 Queensway, W2 • 020 7792 9767
Open noon–10:30pm daily

Queensway has long been a centre for Chinese
culinary excellence, and Magic Wok has been in its
vanguard for many years. The decor is thoroughly
undistinguished, but the food shines out. Stick to
the specials menu and you can't go wrong; the rich,
flavourful hot pot dishes are especially good. **Cheap**

Satay House *traditional Malaysian*   `7 H2`
13 Sale Place, W2 • 020 7723 6763
» www.satay-house.co.uk
Open lunch & dinner daily

For toothsome, freshly cooked Malaysian food you
can't beat this modest little Paddington restaurant. A
lively, multinational crowd heads here for classic rice
and noodle dishes, and such delicacies as deep-fried
sea bass cooked in salted beans. **Moderate**

Chain Restaurants

For conveyor-belt sushi head for **Yo! Sushi** or
venture a little further upmarket at **Itsu**. Noodle bar
group **Wagamama** is still the business for huge
bowls of *ramen* (noodle soup) in a canteen
atmosphere, while there's a more intimate vibe at
pan-Oriental mini-chain **Busaba Eathai**. Venturing
further west across the globe, **Masala Zone** has
done for Indian food what Wagamama did for
Japanese. Reaching Europe, you can't beat **Strada**
for wood-fired pizza. More unusual is idiosyncratic
Belgian *moules-frites* specialist **Belgo**, while the
dishes served at **Giraffe** span the world. The newest
mini-chains are devoted to the "gourmet burger".
Check out **Hamburger Union** and the **Gourmet
Burger Kitchen**. For restaurant details, *see pp224–5*.

» *You may have to queue at canteens and conveyor-belt restaurants such as Wagamama and Yo! Sushi*

Restaurants

Moro *Spanish & North African* `4 A5`

34–6 Exmouth Market, EC1 • 020 7833 8336
>> www.moro.co.uk Open lunch & dinner Mon–Sat
(private functions only on Sun)

Few restaurants have attracted plaudits as unanimous and enthusiastic as those applied to Moro since it opened in 1997. Confusingly named husband-and-wife team Sam and Sam Clark shared their culinary schooling at the pioneering Eagle gastropub *(see below)* just down the road, and also at the celebrated River Café *(see p45)* in Hammersmith. From these two gastronomic beacons they've adopted the sensible policy of letting the quality of fine ingredients shine through in simple dishes. Their unique contribution to both the concept and the London food scene comes from applying these principles to an inspired crossover of Spanish and North African cuisine (as the name Moro, meaning "Moor" in Spanish, implies). The results can be sampled in, say, a meal of *ajo blanco* (Spanish garlic and almond soup), followed by quail baked in flatbread, with rosewater and cardamom ice cream to finish.

If you're more in the mood to snack than to feast, tapas are available from the long zinc bar that runs along one side of the bright and casual, though often frenetically noisy, dining room. **Expensive**

The Eagle *the original gastropub* `10 A1`

159 Farringdon Road, EC1 • 020 7837 1353
Open all day from noon Mon–Sat, lunch only Sun

Credited with starting the gastropub revolution that has now swept the country, The Eagle is still up there with the best of its progeny more than a decade later. Garrulous media folk pack out the tightly packed tables and feast on perfectly cooked rustic stomach-fillers and grilled meats. **Moderate**

Fish Central *fish & chips in style* `4 C5`
149–51 Central Street, EC1 • 020 7253 4970
➤➤ www.fishcentral.co.uk
Open lunch & dinner Mon–Sat

An oasis of value and charm in the overpriced City,
Fish Central was converted in 2003 from a takeaway
into a swish, minimalist restaurant. Yet the prices are
still low, the welcome cheery and the food superb –
haddock in matzo is a slice of piscine heaven. **Cheap**

Flâneur Food Hall *modern European* `10 A1`
41 Farringdon Road, EC1 • 020 7404 4422
➤➤ www.flaneur.com
Open 9am–10pm Mon–Sat, 9am–6pm Sun

High-ceilinged Flâneur is a superior seller of choice
comestibles, and its restaurant offers a similarly
elevated menu of dishes such as roast cod with pak
choi, pickled cucumber and soy reduction. Emphasis
is placed on fresh, well-sourced ingredients. **Moderate**

Smiths of Smithfield *modern European* `10 B2`
67–77 Charterhouse Street, EC1 • 020 7251 7950
➤➤ www.smithsofsmithfield.co.uk Café open breakfast & lunch
daily; dining room open lunch & dinner Sun–Fri

Revelling in the industrial chic of bare brick and raw
concrete, Smiths is a multi-floor venue successfully
combining a buzzing bar-café (brunch is a must), a
lively dining room, and a polished restaurant catering
to City high-flyers. **Moderate/Expensive**

The White Swan *proper gastropub* `10 A2`
108 Fetter Lane, EC4 • 020 7242 9696
➤➤ www.thewhiteswanlondon.com
Open lunch & dinner Mon–Fri

While maintaining the spirit of a boozer on the
ground floor, the pub's first floor is a surprisingly
polished dining room, serving smart gastropub
dishes, such as partridge with juniper gravy and
braised pork belly with pickled cabbage. **Moderate**

Restaurants

St John *iconic British restaurant* `4 B5`

26 St John Street, EC1 • 020 7251 0848
➤➤ www.stjohnrestaurant.com
Open lunch & dinner Mon–Fri, dinner only Sat

Chef Fergus Henderson has been in the vanguard of modern British cooking since this unique restaurant opened in 1994. His philosophy of "nose to tail eating" – no part of an animal is off limits – has led to the creation of classic, no-compromise dishes such as roast bone marrow and parsley salad, and veal tongue, beetroot and pickled walnut. But faint hearts need not fear: less offbeat gems include boiled ham, carrots and parsley sauce, and veal chop with chicory and anchovy. Desserts are straight from the nursery: apple crumble and custard, and hot chocolate pudding. There are no decorative frills to detract from the supreme quality of the food in this eccentric building that is part Georgian townhouse, part former smoke-house. An on-site bakery and bar offer snacks such as welsh rarebit, and tripe and chips. **Expensive**

Café Spice Namaste *pioneering Indian* `11 F3`

16 Prescot Street, E1 • 020 7488 9242
➤➤ www.cafespice.co.uk Open lunch & dinner Mon–Sat

No-one has done more than Bombay-born chef Cyrus Todiwala to revitalize British Indian restaurants for the 21st century. He opened Café Spice Namaste in 1995, and it remains one of the capital's premier Subcontinental dining destinations a decade later. A central bar separates the two dining rooms, which are decorated in fiery colours to reflect the zip of a menu that marries traditional Indian culinary techniques with unusual ingredients. Sample the delights of venison tikka flavoured with roasted fennel, star anise and cinnamon, and fresh buffalo mozzarella served with Parsee-style pickle and *sarias* (crackers). Or experience the depth of flavour in a classic lamb dhansak. Even the home-made pickles and chutneys that accompany the pre-meal pappadoms are exceptional. You can enjoy Indian nibbles and bottles of icy Cobra lager in the beer garden, too. **Moderate**

Club Gascon *hearty French* `10 B2`

57 West Smithfield, EC1 • 020 7796 0600
Open lunch & dinner Mon–Fri, dinner only Sat

The earthy flavours of Southwest France are Club Gascon's speciality, with foie gras prominent on a menu that features a range of small courses rather than the traditional starter-main-dessert. Some of the dishes raise a smile: wild sea bass might come with a "surprised" turnip (a tiny root veg topped with foam), or your apple pie could arrive seemingly empty, only for you to realize that the filling is within the accompanying ice cream. The presentation is as imaginative as the food, with courses appearing on slate, glass and ceramic tiles as well as china. If your budget will stretch to it, order the five-course degustation menu; each dish is paired with a different glass of wine. A couple of doors away, Cellar Gascon serves up cheaper, but equally fine, bistro food to accompany a superb selection of Gallic wines. Staff are cheery, confident and utterly professional. **Expensive**

Les Trois Garçons *characterful French* `5 F5`

1 Club Row, E1 • 020 7613 1924
» www.lestroisgarcons.com
Open lunch & dinner Mon–Fri, dinner only Sat

This joyously over-the-top Gallic eaterie heaves with stuffed animals, Murano glass chandeliers and baroque bric-a-brac (all for sale). Yet the classic French food is straight down the line and of a high order. A unique dining experience. **Expensive**

Cantaloupe *trend-setting Mediterranean* `5 E5`

35 Charlotte Road, EC2 • 020 7613 4411
» www.cantaloupe.co.uk
Open lunch & dinner Mon–Fri, dinner only Sat

This versatile bar-restaurant is still a trailblazer of the trendy Hoxton/Shoreditch scene, but doesn't sacrifice substance for appearance. The setting is revamped industrial, and there's plenty of fire and imagination on the short, Mediterranean-slanted menu. **Moderate**

Great Eastern Dining Room *Oriental* `5 E5`
54–6 Great Eastern Street, EC2 • 020 7613 4545
>> www.greateasterndining.co.uk
Open noon–midnight Mon–Thu, noon–1am Fri, 6pm–1am Sat

The lively, noisy GEDR draws in a young, fashionable crowd for artfully conceived oriental treats like pork and prawn dumplings, rare beef salad with red chilli dressing, and lemongrass and ginger pannacotta. *(See also E&O, p46.)* **Moderate**

Real Greek *real Greek* `5 E5`
14–15 Hoxton Market, N1 • 020 7739 8212
Branch: 140–42 St John St, EC1 • 020 7253 7234
>> www.therealgreek.co.uk Open lunch & dinner Mon–Sat

The moribund London Greek restaurant scene was given a life-saving shot in the arm when Theodore Kyriakou opened this stylish place in 1999. Dishes rarely encountered outside Greece are cooked with conviction and served with a smile. **Moderate**

Viet Hoa *the original Vietnamese* `5 E4`
70–72 Kingsland Road, E2 • 020 7729 8293
Open lunch & dinner daily

Hoxton has a sizeable and vibrant Vietnamese community, and this airy, one-time local canteen was the first place in London to bring the sharp, clean flavours of their cuisine to a non-native audience. It's still packing the crowds in, and you won't find a better bowl of *pho* (meat and noodle soup) in town. **Cheap**

Green Papaya *neighbourhood Vietnamese* `5 H1`
191 Mare Street, E8 • 020 8985 5486
Open dinner Tue–Sun

Hackney is home to a great mix of ethnicities, a fact reflected in its diverse community cafés. Green Papaya is a step up in terms of decor (stripped floorboards, crimson walls, candlelight and a lovely garden) and cooking. Try a classic noodle soup or go for something more unusual from the daily specials menu. **Cheap**

Gallipoli *day-long meze*

4 B2

102 Upper Street, N1 • 020 7359 0630
>> www.gallipolicafe.com Open 10am–11pm
Mon–Thu, 10am–midnight Fri & Sat

This cracking Turkish bistro has a lively atmosphere
and serves generously proportioned, moderately
priced food. As well as a fine all-day breakfast, there's
a long menu of authentic Turkish dishes, especially
meze and grilled meats. **Moderate**

The Drapers Arms *great gastropub*

4 A2

44 Barnsbury Street, N1 • 020 7619 0348
>> www.thedrapersarms.co.uk
Open lunch & dinner Mon–Sat, lunch only Sun

Of all the Islington gastropubs, none provides a better
all-round package of great food, convivial ambience
and willing service than the Drapers. You'll pay West
End prices in the airy first-floor restaurant, but the
globe-trotting menu is top-notch. **Moderate**

The House *prize-winning gastropub*

4 B1

63–9 Canonbury Road, N1 • 020 7704 7410
>> www.inthehouse.biz
Open lunch & dinner Tue–Sun, dinner only Mon

North London is awash with gastropubs, but few
come close to matching the award-winning House for
quality of food. The setting is relaxed and friendly,
with a modern, stripped-down bar area, an open fire
in winter and a decked terrace and beer garden for
when the sun shines. It's only when you start
exploring the menu, though, that you understand
why this place has become many Islingtonians'
favourite spot to eat. There's a French emphasis to
the dishes, such as roast sea bass with *piperade*
(sauté peppers), olive tapenade and langoustine oil,
and terrine of chicken, sweetbreads, Grelot onions
and foie gras wrapped in Parma ham. There's also a
superb, varied brunch menu at weekends and good-
value lunch and pre-theatre set meals. Not cheap,
but absolutely worth it. **Moderate**

Restaurants

Odette's *romantic modern European* 2 B2
130 Regent's Park Road, NW1 • 020 7586 5486
Open lunch & dinner Tue–Sat, lunch only Sun

One of North London's best-loved restaurants, Odette's is a prime spot for a romantic dinner *à deux*. It was given a sensitive renovation a few years back, yet it retains all the old-fashioned idiosyncrasy that has long endeared it to the moneyed media folk of Primrose Hill. Scores of gilded mirrors reflect candlelight around the intimate dining rooms, providing a seductive setting for adventurous but not over-fussy contemporary cooking.

Pithivier of rabbit with white bean cream would be a typical starter; for mains, chargrilled leg of lamb with Italian seasoning, roasted artichokes and fondant potatoes, or loin of veal with herb gnocchi and fresh peas. The wine list is also notable, and features an impressively international spread of vintages. Service can be a touch uneven, but overall Odette's is a North London jewel. **Expensive**

El Parador *superior tapas* 3 E4
245 Eversholt Street, NW1 • 020 7387 2789
Open lunch & dinner Mon–Fri, dinner only Sat & Sun

An oasis of Iberia in the unpromising area between Euston station and Camden Town, El Parador is at its best in the summer, when the dining room and basement are augmented by a small garden. The tapas are better than the London norm, with fresh, high-quality ingredients to the fore. **Cheap**

Café Corfu *Greek delights* 3 E2
7 Pratt Street, NW1 • 020 7267 8088
>> www.cafecorfu.com Open all day from noon Tue–Sun

Many Greek restaurants in London are lacklustre. Not so Café Corfu, which offers an excitingly varied menu of rarely encountered specialities from the Greek mainland and islands, as well as classic roast lamb dishes. The setting is lively, with music and dancing at weekends, and the service is spot-on. **Moderate**

Manna *vegetable dishes from heaven* `2 B2`
4 Erskine Road, NW3 • 020 7722 8028
>> www.manna-veg.com
Open dinner only Mon–Sat, lunch & dinner Sun

Serving well-crafted dishes for more than 40 years, Manna is still noteworthy among vegetarian restaurants. Tuck in to a meal of, say, soba noodle salad, organic fennel schnitzel, and star anise brûlée accompanied by a fine organic beer or wine. **Moderate**

The Lansdowne *reliable gastropub* `2 C2`
90 Gloucester Avenue, NW1 • 020 7483 0409
Open dinner only Tue–Sat, lunch & dinner Sun

The Lansdowne has long been one of the capital's premier gastropubs, and its standards remain as high as ever. Snacks can be ordered from the chalkboard in the lively downstairs bar, or go for something more substantial on the short, reliable menu in the posher red-and-black-clad first-floor restaurant. **Moderate**

Mango Room *the best Caribbean in town* `2 D1`
10 Kentish Town Road, NW1 • 020 7482 5065
>> www.mangoroom.co.uk Open dinner only Mon, lunch & dinner Tue–Sat, lunch only Sun

First-class Caribbean food is scarce in London and almost never found in a restaurant as stylish and buzzy as this. Jerk chicken and curried goat are classics. Creole snapper with mango and green peppercorn sauce is an unusual alternative. **Moderate**

The Wells *gastropub with a view* `1 B4`
30 Well Walk, NW3 • 020 7794 3785
>> www.thewellshampstead.co.uk Open lunch & dinner daily

Enjoy the views of leafy Hampstead from the spacious, streamlined first-floor restaurant of this pub, while you savour the menu of well-honed comfort food – rich, calorie-packed and utterly irresistible. For a blow-out, try the classic Chateaubriand with thrice-cooked chips, followed by custard tart. **Moderate**

>> *For an index of restaurants by cuisine, see pp224–6*

Restaurants

Holly Bush *proper pub grub* 1 A5
22 Holly Mount, NW3 • 020 7435 2892
Open noon–11pm daily

A pub since the early 1800s, this building retains the feel of Hampstead when it was a village on the edge of London. There's a log fire, low beams and excellent real ales on tap. Although it's not a gastropub, the pub fare – pies, sausage and mash, fresh prawns – is substantial and of good quality. **Moderate**

Kovalam *great-value, high-quality Indian*
12 Willesden Lane, NW6 • 020 7625 4761
⊖ Kilburn Open lunch & dinner daily

Willesden Lane in Kilburn is something of a mecca for fans of good, cheap South Indian food, and Kovalam is probably the pick of the bunch. The decor may be humble, but the depth of flavour in its superb Keralan dishes is regal – try the breadfruit curry. Many dishes are suitable for vegetarians. **Cheap**

Blueprint Café *European by the river* 11 F5
Design Museum, Shad Thames, SE1 • 020 7378 7031
≫ www.conran.com Open lunch & dinner Mon–Sat, lunch Sun

The twin attractions of this classy restaurant – it's certainly no café – within the Design Museum are expansive views of the Thames and a daily-changing, Italian-leaning menu. The room is a no-nonsense setting for superior peasant food, such as roast partridge with cabbage and bacon. **Expensive**

Champor-Champor *Malaysian fusion* 10 D5
62 Weston Street, SE1 • 020 7403 4600
≫ www.champor-champor.com Open dinner Mon–Sat

Primary colours burst from the walls of this lively little restaurant, reflecting the zesty flavours on the inventive menu. The essence is Malaysian, but with pan-Asian influences. Typical dishes include steamed tilapia with turmeric leaf, crab and coconut bisque, and masala lamb fillet with aubergine mousse. **Moderate**

Tas *uncommonly good Turkish* 10 A5
33 The Cut, SE1 • 020 7928 1444
>> www.tasrestaurant.com
Open all day from noon daily

Here is proof that high-quality Turkish cooking and a contemporary setting can harmonize. The menu is strong on grilled meats and perkily fresh meze, with a huge choice for vegetarians. Add in friendly staff and fair prices, and you have a winner. **Moderate**

Livebait *fish in myriad forms* 10 A5
41–5 The Cut, SE1 • 020 7928 7211
>> www.santeonline.co.uk/livebait
Open all day from noon Mon–Sat

With its cheery tiled interior and booth seating, Livebait looks like a classy fish-and-chip shop. But this won't prepare you for the wonderful menu roving from the simple pleasures of a bowl of cockles to the epicurean heights of oven-roast halibut. **Moderate**

Mesón Don Felipe *authentic Spanish* 10 A5
53 The Cut, SE1 • 020 7928 3237
Open all day from noon Mon–Sat

For many hispanophiles this perennially packed little tapas bar is as close as you can get in London to the real thing. Regulars perch at the huge bar in the middle of the room, while friendly staff distribute melting *bacalao* (deep-fried salt cod), broad beans with ham, and perfect tortilla. **Cheap**

Masters Super Fish *fish & chips* 10 A5
191 Waterloo Road, SE1 • 020 7928 6924
Open dinner Mon, lunch & dinner Tue–Sat

Clad in dark wood and exposed brick, this is much better than the average "chippie". True, you can get a classic cod'n'chips with mushy peas, but there's also fresh Cromer crab and crisp, mustard-coated haddock for the more adventurous. A favoured haunt of London cab drivers – who know a thing or two. **Cheap**

Restaurants

Oxo Tower *fine food and fabulous views* `10 A4`
Top floor, Oxo Tower Wharf, Barge House St, SE1
020 7803 3888
» www.harveynichols.com Open lunch & dinner daily

There are few locations in London as spectacular as the top floor of the Oxo Tower. Floor-to-ceiling glass walls and a 250-ft (90-m) long terrace allow uninterrupted views over the Thames. It's stunning, and yours to admire for the price of a drink at the sleek bar.

Eating here will make a greater dent in your wallet, though the cost is justified by the high standard of modern European food served at the relaxed Brasserie and more formal Restaurant. Lunch at the Brasserie might consist of chilli crab with egg linguine, followed by sea bass and warm halloumi, and a coconut parfait with passion fruit dessert. The refinement of the menu rises in the Restaurant, with such delicacies as warm salad of quail with foie gras and truffle, monkfish with oxtail or pink grapefruit with Campari sorbet. Both venues serve more affordable set lunches. **Expensive**

Roast *British favourites* `10 D5`
The Floral Hall, Borough Market, SE1 • 020 7940 1300
» www.roast-restaurant.com • Open breakfast, lunch & dinner Mon–Fri, 7am–4pm & 6–11pm Sat

Overlooking Borough Market, Roast specializes in modern dishes using traditional produce, such as ox heart with onions, bone marrow and herbs, or pollack with melted shrimp and crab butter. Breakfasts include mulled fruits and excellent kedgeree. **Expensive**

Ransome's Dock *modern European*
35–7 Parkgate Road, SW11 • 020 7223 1611
Train to Clapham Junction
» www.ransomesdock.co.uk
Open lunch & dinner Mon–Sat, lunch only Sun

Perched on the edge of a small inlet off the Thames, Ransome's Dock is noted for its well-sourced ingredients and simple dishes such as slow roast pork belly with raisins and sherry. **Expensive**

Tsunami *way-out Japanese*
5–7 Voltaire Road, SW4 • 020 7978 1610
⊜ Clapham North
Open dinner Mon–Fri, all day (12:30–11:30pm) Sat

Tsunami is one of that rare breed of restaurants that thrill and satisfy in equal proportions. The first surprise is finding such a smart, stylish space just off Clapham's workaday high street. With its ascetically plain decor and nattily attired staff, it has an air of both simplicity and sophistication. A similar balance is found on the menu, which combines classic Japanese cooking – excellent, biting-fresh sashimi, sushi and tempura – with originality and imagination. Witness the mingling of sautéed foie gras with Asian pear and truffle, quail with ginger honey soy, and the green tea tiramisu.

There are parallels between Tsunami and ultra-chic Nobu *(see p38)*, where some of the staff trained, but Tsunami is free of "attitude", and there's no need to book months in advance. **Moderate**

Chez Bruce *bistro by the common*
2 Bellevue Road, SW17 • 020 8672 0114
Train to Wandsworth Common
》 www.chezbruce.co.uk Open lunch & dinner daily

The traditions of French cuisine provide the framework at Bruce Poole's Chez Bruce, which is regularly voted one of London's favourite neighbourhood restaurants. Also expect inspired borrowings from elsewhere in Europe, though, and a sound focus on seasonal ingredients. The menu might include fillet of sea bass with lobster ravioli, beurre blanc, samphire and chives, or rump veal with artichokes, morels, salsa verde and roasting juices. Offal lovers should be delighted with dishes such as lamb's tongue, kidney and sweetbread, but there's always an interesting vegetarian choice too. The seasonal menu is fixed price, but drinks and extras can bump up the bill. The staff are knowledgeable and relaxed, and the sommelier will guide you through the wines, many of which are sold by the glass. **Expensive**

shopping

London's retail landscape is as diverse as the city itself, yielding up traditional tailors and radical fashion designers, antiquarian booksellers and alternative record shops, luxury department stores and gritty markets. Of course, it has its fair share of international chains, but you don't have to travel far off the beaten track to find quirky contemporary boutiques and time-honoured delicatessens.

SHOPPING

In fashion terms, London is known both for its traditions of craftsmanship and for its radical designs, which makes for the kind of eclectic shopping experience I love. I always advise visitors to take a peek inside the historic shops, to sample the period atmosphere and beautifully made goods, but it's the independent boutiques that really get my pulse racing. They have taken off in recent years, offering hot new labels and one-off items made by cutting-edge designers.

Lisa Ritchie

London Classics

Traditional British wares are known for impeccable craftsmanship, and stores such as umbrella purveyor **James Smith & Sons** *(see p67)* are loved for their level of service and knowledge. Established London designers such as **Paul Smith** *(see p88)* and **Margaret Howell** *(see p76)* draw on tailoring heritage to create new British styles.

Shoes and Accessories

London has a long pedigree of shoemaking, and some of the most famous names in footwear – **Jimmy Choo** *(see p81)* and **Patrick Cox** *(see p79)* among them – started here. It also has a history of creating fine leather goods and accessories: try **Smythson** *(see p73)* for diaries, and **Bill Amberg** *(see p85)* and **J&M Davidson** *(see p85)* for well-crafted bags.

Books and Records

London rocks. Head to Notting Hill for shops specializing in rare vinyl, indie rock, reggae and soul, such as **Rough Trade** *(see p85)* and **Honest Jon's** *(see p87)*, or to Soho for dance music. The atmospheric antiquarian bookshops of **Charing Cross Road** and its offshoot **Cecil Court** *(see pp68–9)* welcome collectors and casual browsers alike.

choice shops

Cutting-Edge Fashion

London designers have a reputation for innovation and irreverence alongside a respect for craftsmanship – a case in point is 70s punk stylist Vivienne Westwood. Hot London labels can be found at **b Store** *(see p71)*, **aQuaint** *(see p65)* and **Dover Street Market** *(see p73)*, while, for budding design talent, check out **Portobello Green** *(see p87)*.

Funky Design Finds

Mint *(see p77)* brings together unusual interior goods, much of them British-designed, in a compact space. **Neisha Crosland's** *(see p81)* home and fashion accessories are embellished with her graphic prints, and idiosyncratic **Story** *(see p91)* displays an array of furniture, fabrics, reclaimed items and vintage pieces in an airy studio setting.

Vintage and Retro

Fans of vintage fashion will find a well-stocked hunting ground, especially in Notting Hill and around Brick Lane in the East End. **Rellik** *(see p89)* is one of the capital's best places to find immaculate, high-fashion pieces. The boutiques at **Dover Street Market** *(see p73)* and high street chains such as **Topshop** *(see p72)* have vintage sections.

Floral Street *big names & small boutiques* 9 G3
Cobbled pedestrian street in Covent Garden, WC2
For individual shop details, *see pp214–15*

This winding lane tucked behind Covent Garden Market is packed with well-known fashion stores ranging from young, trendy labels such as **Full Circle**, with their skinny-legged Cult of Men and Cult of Women ranges, to established designer names that include **Paul Smith, Ted Baker, Agnès B, Nicole Farhi** and purveyors of comfy footwear **Camper**. Dotted among these are some one-off shops, such as **Kirk Originals**, which sells colourful, retro-inspired eyewear (at No. 29). Posh combatwear is the theme at **Maharishi**, where a jungle-like interior comes complete with palm trees and mini military helicopters (No. 19a). The clothes mix contemporary styling with inventive variations on camouflage prints. **The Tintin Shop** (No. 34) is devoted to the famous Belgian comic strip, selling books in several languages, posters, T-shirts and other themed items.

Vertigo *original film posters* 9 G3
22 Wellington Street, WC2 • 020 7836 9252
➤➤ www.vertigogalleries.com Open 11–6:30 Mon– Fri, 11–5:30 Sat

This light-filled little gallery showcases original movie posters and "lobby cards" (small posters displayed in American cinemas). The selection and prices range from affordable modern items to rarities going for thousands. For an original gift idea, choose a film from someone's birth year, or one with a British theme.

Aram *iconic modern furniture* 9 G3
110 Drury Lane, WC2 • 020 7557 7557
➤➤ www.aram.co.uk Open 10–6 Mon–Sat (to 7 Thu)

A champion of contemporary design since the 1960s, Aram now has a vast converted warehouse to show off its modern-classic furniture to stunning effect. Wandering around its five floors, admiring iconic pieces by Le Corbusier and Eileen Gray, is like visiting a museum. Indeed, the shop hosts regular exhibitions.

Monmouth Street *girls' pampering zone* `9 F3`

Covent Garden, WC2

For individual shop details, *see pp214–15*

Monmouth Street is rapidly turning into Boutique Central, with a line-up of classy shops. At No. 23 is London's chicest sex shop, **Coco de Mer**, selling beautiful lingerie (some emblazoned with discreet pornographic prints), a range of tasteful sex toys such as arty, coloured-glass dildos, and erotic books. The decor is neo-Victorian with crimson floral wallpaper, and the dressing rooms have a peephole concealed behind a picture through which your partner can spy on you from a hidden chamber next door – very kinky.

American skincare supremo **Kiehl's** is at No. 29. The company's excellent products, based on natural ingredients, are instantly recognizable in their no-frills packaging. Be warned, however – they're far more expensive here than in the US. **Poste Mistress** at Nos. 61–3 has the feel of a 1970s boudoir, with designer shoes from the likes of Angelo Figus and Pucci perched amid kitsch, framed photos and burgundy velvet pouffes.

The talented buyer at **Koh Samui** (Nos. 65–7) always selects exciting pieces from well-known designers (Dries Van Noten, Miu Miu, Clements Ribeiro), plus cutting-edge offerings by up-and-coming talent. The jewellery and accessories are especially creative. Across the street at **aQuaint** (No. 38), Ashley Isham's grown-up, tailored-yet-feminine womenswear hangs side by side with neat modern clothing by British designers Emma Cook and Boyd, and exquisite, expensive frocks by Lanvin.

Earlham Street *bustling street markets* 9 F3

At the Seven Dials intersection, Covent Garden, WC2
For individual shop details, *see pp214–15*

The west end of Earlham Street is packed with market stalls hawking cheap T-shirts and casual clothes. Sprawling over several stalls is **The Wild Bunch** florist, which offers a wide array of good-quality blooms. The shops lining the street are mainly funky fashion chains, including global surf-skate-style brand **Stüssy** at No. 19, futuristic club label **Cyberdog** at No. 9 and expanding British chain **All Saints** at No. 5, which sells cool clothes and jeanswear for men and women.

Adding to the mix is traditional ironmonger **F W Collins & Son** at No. 14, which opened in 1835 when the area still had a reputation as a meeting-place of criminals. A branch of design bookshop **Magma** is at No. 8 *(see also p90)*. At the east end of Earlham Street are the surf/skatewear shops of the **Thomas Neal Centre** and hip young American clothing/home emporium **Urban Outfitters**, at Nos. 42–56.

Neal's Yard Dairy *British cheeses* 9 G3

17 Shorts Gardens, WC2 • 020 7240 5700
▶▶ www.nealsyarddairy.co.uk
Open 11–6:30 Mon–Thu, 10–6:30 Fri & Sat

The very smell of this tiny shop will have cheese-lovers swooning. The counter and shelves groan under the weight of massive whole cheeses. Regional gems by independent producers include Colston Bassett Stilton, Lincolnshire Poacher and Montgomery's Cheddar.

Size? *trendy trainer store* 9 G3

17–19 Neal Street, WC2 • 020 7240 1736
Open 9:30–7:30 (to 8 Thu), noon–6 Sun

Sneaker freaks will be in their natural habitat at this always-busy shop, which sells big names such as Converse, Nike and Lacoste – including limited-edition styles – alongside elusive cult brands. Adidas fans should head for the basement and one of the UK's few official shops dedicated to the label.

Forbidden Planet *sci-fi/fantasy megastore* `9 F2`
179 Shaftesbury Avenue, WC2 • 020 7420 3666
>> www.forbiddenplanet.com Open 10–7 (to 8 Thu), noon–6 Sun

For shoppers with an unhealthy obsession with *Lord of the Rings* or *Star Trek*, this is the place to come for the full range of action figures and videos. Forbidden Planet is the world's largest sci-fi and fantasy retailer, and the London megastore is packed with books and comics. There is even an "adults only" section.

James Smith & Sons *umbrellas* `9 G2`
53 New Oxford Street, WC1 • 020 7836 4731
>> www.james-smith.co.uk Open 9:30–5:25 Mon–Fri, 10–5:25 Sat

This family business has been making umbrellas and canes for over 170 years. The Victorian shop, still with its original signs and fittings, is an attraction in itself. Inside are racks crammed with umbrellas in every pattern – stripes, checks, paisley, frilled parasols – and walking sticks with curious carved handles.

Falkiner Fine Papers *paper supplies* `9 G1`
76 Southampton Row, WC1 • 020 7831 1151
Open 9:30–5:30 Mon–Fri, 10:30–5:30 Sat

Located near St Martins College of Art, Falkiner sells all manner of products relating to paper. There's equipment for making it, quill pens, sketchbooks and shelf upon shelf of individual sheets, from marbled patterns to parquet and bricks for dolls' houses. Japanese silkscreen prints are another line.

Contemporary Wardrobe *vintage wear* `9 G1`
The Horse Hospital, Colonnade, WC1 • 020 7713 7370
>> www.thehorsehospital.com
Open noon–6 Mon–Sat, by appointment

Thousands of vintage street fashions can be found at this hire shop, which shares its site with a venue for avant-garde art and film. Rooting around here could turn up a piece used in the film *Quadrophenia* or a video shoot with Kylie. Some garments are for sale.

Gay's The Word *specialist bookshop* `3 G5`
66 Marchmont Street, WC1 • 020 7278 7654
>> www.gaystheword.co.uk Open 10–6:30 Mon–Sat, 2–6 Sun

The UK's largest gay bookshop has been in business since the late 1970s. Titles cover fiction, philosophy, history, politics, erotica, relationships and emotional issues. Gay detective novels have a section to themselves. Videos and second-hand books are also on sale in this friendly shop.

Eatmyhandbagbitch *cool design* `9 G3`
37 Drury Lane, WC2 • 020 7836 0830
>> www.eatmyhandbagbitch.co.uk
Open 11am–6pm Mon–Sat, or by appointment

An array of original furniture and objects for the home, ranging from 1900 right up to the 1980s, can be found in this wonderful shop. Eatmyhandbagbitch is a real treat for serious collectors of classic and less well-known 20th-century interior design.

Cecil Court *antiquarian books & prints* `9 F3`
Pedestrian lane off Charing Cross Road, WC2
For individual shop details, *see p215*

This narrow street, lined with quirky little shops, is a collector's paradise. **Nigel Williams** at No. 25 special-izes in first editions, with lots of Enid Blyton and P G Wodehouse, while, across the street, **Marchpane** also deals in antique children's titles, especially sumptuously illustrated fairy stories. **P J Hilton** has a good selection of beautifully bound 19th-century literature, and **David Drummond** sells books and ephemera relating to the performing arts.

Continuing the dramatic theme, **Stage Door Prints** (No. 9) has signed photos of stars such as Laurence Olivier, Vivien Leigh, Edith Piaf and Anna Pavlova, plus theatre-related prints. You'll find a wider selection of antiquarian prints – encompassing fish, fashion, maps, the military and much more – at **Storey's** (No. 3). Opposite, **Tindley & Chapman** deals in immaculate first editions of 20th-century fiction.

Charing Cross Road *bookshops* `9 F3`
Road bordering Covent Garden & Soho, WC2
For individual shop details, *see p215*

The name "Charing Cross Road" gets bibliophiles' pulses racing. Together with offshoot Cecil Court *(see left)*, it is London's main centre of new, second-hand, specialist and antiquarian bookshops. Check out the commemorative plaque on the site of the defunct Marks & Co, whose address gave its name to the book and film *84 Charing Cross Road*.

Recently refurbished, the famous **Foyles** stocks everything from popular fiction to academic texts on its five floors. It now also houses London institution **Ray's Jazz** – a music shop, with a café attached where you can dig the tunes – and renowned women's bookshop **Silver Moon**. There's also an art gallery on the premises. Even if you're not buying for children, go and have a look at the live piranhas in the children's department. Across the street is a massive branch of **Borders** with the chain's usual all-embracing selection of magazines, books and CDs. It has a café and comfy chairs for lounging in, too. A large branch of **Blackwell's** bookshop is at No. 100.

Of the second-hand bookshops on Charing Cross Road, many are appealingly ramshackle emporiums, where the pleasure comes from rooting out treasures from the packed, dusty shelves. **Quinto** at No. 48A and **Henry Pordes** at Nos. 58–60 are well reputed. For coffee-table art tomes and scholarly subjects, visit **Shipley** at No. 70. Its sister shop, **Shipley Media**, at No. 80, specializes in photography, film and fashion.

Any Amount of Books *great bookshop* `9 F3`
56 Charing Cross Road, WC2 • 020 7836 3697
>> www.anyamountofbooks.com
Open 10:30am–9:30pm daily

This bookshop sells second-hand books from around the world, the owners making occasional trips to far-flung places to find exciting titles. Some books can be found for as little as £1, while rare editions are worth hundreds. Once inside you'll browse for hours.

Kokon To-Zai *sounds & style* `9 F3`
57 Greek Street, W1 • 020 7434 1316
>> www.kokontozai.com Open 11–7:30 Mon–Sat, noon–6 Sun

Revamp your record collection and your wardrobe at this compact one-stop shop selling cutting-edge clothes and music. Staff man the decks so you can browse to the electro beat. On the rails are street designs for both sexes by local and global talent, as well as the store's own sportswear-influenced line.

Gerry's *wines & spirits* `9 F3`
74 Old Compton Street, W1 • 020 7734 4215/2053
Open 9–6 Mon–Fri, 9–5:30 Sat

This is the place to come if you're looking for an obscure liqueur or spirit – there are over 100 varieties of vodka alone. The shop is crammed with a huge variety of booze from all over Europe, South America and elsewhere, from strawberry-flavoured tequila to absinthe in a bottle shaped like the Eiffel Tower.

The World According To... *hip lines* `9 E3`
4 Brewer Street, W1 • 020 7437 1259
Open 10:30–6:30 Mon–Fri, 11–6:30 Sat

Blink and you'll miss this tiny basement shop in the heart of the red-light district. The names inside couldn't be further from the scene on the street, with Eley Kishimoto, Cacharel and Sonia Rykiel's SONIA line rubbing shoulders with Vivienne Westwood, new London labels and urban sportswear.

Vintage *memorabilia & mags* `9 E3`
39–43 Brewer Street, W1 • 020 7439 8525
>> www.vinmag.com Open 10–8 (to 10pm Fri–Sat), noon–8 Sun

The ground floor is devoted to entertainment memorabilia (Charlie's Angels T-shirts, Bond mousepads). The basement holds 75,000 vintage magazines, organized by decade and theme. In addition to *Picture Post* and *Vogue*, you'll find such obscurities as *The Naturist* and a *Dr Kildare Annual*.

Agent Provocateur *kitsch-sexy lingerie* `9 E3`
6 Broadwick Street, W1 • 020 7439 0229
➤➤ www.agentprovocateur.com
Open 11–7 Mon–Sat (11–8 Thu), 12–5 Sun

The original Soho branch of Agent Provocateur is the best, as it maintains a slightly seedy air that befits the shop's porn-chic image. Staff in pink uniforms sell 1950s pin-up-style underwear as well as accessories such as diamanté-handled riding crops.

Phonica *vinyl-lovers' paradise* `9 E3`
51 Poland Street, W1 • 020 7025 6070
➤➤ www.phonicarecords.com
Open 11:30–7:30 Mon–Wed & Sat, 11:30–8 Thu & Fri

Here there's a counter lined with record decks and 70s lounge chairs to relax on while leafing through back copies of *Jockey Slut*. Among the vinyl, you'll find Afro-beat, electronica, hip hop, nu jazz from the Jazzanova-Compost label and Donna Summer disco heaven.

Lina Stores *traditional Italian deli* `9 E3`
18 Brewer Street, W1 • 020 7437 6482
Open 8–6:30 Mon–Fri, 8–5:30 Sat

A wonderful family-run deli, Lina Stores is a Soho institution. Besides selling traditional Italian stock items such as olive oil, parma ham, salami, a great variety of cheeses and *bottarga* (flakes of dried fish roe for sprinkling on pasta), they also make their own fresh pasta, pesto and sausages.

b Store *radical designer fashion* `8D3`
24A Savile Row, W1 • 020 7734 6846
➤➤ www.buddhahood.co.uk Open 10:30–6:30 Mon–Fri, 10–6 Sat

This small boutique for men and women sells its own range of funky footwear – Buddhahood – alongside cutting-edge designs from Peter Jensen, Boudicca and Michelle Lowe-Holder. Although the shop attracts such lofty clientele as model Kate Moss and pop princess Kylie, the mood is pleasantly down to earth.

Shopping

Newburgh Street *Carnaby's cooler cousin* `9 E3`
Cobbled pedestrian street, W1
For individual shop details, *see p216*

Running parallel to brash Carnaby Street, this little strip has a more independent spirit. Among the line-up of small street-fashion outlets is **Bond**, which stocks a range of urbanwear from labels such as Alife, Stüssy, Obey and Adict. Neighbouring **Onitsuka Tiger** sells classic sportshoes, like the Mexico 66. **Jess James** offers modern jewellery from up-and-coming and well-known designers – displayed in innovative ways, such as in a long leather case with portholes which light up as you approach. **The Dispensary** sells laid-back clothes on the wearable side of fashionable for both sexes, from designers local and far-flung. Tiny perfumery **Scent Systems** stocks unusual fragrances and skincare, many of them not available elsewhere in the UK. These include the German products Just Pure, to be used in accordance with the cycles of the moon.

Liberty *English-eccentric department store* `8 D3`
210–20 Regent Street, W1 • 020 7734 1234
>> www.liberty.co.uk
Open 10–7 Mon–Sat (to 8 Thu), noon–6 Sun

London's quirkiest department store maintains its rich history while embracing the 21st century. Tudor House contains the global furniture, Oriental rugs and printed fabrics that made Liberty's name, while Regent House has extravagant lingerie and ultra-fashionable shoes.

Oki-ni *limited-edition designs* `9 E3`
25 Savile Row, W1 • 020 7494 1716
>> www.oki-ni.com Open 10–6 Mon–Sat (to 7 Thu)

A totally original concept, Oki-ni is a British-Japanese design group that collaborates with such diverse labels as Duffer of St George, Adidas, Paul Smith, Levi's, Evisu and Zakee Shariff to create exclusive garments. The shop is more a showroom than a retail site, as most items have to be ordered from the website.

Topshop *fashion superstore* `9 E2`
36–8 Great Castle Street, W1 • 020 7636 7700
>> www.topshop.co.uk
Open 9–8 Mon–Sat (to 9 Thu), noon–6 Sun

"The world's largest fashion store" attracts 180,000 shoppers a week. Blaring music and video screens may be for kids, but stylists trawl it for cheap garments. The basement Boutique has affordable pieces by Preen, Maria Chen-Pascual and others.

Georgina Goodman *unique shoes* `8 D5`
12–14 Shepherd Street, W1 • 020 7499 8599
>> www.georginagoodman.com Open 10–6 Mon–Sat

Goodman's sculptural, hand-painted shoes (created to individual specifications in the workshop downstairs) are wearable works of art with pricetags to match, but there is a more affordable, ready-to-wear line, too. Also on sale in the airy, gallery-style space are baby bootees, bags and other leather goods.

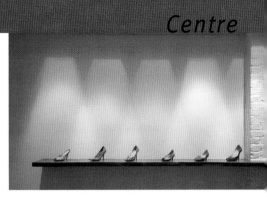

Smythson *impeccable stationery* `8 D3`
40 New Bond Street, W1 • 020 7629 8558
>> www.smythson.com
Open 9:30–6 Mon, Tue, Wed & Fri, 10–7 Thu, 10–6 Sat

This posh stationer is great for gifts, especially leather-bound notebooks in a range of classic colours, some embossed with witty titles such as *Blondes Brunettes Redheads*, as well as the more practical *Travel Notes*. Other wonderfully traditional accessories include visitors' books and travel wallets.

REN *British natural body products* `8 D4`
19 Shepherd Market, W1 • 020 7495 5960
>> www.renskincare.com
Open 11–6:30 Mon–Sat (often closed 3–4)

Ren means "clean" in Swedish, reflecting the philosophy behind this British hair- and skincare brand. Products such as the Moroccan rose otto shower wash and the grapefruit and jojoba cream are made without pore-blocking additives and have lovely scents.

Dover Street Market *high/low fashion* `8 D4`
17–18 Dover Street, W1 • 020 7491 8460
Open 11–6 Mon–Sat (to 7 Thu)

A new concept by Comme des Garçons designer Rei Kawakubo, this six-floor space has the rough-edged feel of an indoor market. Comme collections are displayed alongside other upmarket labels such as Alaïa and Lanvin, a vintage concession and curiosities which include Victorian taxidermy.

Traditional British Brands

Some bastions of British conservatism have recently been given the kiss of life. **Burberry** has been transformed from staid raincoat manufacturer to "it" label. And, although the hallowed check has gained popularity among football fans, the macs are still top-quality, and the more exclusive catwalk line, available at the New Bond Street flagship, exudes urban chic. The traditional knitwear brand **Pringle** now has cool variations on its famous argyle sweaters and neat, classic separates. **Mulberry** has shaken off its former frumpiness with contemporary takes on English country style: the renowned bags in mock-croc leather and durable, synthetic Scotchgrain are now streamlined with modern shapes. All outlets on New Bond St; *see p227.*

Shopping

Poste *trendy men's shoes* `8 D3`
10 South Molton Street, W1 • 020 7499 8002
Open 10–7 Mon–Sat, noon–6 Sun

With its Chesterfield sofa and framed pictures of vintage pin-ups and sporting heroes, Poste has the air of a gentlemen's club. Most of the shoes are updates of classics by designers such as Jeffery-West, Paul Smith and Dries Van Noten, with a selection of fashionable trainers by the likes of Adidas and Puma.

Browns *international designer boutique* `8 D3`
23–7 South Molton Street, W1 • 020 7514 0000
» www.brownsfashion.com Open 10–6:30 Mon–Sat (to 7 Thu)

The mother of all London boutiques has been in business for over 30 years, occupying five inter-connecting shops. The mood is decidedly grown-up, with Dries Van Noten, Lanvin, Alaia and an entire floor devoted to Jil Sander. Across the street, black-mirrored Browns Focus showcases young hip labels.

Spymaster *espionage emporium* `8 C2`
3 Portman Square, W1 • 020 7486 3885
» www.spymaster.co.uk Open 9:30–6 Mon–Fri, 10–5 Sat

Aspiring James Bonds will love this store, which caters to amateur sleuths, government departments and law-enforcement agencies. All your espionage needs are catered for, from trained sniffer dogs and armoured cars to shark repellent and a nifty bug detector disguised as a pen. Eat your heart out, Q.

N Peal *indulgent cashmere* `9 E4`
37 & 71–2 Burlington Arcade, W1 • 020 7493 5378
» www.npeal.com Open 9:30–6 Mon–Sat

A resident of London's famous Burlington Arcade since 1936, N Peal has managed to move with the times. The range of cashmere in its two tiny shops (women's at No. 37, men's at 71–2) is impressive, from classic rollnecks and cardies to younger, street-inspired styles in the more affordable npealworks collection.

Stella McCartney *cool designerwear* `8 D4`
30 Bruton Street, W1 • 020 7518 3100
» www.stellamccartney.com Open 10–6 Mon–Sat (to 7 Thu)

A spacious Mayfair townhouse is a suitably glamorous setting for McCartney's figure-skimming dresses, slim-fitting suits and separates in seductive fabrics. The non-leather shoes are displayed in a parlour deco-rated with wallpaper created by the designer herself. Vegetarian footwear has never been so sexy.

Selfridges *department store heaven* `8 C3`

400 Oxford Street, W1 • 0870 837 7377
>> www.selfridges.com Open 10–8 Mon,
9:30–8 Tue, Wed, Fri & Sat, 9:30–9 Thu, noon–6 Sun

Look out, Harrods; watch your back, Harvey Nicks, because Selfridges is a serious contender for London's best department store. Constantly introducing new labels and innovations, the Oxford Street giant can truly be said to have all the bases covered. Whether you're looking for the latest bestseller, a new iBook or a vintage frock, you're likely to find it in this retail universe.

The fashion department embraces almost every high street brand as well as emerging design talent. The cosmetics hall on the ground floor takes in the big names and cult imports from Europe and the US, while a branch of modern holistic chemist **Farmacia** offers organic options on the fifth. The food hall features cuisine from around the globe; the shoe department has been revamped with glamorous mini salons of exclusive labels **Jimmy Choo** *(see also p81)* and YSL; there's an **Agent Provocateur** outpost *(see also p71)* in the massive lingerie section; and the expanded sports department includes must-have surfing and skateboard labels.

The slick Superbrands section has also created a buzz. Accessed through a red resin tunnel, it consists of eight hot designers, including **Stella McCartney**, **Alexander McQueen** and **Balenciaga**, grouped around a branch of sumptuous, souk-style Moroccan restaurant **Mômo** *(see also p38)*, which provides respite from traipsing round the store's six massive floors.

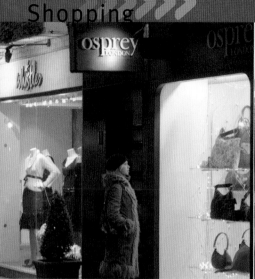

St Christopher's Place *shopping oasis* `8 C3`
Pedestrian square, W1
For individual shop details, *see pp226–9*

Opposite Bond Street Tube station, a narrow alleyway leading off Oxford Street (Gees Court) widens into a hidden square with shops and eateries. This appealing enclave features a modern fountain and is dominated by a large branch of Italian gourmet café chain **Carluccio's,** where you can also pick up all manner of tasty Italian ingredients and snacks to take away from the deli counter. Drinkers from the pub opposite spill out onto the pavement, and you can often catch live jazz on summer nights. Shopping

highlights include a branch of **Mulberry** (11–12 Gees Court; *see also p73*), for classic English attire with contemporary styling, and the spacious flagship of women's chain **Whistles** (12 St Christopher's Place), which stocks hot designers alongside the shop's own-label – signature styles include bias-cut dresses and modern tailoring.

Next door, **Osprey** is the place for mid-priced, classic British-designed handbags (structured shapes in mock croc are a key look). There's also a branch of Scandinavian fabric company **Marimekko** (Nos. 16–17), which is known for its bright abstract patterns, featuring on everything from bags to bedding.

Margaret Howell *updated British classics* `8 C2`
34 Wigmore Street, W1 • 020 7009 9009
»» www.margarethowell.co.uk Open 10–6 Mon–Sat (to 7 Thu)

This vast, gallery-style space showcases the designer's collections for men and women, and a selection of simple tableware and vintage and reissued post-War furniture. The clothes are best described as relaxed modern classics, made of quality British fabrics suited to the national climate, such as tweed and cashmere.

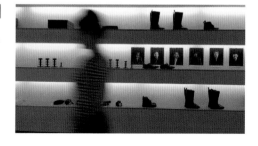

Mint *unusual designer homewares* `8 C2`
70 Wigmore Street, W1 • 020 7224 4406
Open 10:30–6:30 Mon–Sat (to 7:30 Thu)

Mint brings together an international collection of furniture and homewares, a mix of the ultra-modern and the antique, made by both established designers and recent graduates. Pottery and glassware are hand-made and appealingly asymmetrical. Even tea towels are elevated from the ordinary by lovely prints.

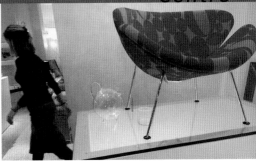

Paul Rothe *traditional delicatessen* `8 C2`
35 Marylebone Lane, W1 • 020 7935 6783
Open 8–6 Mon–Fri, 11:30–approx 5:30 Sat

Established in 1900, this old-fashioned deli is run by the original Rothe's grandson and great-grandson, who wear dapper white coats. Chunky soup and neatly cut sandwiches are served on proper china, while the "English and foreign provisions" include preserves, traditional sweets and Scottish biscuits.

Calmia *yoga emporium & spa retreat* `8 C1`
52–4 Marylebone High St, W1 • 020 7224 3585
›› www.calmia.com
Open 10–7 Mon–Sat, 10–6 Sun

Yoga has never been so chic. While achieving inner peace, you can look fabulous in expensive gear from supermodel Christy Turlington's Nuala range or DKNY Pure. Everything related to yoga is here, from mats and relaxation tapes to candles and organic skincare. Luxurious spa treatments are available downstairs.

Sixty 6 *creative mix 'n' match for women* `8 C1`
66 Marylebone High Street, W1 • 020 7224 6066
Open 10:30–6:30 Mon–Sat, 1–5 Sun

Embroidery and beading abound at this shop celebrating eclectic, feminine style. Separates are often paired up in unusual combinations, providing plenty of inspiration. Designs by the likes of Temperley, Megan Park and Roland Mouret are supplemented by pretty scarves and bags.

›› *Newly fashionable Marylebone High Street also has a branch of the Conran Shop (see p82)*

Shopping

Daunt Books *elegant shop for travellers* `8 C1`
83 Marylebone High Street, W1 • 020 7224 2295
Open 9–7:30 Mon–Sat (to 7 Thu), 11–6 Sun

Arguably London's most beautiful bookshop, Daunt
retains its original Edwardian character, with oak
shelves and green-shaded lamps. General titles are in
the front; the galleried rear conservatory is devoted
to travel and related fiction organized by country. It's a
great place to browse even if you're not planning a trip.

Skandium *nordic interiors* `8 C1`
86–7 Marylebone High Street, W1 • 020 7935 2077
›› www.skandium.com Open 10–6:30 Mon–Wed,
Fri & Sat, 10 –7 Thu, 11–5 Sun

This flagship shop offers the best of Scandinavia's
clean, contemporary design under one roof. Compare
the modern-classic furniture by Alvar Aalto and Arne
Jacobsen with the functional yet fashionable tableware, accessories, books and jewellery.

Kabiri *diverse jewellery* `8 C1`
37 Marylebone High Street, W1 • 020 7224 1808
›› www.kabiri.co.uk
Open 10–6:30 Mon–Sat, noon–5 Sun

An exciting collection of contemporary jewellery, much
of it the work of British designers, is packed into this
small shop. Jewellery by sought-after designers is
displayed alongside pieces by recent graduates, so
prices vary from £30 to several thousand.

La Fromagerie *divine deli* `8 C2`
2–4 Moxon Street, W1 • 020 7935 0341
›› www.lafromagerie.co.uk Open 10:30–7:30 Mon,
8–7:30 Tue–Fri, 9–7 Sat, 10–6 Sun

Known for its "cave" packed with cheeses from
independent producers across Europe, this rustic-
modern shop also sells condiments, bread, coffee,
wines and charcuterie. Sample these at the in-store
café, or ask for a picnic box to take to Regent's Park.

Prestat *high-class chocolatier* `9 E4`
14 Princes Arcade, SW1 • 020 7629 4838
» www.prestat.co.uk Open 9:30–6 Mon–Fri, 10–5 Sat

This tiny shop looks like a chocolate box itself, its shelves covered in fabulously packaged, handmade confectionery. Choose from traditional mint wafers, rose and violet creams and fondants, or such new-fangled sweet treats as banoffee truffles, presented in old-fashioned boxes with flamboyant hues.

Patrick Cox *slick designer shoes* `14 B2`
129 Sloane Street, SW1 • 020 7730 8886
» www.patrickcox.co.uk Open 10–6 (to 7 Wed), noon–6 Sun

The Canadian designer launched his label in London in the 1980s and has recently revitalized the French brand Charles Jourdan. Shoes for men and women are on the flashy side, with mod and punk influences, bright colours and glitzy trims. The diffusion range, Wannabe, offers basics with a designer edge.

Jo Malone *luxury skincare & fragrances* `14 B2`
150 Sloane Street, SW1 • 020 7730 2100
» www.jomalone.co.uks Open 9:30–6 Mon, Tue & Sat, 9:30–7 Wed–Fri, noon–5 Sun

Gorgeous scents greet you upon entering this classy store. The skincare range is simple yet effective, while fragrances are based on delectable ingredients such as orange blossom, nutmeg, ginger – even coffee. Enjoy a sample with a complimentary hand massage.

Maria Grachvogel *glamorous dresses* `14 B2`
162 Sloane Street, SW1 • 020 7245 9331
» www.mariagrachvogel.com Open 10–6 Mon–Sat (to 7 Wed)

Popular with the crème of Hollywood, Grachvogel's sophisticated evening dresses celebrate the female form with simple, body-skimming lines, sensuous fabrics and subtle detailing of feathers or sequins. In this glamorous, pink-walled shop, you'll also find the designer's collection of understated yet sexy daywear.

Shopping

Elizabeth Street · *sophisticated shopping* · `14 C2`

Off Eaton Square, SW1
For individual shop details, see pp227–9

A short stroll from Knightsbridge is this attractive street with a diverse selection of appealing shops. The friendly perfumery **Les Senteurs** at No. 71 sells unusual European fragrances, such as Annick Goutal and Parfums Caron. If you've bagged a ticket to Ascot or just want to turn heads with an exquisite trilby or extravagant, feathered creation, visit celebrated hatter **Philip Treacy** at No. 69. Across the street at No. 46 is wonderful French bakery **Poilâne**, where you can buy authentic croissants, fruit tarts and rustic loaves

– at a price. At No. 42 is the bright, cheerful shop of British designer **Tracey Boyd**, where girlish strappy dresses, cute short-sleeved blouses and flared skirts in fun patterns are strengths. Jeweller **Erickson Beamon** at No. 38 is a long-standing favourite never long out of the fashion press. Dramatically cascading gold chains and beads make for a strong signature look.

If you're flagging, have a cup of the best hot chocolate you've ever tasted at **The Chocolate Society** shop and café at No. 36 – the society is dedicated to promoting high-quality chocolate. Opposite, at No. 45, is gorgeous modern florist **Woodhams**, which is worth visiting just to breathe the scented air.

Anya Hindmarch · *personalized bags* · `14 B2`

15–17 Pont Street, SW1 • 020 7838 9177
» www.anyahindmarch.com Open 10–6 Mon–Sat (to 7 Wed)

Hindmarch is known for classic bags printed with striking images. You can have one made up with your own photo. She also makes impeccable leather bags, including the popular double-handled Ebury, which you can have embossed inside with a personal message. Dainty shoes are also on offer.

Lulu Guinness *head-turning bags & more* `14 B2`
3 Ellis Street, SW1 • 020 7823 4828
>> www.luluguinness.com Open 10–6 Mon–Fri, 11–6 Sat

With its nostalgic illustrations and vintage fashion ads, this shop's decor is as striking as the witty handbags on display. Guinness's creations include a flower pot bursting with fabric roses and an embroidered circus tent complete with performing seal. Her retro-look cosmetics range is also sold.

Neisha Crosland *contemporary fabrics* `14 A3`
8 Elystan Street, SW3 • 020 7584 7988
>> www.neishacrosland.com Open 10–5:30 Mon–Sat

Neisha Crosland started out designing textiles and has branched out into clothes (through her Ginka fashion label), accessories and home furnishings, including a range of gorgeous wallpapers and quirky furniture. What links such disparate products is the designer's striking semi-abstract, semi-natural prints.

Joseph *high-class urban separates* `13 H3`
77 Fulham Road, SW3 • 020 7823 9500
Open 10–6:30 Mon–Sat (to 7 Wed), noon–5 Sun

Joseph's de luxe basics, especially the well-cut trousers, have devoted fans. This minimalist flagship sells his collection alongside pieces from Prada, YSL and Marni; the basement is devoted to designer shoes. Across Draycott Street, Joseph Essentials, Gigi boutique and Joe's Cafe complete the colony.

Jimmy Choo *celebrated designer heels* `14 A3`
32 Sloane Street, SW1 • 020 7823 1051
>> www.jimmychoo.com Open 10–6 (to 7 Wed), noon–5 Sun

This spacious London flagship, with plush couches for luxurious lounging, is devoted to Jimmy Choo's fabulous footwear and handbags. The sleek styles are subtle enough not to date next season – essential when you're splashing out hundreds. The bridal range caters for those who demand the best on their big day.

>> *Harvey Nichols' top floor restaurant and bar is an ideal stop-off during Knightsbridge shopping* (see p83) `81`

The Conran Shop *Sir Terence's place* `14 A2`

Michelin House, 81 Fulham Rd, SW3 • 020 7589 7401
>> www.conran.com Shop open 10–6 Mon, Tue & Fri, 10–7 Wed
& Thu, 10–6:30 Sat, noon–6 Sun. Bibendum restaurant lunch
& dinner daily; Oyster Bar all day from noon daily

Iconic designer and entrepreneur Terence Conran has housed his London flagship in the magnificent former HQ of Michelin Tyres. This curious Art Deco building, which features stained-glass panels depicting the Michelin Man and is crowned with lights in the form of stacked tyres, is also home to Conran's acclaimed Bibendum restaurant on the first floor (expensive modern European cuisine). For the best views of the architectural curiosity, enter via the front portico with its picturesque flower stall and cart selling crustacea and fresh fish. This entrance is also the setting for the tiled Oyster Bar (less formal, but no cheaper, than the main restaurant).

In the shop, a more affordable line of contemporary furniture, Content by Conran, is now sold alongside the main collection of classic modernist designs. In fact, there are many reasonably priced items for home, garden and office. There's also a selection of high-tech gadgets, including the latest cameras, and a good range of bath products, coffee-table books and high-quality children's toys.

Kate Kuba *high-fashion footwear* `14 B3`
22 Duke of York Sq, King's Road, SW3 • 020 7259 0011
>> www.katekuba.co.uk Open 10–6:30 Mon, Tue, Thu,
Fri & Sat, 10–7 Wed, noon–6 Sun

Stock in this spacious, contemporary branch runs
from basic loafers to jewelled killer heels. Divas
Mary J Blige and Beyoncé are fans of the flamboyant
end of the footwear, while flashy variations on the
cowboy boot are a perennial favourite here.

Oliver Sweeney *men's shoes* `14 B3`
29 King's Road, SW3 • 020 7730 3666
>> www.oliversweeney.com Open 10–7 (to 8 Wed), noon–6 Sun

A combination of comfort, craftsmanship and cool
has made the shoes of choice for David Beckham,
Brad Pitt and Noel Gallagher. A wide range of
traditional and more cutting-edge styles is available
(including smart leather trainers), all made on
Sweeney's supportive Anatomical Last.

Korres *natural Greek skincare* `14 A3`
124 King's Road, SW3 • 020 7581 6455
>> www.korres.com Open 10–7 Mon–Sat, noon–6 Sun

This long, narrow shop is stocked with the Athenian
company's products for skin and hair, all in vivid
packaging. Tantalizing aromas emanate from lotions
based on olives, rosemary and other natural plant
extracts characteristic of Greece. Anti-cellulite creams
and sun milks are part of the range.

Department Stores
London has excellent department stores. In Knightsbridge, you really can buy anything in **Harrods**,
where even the chandeliers are dripping with grapes.
Nearby at sophisticated **Harvey Nichols** the focus is
on designer fashion; ladies who lunch love the Fifth
Floor restaurant at "Harvey Nicks". On Piccadilly,
elegant **Fortnum & Mason** is famous for its food
hall, staffed by frock-coated assistants and selling
such oddities as dried edible insects among the
quaintly packaged teas and jams. A short stroll up
Bond Street leads to **Fenwick**, which has the feel of
a boutique and is renowned for accessories. On
Oxford Street, **John Lewis** has affordable basics,
while **Selfridges** *(see p75)* steals the show. For all
shop details, *see p226.*

Shopping

Designers Guild *modern homewares* `14 A4`
267 & 277 King's Road, SW3 • 020 7351 5775
>> www.designersguild.com Open 10–6 Mon–Sat,
noon–5 Sun (fabric shop closed on Sun) ✓

Who says modern design has to be muted and mini-
mal? Tricia Guild's contemporary emporium explodes
with colour and pattern. There are cushions, bedding,
funky fashion accessories, furniture, a children's
range, stationery, bath products and design books.

Antiquarius *antiques emporium* `14 A4`
131–41 King's Road, SW3 • 020 7351 5353
>> www.antiquarius.co.uk Open 10–6 Mon–Sat

Many of the stalls behind the green awnings of
Antiquarius sell antique furniture, but there are other
smaller treasures to be found, too. A few antique
jewellery stalls at the front are worth a browse; otherwise go to the back room for rare finds such as vintage
Louis Vuitton luggage and original movie posters.

Space.NK *cult cosmetics and a spa* `7 F3`
127–31 Westbourne Grove, W2 • 020 7727 8063
>> www.spacenk.com Open 11–7 Mon, 10–7 Tue, Fri, Sat,
10–8 Wed & Thu, noon–6 Sun

This capacious branch of the beauty-products empire
has a spa on the ground floor, offering luxurious
treatments. Upstairs there is a vast array of cosmetics
from around the world, as well as Space.NK's own
range, which includes grooming for the boys.

202 *lifestyle shop and café* `7 F3`
202 Westbourne Grove, W11 • 020 7792 6888
>> www.nicolefarhi.com Open 8:30–6 (from 10 Mon), 10–5 Sun

Nicole Farhi's "lifestyle" store brings together an airy,
French-style café buzzing with beautiful people, selected pieces from Farhi's collections for both men and
women (trademarks are relaxed separates in natural
fabrics, chunky sweaters and sheepskin coats), home
accessories and a smattering of antique furniture.

Bill Amberg *leather goods* `7 E2`

21–2 Chepstow Corner, W2 • 020 7727 3560
>> www.billamberg.com
Open 10–6 Mon–Sat (to 7 Thu), 11–4 Sun

Long-established leather designer Bill Amberg
produces unfussy, high-quality bags and accessories
in calfskin, suede and bridle leather. There are also
sheepskin-lined baby slings, and, for hunters, gun
cases and a cartridge belt.

Miller Harris *exquisite London perfumery* `7 E3`

14 Needham Road, W11 • 020 7221 1545
>> www.millerharris.com Open 10–4 Mon & Tue, 10–6 Wed–Sat

Lyn Harris trained in Grasse – the perfume capital on
the French Riviera – before opening this London shop.
Her gorgeous scents have a complexity that transcends
most department store fragrances, yet the prices are
comparable. You may even have your own bespoke
perfume created if you can wait several weeks.

Rough Trade *legendary indie record shop* `6 D3`

130 Talbot Road, W11 • 020 7229 8541
>> www.roughtrade.com
Open 10–6:30 Mon–Sat, noon–5 Sun

Established nearly 30 years ago, Rough Trade was an
essential part of the London punk scene. It still flies
the indie flag, offering everything from electro-pop to
alt country. The walls are covered with gig fliers, and
hand-written notes point out staff recommendations.

J&M Davidson *neo-classic bags & clothes* `6 D3`

42 Ledbury Road, W11 • 020 7313 9532
>> www.jandmdavidson.com Open 10–6 Mon–Sat, noon–5 Sun

John and Monique are best known for their beautifully crafted bags. Based on classic shapes such as
the bowling bag, and executed in offbeat colours
and animal skins, they have an air of nostalgia.
The Anglo-French duo also design tasteful, retro-
influenced clothes and home accessories.

>> *When shopping in West London, take a break in Holland Park (see p176)*

J W Beeton *eye-catching apparel*   `6 D3`
48–50 Ledbury Rd, W11 • 020 7229 8874
Open 10:30–6 Mon–Fri, 10–6 Sat, noon–5 Sun

The look is fashionable yet individual at this small boutique, where you'll find Fake London's quirky takes on British classics rubbing shoulders on the rails with unusual patterned pieces from Panepinto, a label by an ex-Marni designer. Accessories from emerging home-grown talent add to the mix.

Simon Finch Art *gallery & shop*   `6 C2`
319 Portobello Road, W10 • 020 8962 8620
>> www.simonfinchart.com Open 10–6 Mon–Sat

The latest venture from one of Britain's most successful rare book dealerships doubles as a gallery in a contemporary space on the northern reaches of Portobello Road. The shop sells art and photography books as well as concert posters, graffiti prints, rare gallery catalogues and graphic novels.

Tonic *laidback clothing*   `6 D3`
276 Portobello Road, W10 • 020 8960 8216
>> www.tonicuk.com
Open 10–6 Mon–Fri, 11–6 Sat & Sun

Tonic is a clothing store with plenty of cool threads for men and women. At their sister store at 291 Portobello Road, you'll find labels like Diesel, John Smedley and G-Star. The look is relaxed with a heavy emphasis on denim.

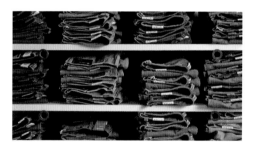

Duchamp *flamboyant men's accessories*   `6 D3`
75 Ledbury Rd, W11 • 020 7243 3970
>> www.duchamp.co.uk Open 10–6 Mon–Sat

Modern dandies will delight in Duchamp's flashy wares. The range of cufflinks is huge, from mini abstract artworks in painted enamel to extravagant creations studded with jewel-bright Swarovski crystals. Ties in contemporary patterns and shirts with flamboyant prints will have peacocks strutting with pride.

Intoxica! *rare vinyl in kitsch setting* `6 D3`

231 Portobello Road, W11 • 020 7229 8010
>> www.intoxica.co.uk
Open 10:30–6:30 Mon–Sat, noon–5 Sun

A Polynesian *tiki*-hut interior with a model hula-dancer provides a bizarre backdrop to rare vinyl pop, jazz, ska, reggae and soul from the 50s to the 90s. Amid the surf, funk and punk are oddities such as *We're the Banana Splits* and the soundtrack to *Vixen*.

Honest Jon's *black music specialist* `6 D3`

278 Portobello Road, W10 • 020 8969 9822
>> www.honestjons.com
Open 10–6 Mon–Sat, 11–5 Sun

This shop has been a fixture of the Portobello scene since 1974, selling a combination of vinyl and CDs. On the ground floor you'll find reggae, funk, soul, hip-hop and R&B; head downstairs for jazz, blues, Portuguese fado, African pop and Indian classical.

Portobello Green *designer enclave* `6 C2`

Arcade at Ladbroke Grove end of Portobello Road
For individual shop details, *see p226–9;*
see also Streetlife *p165*

Nestling under the Westway, this arcade looks uninspiring but is nevertheless home to some very interesting shops. There is also a buzzing market in the courtyard on Fridays and Saturdays, with stalls selling new and vintage clothes. The arcade's most celebrated resident is avant-garde design duo **Preen** at Unit 5 (open Thu–Sat only), whose deconstructed, punky clothes often feature dangling straps and buckles. At **Suite 20** (Unit 20, closed Wed), you'll find retro-inspired separates and bags, some made in original 60s and 70s fabrics. The floaty, patterned chiffon and embroidered silk tops and dresses at **Red Hot** (Unit 9, closed Mon) have been seen on numerous celebrities. **Bedstock** (Unit 26) sells camp cushions and bedlinen decorated with everything from cute kittens to Carmen Miranda and Mao.

Shopping

Bamford & Sons *rich boys' toys* 6 D3
79–81 Ledbury Road, W11 • 020 7792 9350
>> www.bamfordandsons.com
Open 10–6 Mon–Sat, noon–5 Sun

Bamford's updated classic clothes and accessories
for men and boys – in fabrics such as pure linen,
cashmere and "eco leather" – are paired with
gadgets such as customized vintage Rolexes and
limited-edition iPods in a male-centred style fest.

Coco Ribbon *girly emporium* 6 C3
21 Kensington Park Road, W11 • 020 7229 4904
>> www.cocoribbon.com
Open 10–6:30 (to 6 Sat), 12:30–5:30 Sun

Half the stock is Australian, and much is embroidered,
frilled or adorned with feathers. You'll find sequined
cushions, glam costume jewellery, designer dresses
and books such as *The Lazy Girl's Guide to a Fabulous
Body* displayed on antique boudoir furniture.

Paul Smith *all the designer's collections* 6 D4
120 & 122 Kensington Park Road, W11 • 020 7727 3553
>> www.paulsmith.co.uk
Open 10–6:30 Mon–Thu, 10–6:30 Fri & Sat

In this rambling stucco house, Smith's exquisite
classic-with-a-twist men's and women's collections
are draped artlessly over antique tables or hung in
oversized wardrobes. The Playroom displays
children's clothes alongside toys.

Marilyn Moore *funky, feminine knitwear* 6 C3
7 Elgin Crescent, W11 • 020 7727 5577
Open 10–6 Mon–Sat

Marilyn Moore worked for Jaeger before launching her
own label, so it's not surprising her collection includes
modern interpretations of British classics. While the
main focus in-store is on luxurious knitwear – ribbon-
trimmed cashmere, or vintage-look argyle – there's
also a range of updated traditional separates.

Graham & Green *eclectic home stores* `6 C3`
4 & 10 Elgin Crescent, W11 • 020 7727 4594
» www.grahamandgreen.co.uk
Open 10–6 Mon–Sat, 11:30–5:30 Sun

A popular source of inspiration for magazine interior stylists, these two family-run shops are a global jumble of furniture and oddments. Mongolian lambswool cushions, silk kimonos, Venetian mirrors and vintage-style radios are among the offerings.

The Cross *chic lifestyle boutique* `6 C4`
141 Portland Road, W11 • 020 7727 6760
Open 11–5:30 Mon–Sat

This unassuming, white-painted boutique attracts devoted fashion folk. The ground floor is packed with cult-brand toiletries, children's clothes and toys, while downstairs there are feminine separates from such designers as Anna Sui and Rozae Nichols. Sister shop Cross The Road, for interiors and gifts, is at No. 139.

Rellik *vintage designer gear* `6 C1`
8 Golborne Road, W10 • 020 8962 0089
Open 10–6 Tue–Sat

This is an outpost of fabulous vintage in a wasteland of housing estates (the name plays on the Trellick Tower opposite, and spells "killer" backwards). London fashion celebrities are often spotted scanning the 1970s Liberty-print frocks and accessories by Zandra Rhodes, Vivienne Westwood and others.

Chain Stores

Global fashion chains rub shoulders on every major shopping street in the capital, but there are some British labels that stand out from the crowd. Popular **Jigsaw** bridges the gap between budget and designer, with well-made, feminine womenswear. Younger, hipper and cultivating an irreverent image with its double-entendre name is **FCUK**, which offers high-quality casual clothes for both sexes. The **Karen Millen** empire has built on the enduring success of her sharp, sexy suits and figure-flattering dresses. And let's not forget good old **Marks & Spencer:** as well as its excellent lingerie ranges, it has harnessed designer talent to great effect in its Autograph and Per Una collections. For individual shop details, *see pp226–9.*

Saloon *style shop* `4 A4`
23 Arlington Way, EC1 • 020 7278 4497
» www.saloonshop.co.uk
Open 11–7 Mon–Sat

Unusual patterns and colours are the unifying factors in the medley of stock at this boutique. There are clothes by independent designers, handmade jewellery, Marimekko homewares, unusual stationery and one-off pieces by product designers.

Lara Bohinc 107 *super-chic jewellery* `5 E5`
51 Hoxton Square, N1 • 020 7684 1465
» www.larabohinc107.co.uk Open 10–6:30 Mon–Fri only

Slovenian-born designer Bohinc creates unusual jewellery in precious metals ranging from delicate, finely detailed pieces to dramatic geometric styles. Her store is the epitome of arty chic, set in ground-breaking designer Alexander McQueen's former studio next to the cool White Cube Gallery.

Hoxton Boutique *edgy urban chic* `5 E5`
2 Hoxton Street, N1 • 020 7684 2083
» www.hoxtonboutique.co.uk
Open 10–6 Mon–Fri, 11–5 Sat, noon–5 Sun

This boutique fits in well with Hoxton's painfully hip bars. As well as urbanwear by cutting-edge designers such as Vivienne Westwood and Eley Kishimoto, there's the shop's own label, characterized by directional design and printed pieces with a punky feel.

Magma *modern design bookshop* `10 A1`
117–19 Clerkenwell Road, EC1 • 020 7242 9503
» www.magmabooks.com Open 10–7 Mon–Sat

Colourful covers line the walls of this art and design bookshop, which has a leather sofa for relaxed brow-sing. As well as works on graphic design, advertising and photography, there are avant-garde illustrated books that are definitely not for kids, hip stationery and many obscure magazine. *(See also p66.)*

Smallfish Records *quality music*
`5 E5`

329 Old Street, EC1 • 020 7739 2252
» www.smallfish.co.uk
Open 3–8 Mon, 11–8 Tue–Sat (to 5 Sun)

Smallfish Records has such a vast selection of music that it is hard to classify its specialism. With an emphasis on vinyl (although it also stocks CDs), the shop is organized by genre, with areas dedicated to the likes of hip-hop, guitar-based and experimental.

Story *unique shop-cum-gallery*
`11 F1`

4 Wilkes Street, E1 • 020 7377 0313
Open 1–7 Thu–Sun

In a lovely period street, this extraordinary retail space looks like a contemporary gallery and sells an interesting mix of items. Immaculate vintage frocks, antique furniture, reclaimed hotel and airline linen, and simply packaged natural toiletries are set among beautiful dried leaves and shells.

Artcadia *printed wall hangings*
`11 F1`

108 Commercial St, E1 • 020 7426 0733
» www.artcadia.co.uk
Open 10–5:30 Mon–Fri, 10–4 Sat, 10:30–6 Sun

Artcadia's digital prints are an easy way to give a room instant contemporary cred. Buy "off the peg" in the gallery or choose from a wide range of up-to-date patterns and images, from groovy abstracts to flowers, printed up on any size of canvas.

A Gold *British foodstuff*
`11 E1`

42 Brushfield Street, E1 • 020 7247 2487
Open 11–8 Mon–Fri, 11–6 Sat & Sun

This wonderful old shop near Spitalfields Market sells traditional British foods, many in attractive old-fashioned packaging. Wild boar pancetta from Cumbria, Stinking Bishop cheese from Gloucestershire, Yorkshire Brack (fruitbread), English wine and honey made from hives kept on a rooftop in London all make great gifts.

» *The area around Spitalfields comes alive on Sundays* (see p167); *only a few places are open on Saturdays*

Cheshire Street *unusual homewares* 5 F5

Off Brick Lane, E1 Market open Sun; shops Sat & Sun
For individual shop details, *see pp226–9*

A cluster of interesting home accessory shops has appeared on this Brick Lane sidestreet, which on Sundays is lined with market stalls selling everything from bedlinen to hardware. Most shops are only open at weekends – it's best to ring first. **Inexterior** (No. 14) sells an enticing mix of furry cushions, handmade crockery and pretty clothes. At No. 16, **Mar Mar Co** deals predominantly in colourful Scandinavian tableware and interior accessories. **Labour and Wait** (No. 18) is a wonderful source of old-fashioned British household items, from vintage watering cans, earthenware jars and clothespegs to hand-knitted Guernsey sweaters and Welsh blankets. For unique gifts, **Shelf** (No. 40) showcases modern decorative items by British and European artists, such as jokey, illustrated mugs, notebooks and tiles. Next door at **Mimi** there are handmade leather bags.

Tatty Devine *witty trinkets* 11 F1

236 Brick Lane, E2 • 020 7739 9009
>> www.tattydevine.com Open 10–6 Mon–Fri, 11–7 Sat & Sun

Bracelets made of colourful guitar picks, earrings that dangle tiny LPs, and tape-measure belts... Tatty Devine's ironic trashy trinkets have attained cult status. Also for sale at the design duo's shop/studio are fun, punky, printed T-shirts and arty postcards, while the walls are given over to temporary exhibitions.

Rokit *all sorts of second-hand clothes* 11 F1

101 & 107 Brick Lane, E1 • 020 7375 3864
>> www.rokit.co.uk

Open 11–7 Mon–Fri, 10–7 Sat & Sun

From a small second-hand shop in Camden in the 80s, Rokit has expanded, with a store in Covent Garden and these Brick Lane premises. The diverse stock encompasses jeans, leather jackets, army gear, vintage dresses and quirky accessories.

Comfort & Joy *chic & cheap boutique* 4 B3

109 Essex Road, N1 • 020 7359 3898
Open 10:30–6 Tue–Sat

Fed up with chain-store fashion? Try this unpretentious boutique; it sells reasonably priced womenswear designed and made on the premises. Stylish without slavishly following catwalk trends, the simple clothes often sport interesting prints or subtle details such as piping or a crossover neckline.

Upper Street *furnishings & fashion*   `4 B2`
Islington, N1
For individual shop details, *see pp226–9*

As befits one of London's centres of affluent living, Islington has no shortage of stylish interior shops on its main street. Contemporary emporium **Aria** at Nos. 295–6 has wares for every room of the house by the likes of Philippe Starck and Alessi, while its satellite shop across the street at No. 133 stocks cards, leather notebooks, frames and understated designer bags. Heading north, **twentytwentyone** at No. 274 combines immaculate modern-classic and new pieces of furniture. **After Noah** (No. 121) stocks an irresistible jumble of vintage and vintage-style items in a barn-

like space – old-fashioned dial phones, antique metal tins, toys and retro toiletries. The empire of **Gill Wing** spans several diverse, high-quality shops: No. 182 showcases modern jewellery; the cookshop at No. 190 sells all the kitchen paraphernalia you could need, with kitschy touches such as feather-trimmed washing-up gloves; and there are Gill Wing shoe and gift shops nearby, too.

Oliver Bonas at Nos. 147–8 is good for gifts and accessories, and bringing an element of intrigue to the street is **Labour of Love** (No. 193). The boutique sells an assortment of items such as handmade knickers and clothes inspired by classic cinema made by the granddaughter of Italian filmmaker Visconti.

Camden Passage *antiques & curios* `4 B3`

Cobbled lane in Islington, N1 Antiques market Wed & Sat; book market Thu. For individual shop details, *see pp226–9*

This narrow, meandering continuation of Islington High Street is jammed with antiques shops and market stalls, which are busiest on Saturdays, Wednesdays and Thursdays. En route, check out the **Rock Archive** gallery at No. 110 Islington High Street for limited-edition prints of British greats such as Paul Weller and Pete Townshend. Tiny, atmospheric shops are hidden away in the poky Pierrepont Arcade: **Caroline Carrier's** nook is piled high with 18th- and 19th-century porcelain. **Judith Lassalle** sells antique puzzles and games, and **Jubilee Photographica** deals in photographs from the 19th century onwards.

Near the junction of Charlton Place is **Origin**, for 1930s–50s furniture by the likes of Eames, and **Annie's Vintage Clothes**, which has well-preserved flapper dresses. The Victorian **Camden Head** pub is conveniently placed for mid-rummage refreshment.

Primrose Hill Nexus *village shops* `2 B2`

Regent's Park Road, NW1
For individual shop details, *see pp226–9*

An array of inviting shops nestles between the cosy cafés of Regent's Park Road, Primrose Hill's villagey main street. **Anna** at No. 126 serves the area's affluent residents a mix of fashion from designers as diverse as Betty Jackson, Orla Kiely and Maharishi, plus pieces from newly graduated talent and unusual British-made cashmere sweaters. A few doors along, compact **Primrose Hill Books** has many signed copies from local authors. There's a branch of interiors shop **Graham & Green** *(see also p89)* at No. 164, while at No. 170 **Studio Perfumery** offers seductive European scents from Acqua di Parma, L'Artisan Perfumeur, Serge Lutens and others. Around the corner at No. 13 Princess Road, **Rachel Skinner** sells exquisite hats, ranging from trimmed, updated trilbies and cloches for everyday wear to fabulous one-off feathered or floral creations for Ascot and weddings.

Oxo Tower Wharf *craft studios*

Bargehouse Street, SE1 • 020 7401 2255
>> www.oxotower.co.uk Open 11–6 Tue–Sat
For individual shop details, *see p228*

This London landmark on the South Bank is a hotbed
of creativity, housing over 30 designers' studios. The
stylish **Oxo Tower Restaurant, Brasserie and Bar**
(see p58) commands great river views at the top.

There's a diverse assortment of interesting goods,
including jewellery, fashion, accessories and textiles.
Don't miss funky handmade children's clothes by
Bunny London (worn by Madonna's little material girl
Lourdes). **Black+Blum** offers quirky, affordable
designs, such as a lamp in the shape of a figure (the
lightbulb) reading a book (the shade), and a rubber
doorstop in the shape of a man pushing the door
open. **Bodo Sperlein** specializes in elegant bone
china and sculptural lighting. Hip duo **Odie &
Amanda** design bold hand-printed dresses, slinky
tops and tailored tweeds.

Lower Marsh/The Cut *hidden gems*

Roads behind Waterloo Station, SE1
For individual shop details, *see pp223–9*

There's still something of old-fashioned London in
Lower Marsh, a slender side road that feels a world
away from all the pomp and ceremony by the Thames
on the other side of Waterloo. The nostalgia is
especially strong in shops such as **Radio Days** (a real
joy to browse at No. 87) and **What the Butler Wore**
(No. 131), both of which sell a well-selected range of
vintage clothing of the mid- to late 20th century.

The small daily market deals mostly in cheap
fashions and CDs. In contrast, **Grammex** at No. 25, is a
refined shop for classical records and CDs. Cafés
around here offer fry-ups, sushi and Cuban food. Over
on The Cut is the excellent **Calder Bookshop** (No. 51).
This publisher has an impressive list of 20th-century
literary heavyweights, including all the main works of
Samuel Beckett, and the shop is a venue for talks
and poetry readings.

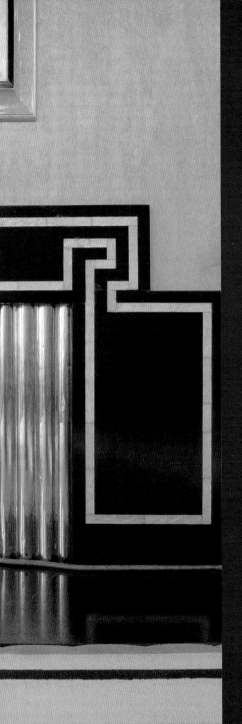

art &
architecture

Some of the world's most treasured cultural artifacts and paintings are gathered in London's blockbuster museums and grand mansions. The city's architecture is a thrilling ad hoc mix of medievalism, stately classicism and dynamic bursts of modernism. And counterbalancing the historical heavyweights is a thriving contemporary art scene, centred on East London.

ART & ARCHITECTURE

In little more than a decade London's art world has evolved from an esoteric, minority-interest scene into one of the key ingredients of London life. In that time, we've witnessed the birth of Tate Modern, seen the Saatchi and White Cube galleries wooing and sparring with a generation of highly profiled artists, and been lured to many smaller galleries that have sprung up or been revamped. The architectural scene has developed too, and London now boasts pioneering contemporary buildings as well as great historic works.

Michael Ellis

Exhibition Spaces

Tates **Modern** and **Britain** and the **RA** have great exhibition spaces *(see pp117, 105, 106)*. Also check out what's happening at the **Hayward** *(see p115)*, **Serpentine** *(see p107)* and **Whitechapel** *(see p110)* galleries, as well as the **ICA** *(see p102)* – all have adventurous programmes and put on some of London's best shows of contemporary art.

Wondrous Churches

In **Westminster Abbey** *(see p12)* and **St Paul's** *(see p12)*, London is blessed with two world-class churches, but the city also boasts lesser-known ecclesiastical treasures in Wren's **St James's Piccadilly** *(see p106)*, **Temple Church** *(see p104)*, **St Bartholomew** *(see p109)* and the 11th-century **Chapel of St John** in the Tower *(see p13)*.

The Big Museums

No city in the world has more museums than London. The major players are the **National Gallery** *(see p101)* for Western paintings, **Tate Modern** *(see p117)* for 20th–21st century art, the **BM** and **V&A** *(see pp104 & 108)* for distinct takes on world culture, and the **Natural History Museum** and **Science Museum** *(see p15 for both)* for life and technology.

choice sights

Treasured Paintings
Besides the major museums, London has many smaller collections with great paintings: Vermeer's *Guitar Player* and a Rembrandt *Self-Portrait* at **Kenwood House** *(see p114)*; Guido Reni's *St Sebastian* at the **Dulwich Picture Gallery** *(see p118)*; Van Dyke's portraits at the **Wallace Collection** *(see p107)* and Rubens' ceiling at the **Banqueting House** *(see p105)*.

Historic Houses
Of the many writers, artists and thinkers who have lived in London, several have had their former homes turned into museums. They include the **Freud Museum** *(see p114)*, opulent **Leighton House** *(see p109)*, the beguiling **Denis Severs' House** *(see p110)* and that treasure-trove of architectural fragments, the **Sir John Soane's Museum** *(see p103)*.

Architectural Highlights
London's mish-mash of architectural styles throws up fantastically diverse buildings, from Inigo Jones's classicism in the **Queen's House** *(see p119)* to the Modernism of **2 Willow Road** *(see p113)*, industrial spaces such as the **Museum in Docklands** *(see p112)*, and such idiosyncrasies as **19 Princelet Street** *(see p109)* and **Eltham Palace** *(see p118)*.

Somerset House *a treasury of culture* `9 H3`

Strand, WC2 • 020 7845 4600
>> www.somerset-house.org.uk
Galleries open 10–6 daily (last entry 5:15)

A stately building set around a grand courtyard, Somerset House contains three galleries. Gloriously free of crowds, the gallery at the **Courtauld Institute of Art** numbers some formidable Impressionist and Post-Impressionist paintings among its superb collection: Gauguin's *Nevermore*, Manet's *Bar at the Folies-Bergère* and Van Gogh's *Self Portrait with Bandaged Ear*, to name a few. It also has some splendid early Flemish and Italian paintings, including Fra Angelico's *Man of Sorrows* and Quentin Metsys's sublime *Virgin and Child with Angels*.

The **Hermitage Rooms** echo the style of the famous namesake museum in St Petersburg and are used to exhibit changing displays on loan from the enormous Hermitage collection. The **Gilbert Collection** was opened in 2000. It focuses on the decorative arts,

with a glittering array of gilt snuff boxes, European silverware and jewel-encrusted objets d'art.

Reminiscent of a European piazza, the courtyard at the centre of Somerset House sparkles with illuminated fountains on summer evenings. In mid-July it is used as the venue for a series of outdoor gigs, with artists such as Goldfrapp, Röyksopp and Calexico performing. Most spectacularly, an outdoor ice rink is installed in the courtyard in winter (late Nov to late Jan), offering skating sessions to the public.

The south wing of the building is home to a plush Modern European restaurant **The Admiralty** (020 7845 4646), which also runs a year-round deli/café and the Summer Café on the River Terrace. The terrace runs the length of the building on the Thames side; you can walk along it whether you've come here for a meal, a coffee or simply for the views. In summer the river is largely obscured by plane trees, but to the east you can glimpse St Paul's, and to the west are the Gothic towers of Westminster. **Adm to galleries**

Theatre Museum *behind the scenes* `9 G3`
7 Russell Street, WC2 • 020 7943 4700
>> www.theatremuseum.org Open 10–6 Tue–Sun

A rambling foray into the past and future of theatre in London. The work of theatrical pioneers such as Edward Gordon Craig and Peter Brook is brought to the fore through archive film, set designs and models. Enthusiastic guides tell stories about famous performers, and there are make-up demonstrations.

Photographers' Gallery *pics & books* `9 F3`
5 & 8 Great Newport Street, WC2 • 020 7831 1772
>> www.photonet.org.uk
Open 11–6 Mon–Sat (to 8 Thu), noon–6 Sun

Occupying two sites – one with a vegetarian café, the other with a great bookshop – the gallery presents London's most concentrated programme of photography exhibitions. Some shows are devoted to new talent, others to high-profile names such as Robert Capa.

National Gallery *old Masters* `9 F4`
Trafalgar Square, WC2 • 020 7747 2885
>> www.nationalgallery.org.uk Open 10–6 daily (to 9 Wed)

The East Wing and main rooms of the National Gallery have been the focus of major changes over the last two years, with a smart new entrance foyer, computer access in the Espresso Bar for exploring and studying the collection, and the Central Hall rehung with sublime works by Titian. These main sections of the gallery are the busiest, however, while the Sainsbury Wing (built in 1991) is relatively quiet and perfectly lit for viewing the Early Renaissance paintings displayed there. Highlights of the Sainsbury Wing include Leonardo's pensive drawing of *The Virgin and Child with St Anne and St John the Baptist* (c. 1500), Botticelli's mighty depiction of post-coitus *Venus and Mars* (c. 1485) and Jan van Eyck's vivid *Arnolfini Portrait* (1434). The National puts on several major exhibitions each year, and has a great new restaurant *(see p35)*.

Art & Architecture

National Portrait Gallery

St Martin's Place, WC2 • 020 7306 0055

>> www.npg.org.uk Open 10–6 daily (to 9pm Thu & Fri)

A large assembly of images of prominent Britons, the collection includes the only known contemporaneous portrait of Shakespeare, delightful miniatures by John Hilliard, and photographs by Cecil Beaton and David Bailey. For a chronological tour, take the long straight elevator to the top floor, where you'll find the earliest works in the gallery's collection, beginning with the 1505 painting of Henry VII. This floor is also where you'll find the Shakespeare portrait, the Hilliard miniatures and the Portrait Restaurant, with its fabulous views across Trafalgar Square to Westminster. On the same level are fascinating portraits of Pepys, Charles I and Nell Gwyn, while moving down to the ground floor brings you ever closer to the most recent works, which include portraits of well-known faces from the worlds of commerce, politics, the arts and science.

ICA *institute of contemporary art*

The Mall, SW1 • 020 7930 3647, 020 7930 6393 (24-hour info)

>> www.ica.org.uk Galleries open noon–7:30 daily

Once the rebellious upstart to the Royal Academy's stuffy old order, the ICA is an institution itself these days. It retains a sense of adventure, however, mixing well-known artists with group shows of the young pre-tenders. It also has two small cinemas, a theatre, a café-bar (open to 1am Tue–Sat) and a bookshop. **Adm**

Along the River

A trip along the Thames is a brilliant means of traversing the city along its east–west axis: the **Houses of Parliament** *(see p12)* show their most elegant side, and the views of the bridges and waterfronts are unparalleled. From central London, boats run downriver from Westminster and Embankment piers to **Greenwich** every 40–45 minutes until early evening. Heading upriver, boats travel from Westminster Pier to **Kew**, a trip of 90 minutes, until mid-afternoon. Of the river websites, **www.transportforlondon.gov.uk/river** gives the best information for river travel, while **www. riverthames.co.uk** has a lively overview of the entire river and associated events, including boat races. For information about **The Art Boat**, *see p106.*

Sir John Soane's Museum `9 H2`

13 Lincoln's Inn Fields, WC2 • 020 7405 2107

>> www.soane.org Open 10–5 Tue–Sat (to 9pm first Tue of the month); tours at 2pm (first come, first served)

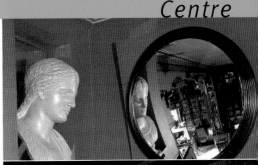

Sir John Soane (1753–1837) was a renowned architect in his day, and the interior of this unique, labyrinthine house is a testament to his passion for the Classical world. On the face of it, you are entering a Georgian terraced house, but Soane's rebuilding throws into disarray the usual neatness of a Georgian interior. A dark, warm corridor gives way to a staircase spiralling up three floors. A succession of skylights – often glazed in yellow to bathe sculptures in what Soane perceived as a Mediterranean light – illuminates the jumbled rooms. At every turn you come across fragments of ancient sculptures and architectural mouldings. Among these are glimpses of an alternative London – beautifully drafted, but unfulfilled plans for betempled bridges, a royal palace for Green Park and a Neo-Classical Houses of Parliament.

The ingenious design of the house reaches its high point in the Picture Room, formerly the stableyard of the house next door. As Soane's painting collection grew, space became a problem, and so he installed hinged screens in the place of solid walls. An attendant will open up panels to reveal works by Turner and Piranesi, and the complete set of original paintings by Hogarth which make up *The Rake's Progress*. In the New Picture Room (added after Soane's death) is one of Canaletto's finest works, *View towards Santa Maria della Salute, Venice*.

RIBA *architectural resource* `8 D1`

66 Portland Place, W1 • 020 7580 5533

>> www.riba.org Open 9–6 Mon–Fri, 9–5 Sat

The Royal Institute of British Architects puts on a range of shows, including homages to architectural greats. The RIBA building itself is a rather lovely 1930s Deco-Classical hybrid, with a café-restaurant and an excellent bookshop, where you can buy all manner of books on architecture and design.

>> *RIBA sells a cheap fold-out map by Architectural Dialogue, which pinpoints modern architecture in London* `103`

British Museum *cultural treasure house* `9 F2`
Great Russell St, WC1 • 020 7323 8000
➤➤ www.thebritishmuseum.ac.uk Museum open 10–5:30 daily
(to 8:30 Thu & Fri); Great Court open to 11pm Thu–Sat

Architect Norman Foster's reworking of the British
Museum's central courtyard created a vast foyer
beneath a curving glass roof at the heart of the BM.
Like a new city square, this is a great meeting area,
with cafés surrounding the gleaming rotunda of
the famous Reading Room, where writers and
philosophers such as Marx, Rimbaud and Verlaine
once studied. From the courtyard, signs point
off north, south, east and west to the various
departments of the museum's massive collection
of artifacts from the world's great cultures and
empires. Obvious highlights include the Rosetta
Stone, the Parthenon sculptures and Ancient
Egyptian mummies, but spare time for other
departments, such as the Japanese collections and
the Enlightenment exhibition in the King's Library.

Dr Johnson's House *literary pad* `10 A2`
17 Gough Square, EC4 • 020 7353 3745
➤➤ www.drjohnsonshouse.org
Open 11–5 Mon–Sat (to 5:30 summer)

The house where the doctor compiled the world's first
proper English dictionary in the mid-18th century was
dutifully restored in the 20th. After a look around, head
round the corner to one of Johnson's favoured watering
holes: Ye Olde Cheshire Cheese on Fleet Street. **Adm**

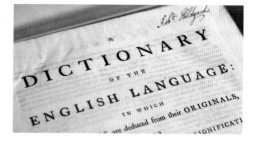

Temple Church *secret history* `10 A3`
Inner Temple off Fleet St, EC4 • 020 7353 3470
➤➤ www.templechurch.com Open Wed–Fri (usually)

This honey-stoned pot of a building dates from the
12th century when it was the church of the Knights
Templar *(see p174)*. Restored after World War II bomb
damage, it has a round form (unusual in Britain) that
echoes the Church of the Holy Sepulchre in Jerusalem.
There are free organ recitals at 1:15pm on Wednesdays.

St Margaret's Church *stained glass* `15 G1`
Sanctuary, Parliament Square, SW1 • 020 7222 5152
>> www.westminster-abbey.org/stmargarets
Open 9:30–3:45 Mon–Fri, 9:30–1:45 Sat, 2–5 Sun

Though often overlooked, St Margaret's Church contains an amazing variety of stained glass. Especially notable are John Piper's abstract designs of 1966, and fragments of the 19th-century Caxton Window (honouring the pioneer of printing) on the north aisle.

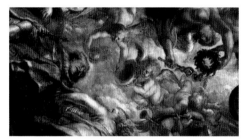

Banqueting House *grandiose building* `9 G5`
Whitehall, SW1 • 0870 751 5178
>> www.hrp.org.uk Open 10–5 Mon–Sat

An epic, heavenly Rubens ceiling and the architecture of Inigo Jones (the artist who brought Renaissance classicism to Britain) lure visitors. The video and audio tour are overly pompous, so it's better to visit the place as part of the lively Old Westminster tour offered by Original London Walks *(see p21)*. **Adm**

Tate Britain *more space for British art* `15 G3`
Millbank, SW1 • 020 7887 8000
>> www.tate.org.uk Open 10–5:50 daily

Ever since more than half of the Tate's collection sailed off down the Thames to set up home in Tate Modern, the original gallery has had to work hard to retain its audience. This it has done with aplomb – sprucing up the interior, creating more viewing space and focusing on British art. There is now more room to wander an excellent, wide-ranging collection, taking in the landscapes of Constable, the world's largest assemblage of Turners (in the Clore Galleries), the Modernism of Hepworth and Moore, and the savage, existential paintings of Francis Bacon.

There is also exhibition space for major shows and, for up-and-coming artists, the Art Now spaces (one of which is used especially for video work). There's a good (and pricey) restaurant in the basement, where the dining area is surrounded by a fantastical mural depicting the "pursuit of rare foods".

Art & Architecture

The Art Boat   *a waterborne Hirst*   `15 G3`
Millbank Pier to Bankside Pier Operates 10–5;
15-minute journey every 40 mins in each direction

Sporting Damien Hirst's trademark coloured dots, the
Art Boat zips between Tates Britain and Modern. The
cost includes as many trips as you like in a day, and
the pier at Tate Modern is useful for other sights –
Shakespeare's Globe, St Paul's (via the Millennium
Bridge), Borough Market and Southwark Cathedral.

Royal Academy   *blockbusters & side shows*   `9 E4`
Burlington House Piccadilly, W1 • 020 7300 8000
>> www.royalacademy.org.uk Open 10–6 daily (to 10 Fri)

While the main gallery of the Royal Academy puts on
blockbuster shows (Monet, the Summer Exhibition),
the Lord Norman Foster-designed Sackler Wing offers
more surprises. Recent exhibitions include Flemish
manuscripts, Jacob van Ruisdael and the minimalist
landscapes of William Nicholson. **Adm**

St James's Piccadilly   *Wren's joys*   `9 E4`
197 Piccadilly, W1 • 020 7734 4511
>> www.st-james-piccadilly.org Open 8–7 daily

This Wren church of 1684 is said to have been the
architect's favourite. It's a little haven from the busy
street outside, with a beautifully structured interior
and astounding 1680s wood carvings by Grinling
Gibbons. There's also an energetic programme of
events, including recitals most afternoons at 1:10pm.

Wren's London

Christopher Wren's influence on London stems from
the Great Fire of 1666, after which he was put in
charge of creating 51 new City churches and a new
cathedral, **St Paul's** *(see p12)*. The building's vast,
exceptionally crafted interior, its crypt lined with
tombs of the famous, and exhilarating views from
the outer dome make St Paul's an essential visit.

St Stephen Walbrook provided a prototype for
St Paul's dome, and the steeple of **St Mary-le-Bow**
shows Wren's appreciation for the Classical architectural orders. **St Bride's** off Fleet Street, meanwhile,
provided inspiration, it is said, for the familiar
tiered wedding cake. For location details, *see p230*.

   Original London Walks *(see p21)* do a Wren-
themed tour on Tuesday afternoons.

Wallace Collection *canvases & militaria*

8 C2

Hertford House, Manchester Square, W1 • 020 7563 9500
➤➤ www.wallacecollection.org
Open 10–5 daily

A stately Georgian house is the setting for this
outstanding collection, left to the nation in 1897.
Highlights include Frans Hals's hugely famous,
flamboyantly moustached *Laughing Cavalier*, and a
touching painting by Rembrandt of his son Titus. Two
brilliant portraits by Van Dyck hang close by. There
are also several lively painted sketches by Rubens,
including an *Adoration of the Magi* and the
celebrated *Rainbow Landscape*.

The Wallace Collection also celebrates the artistry
found in the weaponry of Europe and the Middle East
in past centuries, and includes a pair of pistols with
stocks intricately carved with images of Samson and
Hercules. The glass-roofed central courtyard is where
you'll find The Wallace, a very civilized and relaxing
spot where they serve French brasserie fare.

Serpentine Gallery *contemporary art & architecture*

7 H5

Kensington Gardens, W2 • 020 7402 6075
➤➤ www.serpentinegallery.org Open 10–6 daily

Located in a former tea house in Kensington Gardens, the Serpentine
has built a reputation for putting on solo shows by some of the big guns
of contemporary art. Each year, moreover, a different architect is invited
to create a one-off summer pavilion in the grounds just outside the
gallery – Zaha Hadid, Daniel Libeskind and Oscar Niemeyer have
created brilliant structures in previous years.

Brompton Oratory *Catholic encounter* **14 A2**

Brompton Rd, SW7 • 020 7808 0900
➤➤ www.bromptonoratory.com

Built in the 1880s but looking like a product of
17th-century Italy, the Oratory's façade gives way to
a full-on Baroque interior, with no surface escaping
ornamentation. An arched and many-domed roof
provides a canvas for heavenly images. At ground
level, dark confessionals occupy every corner.

V&A *a refined collection* `13 H2`

Cromwell Road, SW7 • 020 7942 2000

>> www.vam.ac.uk Open 10–5.45 daily (to 10 Wed)

Not only does the V&A put on great temporary exhibitions (such as highly-praised recent shows on Modernism and Leonardo da Vinci), it also offers a truly wide-ranging collection of decorative arts, paintings, sculpture, photography, fashion and furniture. Highlights include the Italian Renaissance sculptures, casts of Trajan's Column, the monumental Raphael Cartoons depicting biblical scenes, and wonderful oil sketches by Constable and canvases by Turner. A newer attraction is the Architecture Gallery, where exhibitions are created from the joint collections of the V&A and RIBA *(see p103)*.

The V&A also contains two great spots for coffee and contemplation: the Madjeski Garden in the museum's courtyard, and the beautiful Morris and Gamble Rooms, clad in stunning arts-and-crafts tiles and inscribed with mottoes on the joys of eating.

Saatchi Gallery `14 B3`

The Duke of York's HQ, Sloane Square, SW3

>> www.saatchi-gallery.co.uk

At the time of writing, the Saatchi Gallery was in the process of moving from the South Bank to premises in Chelsea. The crisp and very spacious new gallery (due to open in 2007) will host around three shows a year of work from Charles Saatchi's ever-changing collection of contemporary art. **Adm**

Linley Sambourne House `13 E1`

18 Stafford Terrace, W8 • 020 7602 3316

>> www.rbkc.gov.uk/linleysambournehouse Tours Sat & Sun

Home makeovers are nothing new, as proved by this beautifully preserved 1870s townhouse, former home of the noted *Punch* cartoonist. Glazed window boxes reflect the Victorian passion for conservatories, while bare patches behind paintings cruelly reveal the Sambournes' frugal use of wallpaper. **Adm**

Leighton House Museum `12 D1`

12 Holland Park Rd, W14 • 020 7602 3316
>> www.rbkc.gov.uk/LeightonHouseMuseum
Open 11–5:30 Wed–Mon

This wonderfully idiosyncratic studio-house was built for the fashionable Victorian painter Frederick, Lord Leighton. Mirroring the success of his career, the house was aggrandized in the late 19th century, when its defining feature, the Arab Hall, was added. This lovely space has a pool with a tiny tinkling fountain, and walls decorated with deep turquoise tiles from Damascus.

The back rooms, overlooking a pleasant garden (open Apr–Sep), are hung with paintings by the main Pre-Raphaelite players – Millais, Burne-Jones, Waterhouse – as well as Leighton's exotic and incredibly detailed Oriental and Classical scenes. Upstairs, light pours into the studio and salon. Here, among paintings of varied success, are small landscape studies and preparatory sketches, which are some of Leighton's most enduring works. **Adm**

St Bartholomew the Great `10 B2`

West Smithfield, EC1 • 020 7606 5171
>> www.greatstbarts.com Open Tue–Sun exc during services

Your imaginative powers are called upon to fully appreciate this 12th-century Norman priory, London's oldest parish church. Much of the nave is now an open churchyard, and the former entrance door is now a gateway leading on to Smithfield Market. But it still has a lot of atmosphere.

19 Princelet Street *a house of refuge* `11 F1`

Spitalfields, E1 • 020 7247 5352
>> www.19princeletstreet.org.uk Open occasional Sun afternoons & Refugee Week (mid-Jun); check website

Now set up as a small museum about immigration in Spitalfields, this terraced house was home to French Huguenots and, later, Jewish émigrés. Beyond the small front rooms is No. 19's most startling secret: a creaking three-storey synagogue of 1869.

Dennis Severs' House *time capsule* `11 E1`

18 Folgate Street, E1 • 020 7247 4013
>> www.dennissevershouse.co.uk Open Mon evenings by
candlelight (booking required) & occasional afternoons

The modern world closes behind you as you enter
this terraced house in Spitalfields. The late artist
Dennis Severs interpreted the history of his home by
furnishing its ten rooms in ways that evoke moments
(more than just periods) in its past. Each room is a
still life: in the front parlour, time seems to have
stopped in the 1700s, with rich pies, half-eaten fruit
and glasses of wine abandoned on the table. The
cold and dusty attic rooms leap straight out of the
early 1900s, with silk-weaving apparatus and crum-
bling damp ceilings. The level of detail is extraordinary. Cracked oyster shells indicate a snack just eaten;
the pungent scent of oranges, cloves and lavender
fills the nostrils. Clocks chime the hour, while a sly
black cat ghosts about. Only by the sight of other
visitors are you reminded of the present. **Adm**

Museum of the Order of St John `10 B1`

St John's Gate, EC1 • 020 7324 4070
>> www.sia.org.uk/museum Tours Tue, Fri & Sat

Be sure to catch the hour-long tour that takes you
down into a hidden 12th-century crypt, then up into a
Tudor gatehouse. The history of the Knights of St John
is fascinating and far-reaching – the Crusades, 14th-
century Poll Tax Riots, Shakespeare, *The Gentleman's
Magazine* and modern first-aid volunteers all appear.

Whitechapel Gallery *contemporary art* `11 F2`

80–82 Whitechapel High Street, E1
020 7522 7888, 020 7522 7878 (recorded info)
>> www.whitechapel.org Open 11–6 Tue–Sun (to 9 Thu)

One of London's largest galleries, the Whitechapel
puts on attention-grabbing exhibitions of modern and
contemporary art. The ongoing series *A Short History
of Performance* and the semi-abstract paintings of
Albert Oehlen were among recent subjects.

Museum of London *history of the city* `5 E4`
London Wall, EC2 • 0870 444 3850
>> www.museumoflondon.org.uk
Open 10–5:50 Mon–Sat, 12–5:50 Sun

From prehistory to the present, the museum takes a historical trawl through this city, plucking out sculptures of Roman gods found buried in temple ruins, metal jewellery from medieval London and photographic documentation over the past 120 years.

Geffrye Museum *homes in history* `5 E4`
136 Kingsland Rd, E2 • 020 7739 9893
>> www.geffrye-museum.org.uk Open 10–5 Tue–Sat, 12–5 Sun

A row of neat little almshouses has been converted into a charming museum on the theme of English domestic interiors and gardens of the last 400 years. The Victorian rooms reach a zenith of clutter before the modern world storms in with the 1930s house. An open loft apartment represents the 1990s.

Wapping Project Space *art, industry, food*
Wapping Wall, E1 • 020 7680 2080 • ⊜ Wapping
>> www.thewappingproject.com
Open noon–10:30 Mon–Sat, noon–6 Sun

WPS showcases contemporary art (especially video), dance and music in a former power station that seems to have remained largely untouched since the time of its industrial death throes in the late 1970s. There's an excellent restaurant too, called Wapping Food.

Victorian Cemeteries

London's great old cemeteries have a poetic equilibrium, the artistry of stonemasons jostling for space with the natural world of brambles and trees. **Highgate Cemetery** is where you'll find the lumpish bust of Karl Marx. **Kensal Green Cemetery** is home to some fanciful Egyptian-style tombs and a chapel built to look like a Greek temple.

Brompton Cemetery is a more civilized affair, with sharp paths and avenues. Like Kensal Green, it has a Neo-Classical temple; its silhouette and golden sandstone are especially striking in the evening light. The wildest cemeteries are **Abney Park** *(see p179)* and the gothic forest of **Nunhead**, where angels and crucifixes seem to sprout from ivy-clad trees. For location details, *see p230*.

Art & Architecture

Docklands *industrial past, commercial future*
Isle of Dogs, E14 • ⊖ Canary Wharf
Museum in Docklands: West India Quay • 0870 444 3857
≫ www.museumindocklands.org.uk Open 10–6 daily

From the driverless trains of the DLR to the pumped-up steel and glass commercial buildings mushrooming all around, there is something exhilarating (albeit not pretty) about Docklands. A shiny new city has all but replaced the wharfs and warehouses of the old port.

The **Museum in Docklands**, set in a beautiful brick warehouse, which once held spices, rum and cotton, tells the 2,000-year tale of London as a place of trade.

That trade continues in the multinational offices at **Canary Wharf**, served by three interconnected shopping malls (Cabot Place, Canada Place and Jubilee Place). There are many pubs and restaurants, most of them chains. Two worth seeking out are **1802**, a smart restaurant and bar next to the museum, overlooking Future Systems' lime-green footbridge; and Conran's stylish **Plateau**, on the fourth floor of Canada Place.

Estorick Collection *Futurism* 4 B1
39 Canonbury Sq, N1 • 020 7704 9522
≫ www.estorickcollection.com Open 11–6 Wed–Sat, 12–5 Sun

Tucked away on a leafy backroad, this gallery is dedicated to the Italian Futurist Movement of the early 20th century. It's the perfect antidote to London's gargantuan museums, a place to quietly peruse Severinis, Boccionis and also works by Modigliani and de Chirico. The House *(see p53)* is nearby for refreshment. **Adm**

Camden Arts Centre *contemporary art*
Arkwright Road, NW3 • 020 7472 5500 • ⊖ Finchley Road
≫ www.camdenartscentre.org Open 10–6 Tue–Sun (to 9 Wed)

Recently refurbished, the arts centre continues to showcase influential artists and Britain's best up-and-coming talent. Art/architectural group MUF created the garden, which features a terrace that traces the "footprint" of two houses destroyed by a bomb during World War II.

For the very latest on London go to ≫ **www.realcity.dk.com**

Lord's *sporting traditions, modern architecture*
Wellington Road, NW8 • ⊜ **St John's Wood**
>> www.lords.org Tours daily (020 7616 8595 to book)

Lord's is more than just a cricket ground: it is the home of the game, the keeper of its beguiling rules and the custodian of its traditions. You may be surprised, then, to discover that it also sports some leading contemporary architecture. The stands surrounding the pitch are by Nicholas Grimshaw and Michael Hopkins – pioneers of High-Tech building design. In playful fashion, the Hopkins Stand has been designed to look like a temporary summer marquee.

The Media Centre was built in 2000 by Future Systems. This sensuous white cocoon, created with the aid of boat manufacturers, rises dramatically from the Mound end, in contrast to the stately Victoriana of Thomas Verity's Pavilion (1890) at the opposite end.

Tours of Lord's are conducted by cricket enthusiasts, and take in the ground's architecture and the MCC Museum, which charts the history of cricket.

Fenton House *17th-century traditions*  `1 A4`
Windmill Hill, NW3 • 020 7435 3471
>> www.nationaltrust.org.uk
Open Apr–Oct: Wed–Fri 2–5 Sat & Sun 11–5

Set in formal gardens, this 17th-century house has displays of early keyboard instruments, fine Chinese porcelain and some precious English and Continental figurines. The Dining Room is the venue for a summer concert series of early music (May–Oct). **Adm**

2 Willow Road *modern living perfected* `1 C4`
2 Willow Road, NW3 • 020 7435 6166
Open Apr–Oct: noon–5 Thu–Sat; Mar & Nov: noon–5 Sat

It's not much to look at from the outside, but the interior of the former home of Modernist architect Ernö Goldfinger is superb: flexible living areas, picture windows and sophisticated colour schemes are defining features. Dotted about are paintings by Henry Moore, Max Ernst and Bridget Riley. **Adm**

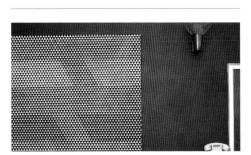

Art & Architecture

Freud Museum *the doctor's final home*
20 Maresfield Gardens, NW3 • 020 7435 2002 • ⊖ Finchley Road
⟫ www.freud.org.uk Open noon–5 Wed–Sun

Preserved as the "Father of Psychoanalysis" left them, the library and study in Sigmund Freud's house contain a great collection of Greek, Roman, Egyptian and Oriental antiquities. But pride of place goes to the original psychoanalytical couch, with its plumped-up cushions and richly patterned Persian rug. **Adm**

Kenwood House *Masters on the Heath* `1 C1`
Hampstead Heath, NW3 • 020 8348 1286
Open Apr–Oct 11–5 daily; Nov–Mar 11–4 daily

Architect Robert Adam's cream Neo-Classical house at the top of Hampstead Heath provides a stately home for the Iveagh Bequest. The often-overlooked collection includes paintings by Turner, Reynolds and Gainsborough, as well as a masterful late *Self-Portrait* by Rembrandt and Vermeer's *Guitar Player*.

Keats House *home of the young Romantic* `1 C5`
Keats Grove, NW3 • 020 7435 2062
⟫ www.corpoflondon.gov.uk/keats Open 1–5 daily

Romantic poet John Keats lived in this genteel house in 1818–20, hoping that the good air and waters of Hampstead would alleviate his tuberculosis. Letters, possessions and manuscripts tell the tale of a sensitive writer who died young. *Ode to a Nightingale* was among the many poems written here. **Adm**

London's Georgian Squares

The most elegant chapter of London's expansion happened during the Georgian era (1714–1830), when homogeneous Neo-Classical streetscapes were created, often set around garden squares. Many of these squares are open to the public. Among the best are the quietish **Golden Square** (Map 9 E3) and thronged **Soho Square** (9 F2); **Berkeley Square** (8 D4) for its magnificent plane trees; **St James's Square** (9 E4) for its exceptional Georgian townhouse surrounds; **Bloomsbury Square** (9 G2) for its jollity; and **Queen's Square** (9 G1) for its tucked-away charm and enticing pubs and cafés on Cosmos Place. Many other squares to which access is normally restricted are open to all on the annual **Open Garden Squares Weekend** *(see p16)*.

Southwark Cathedral *ancient church* `10 D4`
Montague Close, SE1 • 020 7367 6734
>> www.southwark.anglican.org/cathedral/
Open 7:30–6 Mon–Fri, 8:30–6 Sat & Sun

With its stonework cleansed and a flag fluttering from the castellated tower, Southwark Cathedral is an uplifting sight. Inside the church (which dates from the 13th century) are memorials to Shakespeare and Chaucer, and the tomb of Gower, the first English poet.

Jerwood Space *hot competition* `10 B5`
171 Union Street, SE1 • 020 7654 0171
>> www.jerwoodspace.co.uk Open Tue–Sun afternoons (opening times vary depending on the exhibition)

The programme at this contemporary art gallery is based around a series of annual prizes in a variety of media, and the Artists Platform, which showcases new artists. The Jerwood Space also has a great café, with courtyard dining when sunny.

Hayward Gallery *avant-garde shows* `9 H4`
South Bank Centre, SE1 • 020 7960 5226
>> www.hayward.org.uk
Open 10–6 daily (to 8 Tue & Wed)

Arguably London's premier gallery for temporary exhibitions, particularly of contemporary art, the Hayward is a versatile space. It was built in the late 1960s in a Brutalist style, and in recent years the occupiers have been learning to love it again. The interior has been stripped back to the original rough concrete surface that, when empty, gives it the appearance of a multi-storey car park. Brutal it may be, but it is a provoking alternative to the white-box look of many galleries.

Paintings don't necessarily look their best here, but the Hayward is an exceptional space for modern sculpture and multimedia installations. Video works such as Douglas Gordon's *24-Hour Psycho* have been highly acclaimed, as have shows such as Rebecca Horn's *Bodylandscapes* and the Dan Flavin retrospective that was staged in 2006. **Adm**

Art & Architecture

Old Operating Theatre *scary surgery* `10 D5`
9a St Thomas's Street, SE1 • 020 7955 4791
>> www.thegarret.org.uk Open 10:30–5 daily

Accessed via a Herb Garret that lulls you with the idea of quaint botanical potions, the operating theatre of 1822 comes as a shock. An oversize chopping board is set on a stage surrounded by tiered seats for students and onlookers, while in an adjacent room is a vast array of knives and amputation saws. **Adm**

Design Museum *modern design institute* `11 F5`
28 Shad Thames, SE1 • 0870 833 9955
>> www.designmuseum.org Open 10–5:45 daily

Temporary exhibitions take in the breadth of modern designers, from 19th-century engineer Isambard Kingdom Brunel to music-industry graphic artist Peter Saville. On the top floor there is a permanent collection of mass-produced design classics – check out how many you have owned. **Adm**

South London Gallery *big players/new blood*
65 Peckham Road, SE5 • 020 7703 6120
Oval, then bus No. 36
>> www.southlondongallery.org Open 12–6 Tue–Sun

This one-hall gallery stages exhibitions of contemporary artists. International names have included Sherrie Levine, On Kawara and Christian Boltanski; homegrown talent has included Turner Prize winners Simon Starling and and Steve McQueen.

Independent & Commercial Galleries
The most exciting galleries for up-and-coming artists are mainly in East London. There are clusters in Hoxton *(see p168)*, including **White Cube** and **The Agency**, and near Victoria Park (**Matt's Gallery**, **Chisenhale**, **The Showroom** and **Wilkinson Gallery**). There's also a small gallery, **The Approach**, above a friendly pub of the same name. In Central London, on Heddon Street, are **Sadie Coles HQ** and **Gagosian**. Gagosian has also opened a space on Britannia Street at King's Cross. There are many galleries around Cork Street, but don't miss **Stephen Friedman** on neighbouring Old Burlington Street. One of the best is out on its own: the **Lisson** near Marylebone Station. Try www.newexhibitions.com for information. For location details, *see p229*.

Tate Modern *power plant of modern art* `10 B4`
Bankside, SE1 • 020 7887 8000
>> www.tate.org.uk Open 10–6 Sun–Thu, 10–10 Fri & Sat

Since it opened in 2000, Tate Modern has been spectacularly popular. A large part of this success is due to the building itself: a monolithic, brown-brick power station transformed into an elegant Modernist gallery by architects Herzog & de Meuron.

The vast Turbine Hall is the dramatic focus of the building, a challenging space for installations by artists such as Louise Bourgeois, Juan Muñoz, Olafur Eliasson and Rachel Whiteread. The dimensions of the hall are so great – it's 155 m (500 ft) long by 35 m (115 ft) – that works have been increasingly theatrical in an attempt to fill the void. In *Weather Project* (2004), for example, Olafur Eliasson filled the hall with orange light from a giant "sun", covered the entire ceiling with mirrors and pumped in steamy clouds; Whiteread piled the space with hundreds of boxes.

The permanent collection is relatively modest for the size of building, occupying just two of the floors.

The regular rotation of pieces results in compelling displays of work by Matisse, Rodin, Bruce Nauman and other giants of modern art.

Tate Modern has an increasingly strong quota of video work, including Bill Viola's monumental *Five Angels for the Millennium* and Paul McCarthy's seminal *Rocky* (1976), in which the artist beats himself up and collapses into a naked heap. Amid this vastness and energy, however, it is good to know that small paintings can still hold their own, as exemplified by Picasso's exquisite *Girl in a Chemise* (1905).

The Level 4 galleries are given over to invariably brilliant temporary exhibitions, such as 2006's Kippenberger retrospective and the previous year's *Open Systems: Rethinking Art c.1970*; an entrance fee is charged for these exhibitions.

There is a moderately priced café on Level 2, offering good food and efficient, friendly service. The café on Level 7 gets extremely busy – if you want the views, visit before or after the lunchtime rush (12:30–2:30pm) and be prepared to wait.

>> *As well as offering free guided tours daily, the Tate Modern has also introduced Palm Pilot tours*   117

Dulwich Picture Gallery *fine paintings*
Gallery Road, Dulwich Village, SE21 • 020 8693 5254
Train to West Dulwich
➤➤ www.dulwichpicturegallery.org.uk
Open 10–5 Tue–Fri, 11–5 Sat & Sun

Leafy Dulwich is home to a small and perfectly formed collection of European Old Master paintings from the 17th and 18th centuries, housed in a gallery of 1811 by Sir John Soane *(see p103)*.

The quality of the work is extremely high, as exemplified by Guido Reni's *St Sebastian* (two other versions of the composition exist, one in the Prado, the other in the Louvre). There's also a delicate little Rembrandt (*Portrait of Jacob III de Gheyn*), and works by Raphael, Poussin, Rubens, Hogarth and Gainsborough, including the instantly recognisable *Unknown Couple in a Landscape*. An overhaul by architect Rick Mather added a glazed cloister and a moderately priced café-restaurant. **Adm**

Eltham Palace *medieval meets Art Deco*
Court Yard, SE9 • 020 8294 2548 • Train to Eltham
➤➤ www.elthampalace.org.uk
Open Apr–Oct: 10–5 Sun–Wed, Nov–Mar: 10–4 Sun–Wed

Having fallen ungracefully from its status as one of Henry VIII's hunting residences to become a humble barn in the 18th century, salvation finally came for Eltham Palace in the 1930s. By then, all that remained were the Banqueting Hall and parts of the garden, including the moat bridge. Arts patron Stephen Courtauld decided to restore the Hall and build a new, and very modern, country house around it.

Designed by Seely and Paget, the 1930s house is a seductive piece of Art Deco styling, with sweeping, light-filled rooms; curving walls lined with maple, aspen and sycamore panelling; and ocean-liner style furnishings. It's easy to envisage the sophisticated, Martini-sipping party set who would have weekended with the gregarious Courtaulds. Stories abound about Jonggy, the pet ring-tailed lemur who favoured the Flower Room when he wasn't up in his bunk. **Adm**

National Maritime Museum

16 C2

Greenwich Park, SE10 • 020 8312 6565
➤➤ www.nmm.ac.uk Open 10–5 daily

The NMM consists not only of the National Maritime Museum but also the **Queen's House** and the **Royal Observatory, Greenwich**. The National Maritime Museum itself is, as you might expect, devoted to the history of seafaring, and contains a fine collection of beautifully crafted instruments – astrolabes and other navigational tools – as well as charts from early voyages, important manuscripts, models, paintings and ships' figureheads.

Besides some fine furniture and a few paintings of note, the triumph of the neat little Queen's House is its architecture. This is the work of Inigo Jones (1573–1652), and in details such as the Tulip spiral

staircase you can see not only the classicism that this building eventually led to in Britain, but also a foreshadowing of Modernism in its refined simplicity, sense of proportion and feel for light.

The Royal Observatory contains galleries devoted to the measurement of time (the prime meridian, which demarkates the eastern and western hemispheres, bisects the building) and the ways in which we have endeavoured to navigate the globe.

The Royal Observatory is nearing the completion of a major Time and Space project, which has already seen the opening of a new set of galleries exploring developments in astrology, and theories about time and space. The final part of the project is a state-of-the-art planetarium at Greenwich, by architects Allies & Morrison, which is due to open in 2007.

➤➤ *For more about visiting Greenwich,* see p180

performance

London's theatres in the West End and on the South Bank are world famous, but cutting-edge drama is increasingly found further afield, in places such as the Tricycle in Kilburn and the Almeida, Islington. The city's musical stage stretches from the cupboard-sized 12 Bar Club to the majestic Royal Opera House. A lively comedy circuit is found in a host of pubs and clubs, while cinemas dotted around the city compete for coolness.

PERFORMANCE

London is the undisputed world capital of theatre, with a lineage stretching back to the Elizabethan drama of Jonson, Marlowe and Shakespeare. Now, as then, the city offers exciting, affordable drama for the masses. The city is also known for nurturing radical musical talent (through the pub and club circuit) and is an essential stop on any band's European tour. Recently, cabaret has returned to the spotlight with postmodern variations on the genre.

Lisa Ritchie

Concert Venues

London caters to every possible musical taste. The **South Bank Centre** *(see p135)* offers a diverse programme of classical, jazz and contemporary music. The opulent yet intimate **Wigmore Hall** *(see p128)* is a wonderful place to hear chamber music or a recital, while opera fans should make a beeline for the **Royal Opera House** *(see p124)*.

Dance

Avant-garde companies and contemporary dance stars from around the globe strut their stuff at **Sadler's Wells** *(see p132)*. At renowned training centres **Laban** *(see p136)* and **The Place** *(see p128)*, you can see performances by the bright young stars of tomorrow, as well as exciting works by resident and visiting companies.

Cutting-Edge Theatre

The **Donmar Warehouse** *(see p124)* attracts big names from Hollywood and closer to home with its stimulating programme, but generally for the most ground-breaking productions you'll need to venture away from the West End to the **Almeida** *(see p132)* or further afield to the **Tricycle** *(see p135)*, which is noted especially for political drama.

choice acts

Gigs

Pop and rock are the lifeblood of London culture. The **Borderline** *(see p125)* is a prime place to catch up-and-coming British bands or, for a quirkier atmosphere, check out tiny **12 Bar Club** *(see p125)*. There's also a thriving jazz scene, and London's best club for this genre, **Ronnie Scott's** *(see p127)*, has recently been refurbished.

Independent Cinemas

A recent revamp of the incomparable archive that is the **NFT** *(see p136)* has added a walk-in digital cinema and individual viewing stations. With its period features and comfy leather armchairs, the **Electric** *(see p129)* is the most hospitable of cinemas, while the **Curzon Soho** *(see p126)* offers a truly eclectic art-house programme.

Comedy and Cabaret

Long a breeding ground for taboo-busting comedians, London is now in the midst of a cabaret revival. The latest irreverent cabaret acts from Britain and abroad can be seen at the **Soho Theatre** *(see p126)* or the **Drill Hall** *(see p125)*, while the **Comedy Store** *(see p127)* is one of the best clubs for stand-up and draws in the funniest acts on the circuit.

Royal Opera House *ballet & opera* `9 G3`
Bow Street, Covent Garden, WC2 • 020 7304 4000
>> www.royaloperahouse.org
Tours: three daily at 10:30, 12:30 and 2:30

Shared by the Royal Ballet and Royal Opera, the Opera House is a magnificent theatre, the tiers of its auditorium rising to precipitous heights, topped off with a richly decorated ceiling. The ballet programme offers classical pieces with a few modern works. *Swan Lake*, *The Dream* and *The Rite of Spring* were recent productions. Operatic performances of late have included *Rigaletto*, *Die Walküre* and *La Bohème*. Tickets range from under £5 (restricted view bench seats up in the gods) to more than £150. On Mondays, some seats are offered at huge discounts.

The Linbury Studio is a modest alternative for experimental dance and small ensemble concerts. On Mondays, free lunchtime recitals are held here or in the Crush Room, one of the Opera House's many spaces for eating, drinking and socializing.

Poetry Café *hub of poetry life in London* `9 G3`
22 Betterton Street, WC2 • 020 7470 9880
>> www.poetrysociety.org.uk Open 11–11 Mon–Fri, 6:30–11 Sat

This is a good café in its own right, the fare ranging from Marmite on toast and a cup of tea to decent wine. It's also the venue for readings, poetry and jazz nights, open-mike slots and poetry slams. Come here to find out about the more itinerant poetry events around town, too.

Donmar Warehouse *innovative theatre* `9 F3`
41 Earlham St, WC2 • 0870 0606624
>> www.donmarwarehouse.com

Now under the directorship of Michael Grandage, the Donmar continues the success it achieved under Sam Mendes, who persuaded Nicole Kidman and other stars to perform on stage here. Productions have included Jonathan Kent's *Hecuba* and *Grand Hotel* directed by Michael Grandage.

12 Bar Club *live gigs in a tiny room* `9 F2`
22–3 Denmark Street, WC2 • 020 7240 2622
➤➤ www.12barclub.com Club open from 7:30pm daily

Hosting several acts each night in an upstairs room accessed via a tight alley, the 12 Bar is a great place to hear the ballads of an accomplished singer-songwriter. That said, it also puts on a frenetic London Callin' night (last Sat of the month), which draws on the capital's punk and ska heritage.

Drill Hall *offbeat drama, comedy & opera* `9 F1`
16 Chenies Street, WC1 • 020 7307 5060
➤➤ www.drillhall.co.uk

This alternative arts venue offers a great range of fringe drama, comedy and even opera in its 200-seat theatre. The Drill Hall also has a 50-seat studio for cabaret, a lively bar and a roster of courses and workshops that cover all aspects of performing arts. There's even a photographic dark room for public use.

ENO @ The Coliseum *opera in English* `9 G4`
St Martin's Lane, WC2 • 020 7632 8300
➤➤ www.eno.org

In its superbly revamped building, the English National Opera continues with its mission to present opera in the English tongue. To further popularize the art form, 500 seats are available for just £10 on weekdays. There are great views across Trafalgar Square from the public area on the top floor.

Borderline *tomorrow's rock stars today* `9 F3`
Orange Yard, Manette Street • 020 7734 5547
➤➤ www.meanfiddler.com

A small venue (capacity under 300) with a big reputation – bands such as REM, Oasis, Blur and Pulp have played at this hot and sweaty little club. More than this, though, it's a place for new bands to break through and for stalwarts of the US circuit to find a British audience.

Mean Fiddler *small venue, great sound* 9 F3
165 Charing Cross Road, WC2 • 020 7434 9592
>> www.meanfiddler.com

The Mean Fiddler puts on fewer gigs and more obscure names than the famous Astoria next door, but the proximity of musicians and audience, and the quality of the sound system ensure that it's an ideal place to catch up-and-coming bands. "Rock" is the capital's premier rock night held every Fri 11pm–3:30am.

Soho Theatre *literary haunt* 9 F3
21 Dean Street, W1 • 0870 429 6883
>> www.sohotheatre.com

Not only a theatre but also a scriptwriting centre, this modern venue in the heart of Soho takes plenty of risks with new writers. Expect the work to be fresh, enthusiastic and maybe rough around the edges. It's also a comedy venue, with leading performers such as Ricky Gervais and Kiki and Herb gracing the stage.

Curzon Soho *art-house cinema* 9 F3
99 Shaftesbury Ave, W1 • 0870 756 4620
>> www.curzoncinemas.com

The Curzon screens the best international releases and special features, such as seasons of Eastern European films or short art films. Few other cinemas would screen Eduardo Paolozzi's *14-minute History of Nothing*. Sunday is repertory day, offering such classics as *Alphaville* and *Rear Window*.

Buying Tickets for West End Shows

As a general rule, the cheapest tickets are sold at theatre box offices. If a show is sold out, you might be able to buy returns just before a performance. More expensive seats will usually be available through a STAR-regulated ticket agent. London has just one official discounted tickets booth, in the middle of **Leicester Square**, offering tickets on the day of the performance (open 10–7 Mon–Sat, 12–3:30 Sun). For further information: **www.official londontheatre.co.uk** has play summaries and tickets (it's linked with a pamphlet available at most theatres); **www.thisistheatre.com** provides details about performances and the history of venues; **www.londontheatre.co.uk** has seating plans and links to booking agencies.

Ronnie Scott's *revamped jazz institution*
47 Frith Street, W1 • 020 7439 0747
>> www.ronniescotts.co.uk Open 8:30pm–3am Mon–Sat
(music starts 9:30), Sun 7:30–11pm

Some of the big jazz names from the US may now favour larger venues such as the Festival Hall or the Barbican, but you can't beat the intensity of being just a few feet away from a group of musicians when they hit a groove. On a good night, Ronnie Scott's offers just such an experience and thereby maintains its reputation as the best jazz club in London.

There are two music sessions most nights; food is served during the first. With the audience's hunger sated, the late-night session focuses more fully on the music, drawing out the best performances.

At the time of writing, Ronnie's was undergoing a major revamp to upgrade its facilities, improve the food side of the operation and generally spruce the place up a bit – hopefully without losing too much of its old laid-back, easy-going charm.

Prince Charles Cinema *cut-price tickets* `9 F3`
7 Leicester Place, W1 • 0870 811 2559
>> www.princecharlescinema.com

It has been operating a cheap-tickets policy (£3–4 and super-cheap £1 Friday night specials) since 1991, but recently the Prince Charles has had a redesign to elevate its status. Plush seats and a glitzy bar now add to the enjoyment of a night out at this repertory cinema, which screens recent releases and classics.

Comedy Store *radical club comes of age* `9 F4`
1a Oxendon St, SW1 • 0870 060 2340
>> www.thecomedystore.co.uk

The Store opened in 1979 as a punkish riposte to the gag-merchants who then dominated Britain's comedy landscape, and it helped to create a new genre of free wheeling stand-up. It's a more conventional venue these days, but something of that initial spirit persists with the Sunday and Wednesday improv nights.

Performance

The Place *thrilling moves* 3 F5
17 Duke's Road, WC1 • 020 7121 1100
>> www.theplace.org.uk

The Place is home to the London Contemporary
Dance School and the Richard Alston Dance
Company. The primary stage is the Robin Howard
Dance Theatre, where you can see the work of recent
graduates as well as that of established choreo-
graphers and companies from around the world.

St John's *chamber music* 15 G2
Smith Square, SW1 • 020 7222 1061
>> www.sjss.org.uk

An elegant Baroque church of 1728 provides a
beautiful setting, as well as an acoustically excellent
one, for a programme of classical music. The Academy
of Ancient Music and the London Chamber Orchestra
perform regularly, and there's a reasonably priced
Thursday lunchtime concert series.

Wigmore Hall *supreme classical venue* 8 C2
36 Wigmore St, W1 • 020 7935 2141
>> www.wigmore-hall.org.uk

World-renowned for recitals, Wigmore Hall should be
the first destination for lovers of classical and early
music. The concert hall was built in 1901, its architect
Thomas Collcutt making extensive use of marble and
alabaster for the walls and flooring, which greatly
contributes to the room's acoustics. The fine quality
of resonance has attracted some of the world's most
acclaimed musicians and composers over the
decades, including Saint-Saëns, Prokofiev, Francis
Poulenc, Benjamin Britten and Jacqueline du Pré.

Major artists continue to be drawn here; recent
performers have included the Keller Quartet, Angela
Hewitt and Joanna Macgregor. The Wigmore also
attracts a very loyal audience, especially
appreciative of the hall's intimacy. In addition to daily
evening performances, there are Monday lunchtime
recitals and coffee concerts on Sundays.

Electric Cinema *plush film house* `6D3`
191 Portobello Rd, W11 • 020 7908 9696
>> www.the-electric.co.uk

A beautifully renovated, single-screen cinema, with
the most comfortable audience seating in London.
You can put your feet up on footstools, sit back in a
wide leather chair, and casually reach across to your
drink on a side table. This is Club-Class cinema-going,
with a bar for wine, beer and snacks at the back
(which closes 5 minutes before films begin) and two-
seater sofas on which the romantically inclined can
snuggle up. The programming is excellent too, with
choice films from around the world, as well as the
best of Hollywood's auteurs. On Sunday afternoons,
the cinema screens low-priced double-bill features.

   Another string to the Electric's bow is its next-door
brasserie, which is open from 8am for breakfasts,
then rolls on throughout the day and evening, serving
up perfect brasserie food, from club sandwiches and
whitebait to lamb chops and char-grilled fish.

606 Club *jazz with food and drinks* `13 G5`
90 Lots Rd, SW10 • 020 7352 5953
>> www.606club.co.uk Open nightly

Geared towards the British jazz scene (and, yes, there
is one), this cosy basement bar-restaurant club – with
brick walls, café furniture and low lighting – is open
to non-members if you book for a meal. This is the
only way to get a drink as well, and a fee is added to
the bill for the music.

Shepherd's Bush Empire *hot gigs* `6 A5`
Shepherd's Bush Green, W12 • 020 8354 3300
>> www.shepherds-bush-empire.co.uk

This one-time TV theatre is much loved by musicians
requiring acoustic subtlety. Celebrated artists such
as Beverley Knight and Van Morrison, as well as
relative newcomers such as Neko Case and Nitin
Sawhney, have played here in the last couple of
years. There are usually three or four shows a week.

>> *The BBC Proms concert series is one of the world's largest classical music festivals (see p17)* `129`

Riverside Studios *arts innovation* `12 A4`

Crisp Road, W6 • 020 8237 1111
>> www.riversidestudios.co.uk

Riverside Studios is a small arts centre with great scope and ambition. A repertory cinema offers nightly double bills of world movies, while two performance spaces serve up a wide array of international fare, from Colombian dance to Iranian theatre. The café-bar has a pleasant terrace overlooking the Thames.

Barbican *cultural gathering place* `10 C1`

Silk Street, EC2 • 020 7638 8891
>> www.barbican.org.uk

A major arts centre to rival the South Bank *(see p135)*, the Barbican was hewn from Brutalist concrete in a radical piece of urban planning. Beyond breezy walkways and concourses overlooked by apartments, the interior public spaces are open and welcoming. There's an excellent concert hall, a distinctly loungy cinema (independent, art house and repertory), a theatre and an experimental drama space, the Pit.

The concert hall is home to the accomplished London Symphony Orchestra and also hosts contemporary classical music, rock gigs and jazz – recent artists have included cult American singer Daniel Johnston and the South African jazz legend Hugh Masekela. The Barbican Theatre stages a mix of drama and dance. Gísli Örn Gardarsson's acclaimed production of Büchner's *Woyzeck*, with music by Nick Cave, was a returning hit in 2006.

The Spitz *live bands* `11 F1`

109 Commercial Street, E1 • 020 7392 9032
>> www.spitz.co.uk Open 11am–midnight Mon–Wed, 11am–1am Thu–Sat, 10am–10:30pm Sun

An arty bar and music venue in an increasingly lively part of town, The Spitz is set in a room above Spitalfields Market *(see p167)*. Relax to some rootsy sounds or submit to an acoustic onslaught from some avant-garde electro wizard of the knobs and dials.

Hackney Empire *restored theatrical gem* `5 H1`
Mare Street, E8 • 020 8985 2424
>> www.hackneyempire.co.uk

Having undergone a massive £15 million refurbishment a few years back, the Hackney Empire is now one of London's most impressive venues. The interior, designed by music hall architect Frank Matcham in 1901, is a superb piece of Victorian showmanship. A multicultural hodge-podge of influences from India, Italy and the Middle East is rendered into tiers that subtly reflect the social hierarchy of the time: plenty of curvy ornamentation for the rich; a lick of paint and a side entrance for the poorer patrons.

The setting makes any night out here feel special, but the programme of events deserves equal praise for its mission to bring every kind of entertainment to Hackney. Comedy, which was the strongest element pre-refurb, now vies with opera, jazz, classical, cabaret, drama and dance, with international acts featuring as well as local and national companies.

Comedy Café *food, drinks and laughter* `5 E5`
66–8 Rivington Street, EC2 • 020 7739 5706
>> www.comedycafe.co.uk Open from 7:30pm Wed–Sat

One of London's best places for stand-up. There's usually a couple of established acts such as Nick Revell, Julia Morris or Milton Jones in the line-up. The club's rather American in feel, with orderly table seating, pitchers of beer and burgers rather than pints and packets of crisps. Wednesday is open-mike spot.

Walthamstow Dog Track *fast canines*
Chingford Road, E4 • 020 8498 3300 • ⊖ Walthamstow Central, then bus Nos. 97, 357, 215 or W11
>> www.wsgreyhound.co.uk Racing on Tue, Thu & Sat; lunchtimes Mon & Fri

Even celebrities such as Brad Pitt and Claudia Schiffer have placed a bet down at "The Stow", as it's referred to by regulars. Enjoy the comfort of the Paddock Grill or mix with the commoners in the Popular Enclosure.

>> *For listings of London's many comedy venues, see www.comedyonline.co.uk*

Sadler's Wells *vibrant dance theatre* `4 A4`
Rosebery Avenue, EC1 • 0870 737 7737
>> www.sadlers-wells.com

A superb modern theatre, Sadler's Wells is primarily a dance venue, though it does feature opera as well. Choreographer/dancer Michael Clark has produced acclaimed works here, and the venue has also showcased Argentinian tango, the Rambert Dance Company and the Dance Theatre of Harlem.

Scala *live bands, club nights and more* `3 H4`
275 Pentonville Road, N1 • 020 7833 2022
>> www.scala-london.co.uk

The Scala positions itself as an alternative venue, putting on a mix of live acts (indie, world music and unsigned bands), as well as a staple of adventurous club nights. The Scala's events often have more than one focus on a given night, so live bands may well share the spotlight with DJs and film screenings.

Almeida *pioneering theatre* `4 B2`
Almeida Street, off Upper St, N1 • 020 7359 4404
>> www.almeida.co.uk

The Almeida had a revamp in 2002, acquiring Michael Attenborough as creative director along with a smart new foyer and café-bar. Attenborough's tenure has overseen the hugely acclaimed *Festen* and world premiere of Sebastian Barry's *Whistling Psyche*. The auditorium is a stark, serious and resonant space.

King's Head Theatre Bar *pub-theatre* `4 B2`
115 Upper Street, N1 • 020 7226 8561
>> www.kingsheadtheatre.org

A good pub on Islington's Upper Street has the added attraction of a tiny little theatre out the back. You can order a pre-theatre dinner as well, for a full evening's entertainment. Performances range from newly penned works to well-worn classics. Many stars have played here, including Ben Kingsley and Alan Rickman.

Union Chapel *atmospheric gigs* `4 B1`
Compton Avenue, N1 • Info 020 7226 1686; tickets from
Reckless Records on Upper St or at www.wegottickets.com
>> www.unionchapel.org.uk

The Union Chapel, a working Congregational church, is
a wonderfully Gothic setting for live gigs. Sit beneath
its dramatic arches and soak up the atmosphere with
Hungarian folk groups or creative pop musicians such
as Björk. It also hosts occasional comedy nights.

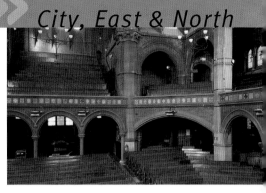

Koko *superb live venue* `2 D2`
1A Camden Road, NW1 • 0870 432 5527
>> www.koko.uk.com

Formerly the Camden Palace, this ornate ballroom
venue re-emerged in 2005 as Koko. It's added a new
spark to Camden, which has for decades enjoyed a
fine live-music reputation. Catch new bands, such
as the Magic Numbers, tried-and-trusted acts like
St Etienne and a contingent of US indie rockers.

Jazz Café *showcase for musical innovators* `2 D3`
5 Parkway, NW1 • 020 7916 6060
>> www.jazzcafe.co.uk Open 7pm–1am Mon–Thu, 7pm–2am
Fri & Sat, noon–4pm (jam session) & 7pm–midnight Sun

Not only jazz, but also soul, funk, world, latin, R&B
and hip-hop are performed here, so the Jazz Café's
remit is broad indeed. What the performers tend to
share is musical inventiveness. So, if it's a hip-hop
night, you're less likely to see a mainstream artist such
as Jäy–Z than you are to witness the lyrical flow of
Q-Tip or Guru (of Gangstarr fame).

As popular with performers as it is with regulars,
the Jazz Café welcomes back time and again the big
names of the jazz/funk/soul world, such as Pharoah
Sanders and Roy Ayers (who's practically made the
place his second home at times). In terms of creature
comforts, the Jazz Café on the balcony offers European
cuisine, while the downstairs bar, located in the
livelier, dancier area right in front of the stage, does a
brisk trade in beers and cocktails.

Performance

Jongleurs *comedy in comfort*
`2 D2`

Middle Yard, Chalk Farm Road, NW1 • 0870 787 0707
>> www.jongleurs.com

The Jongleurs empire started in Battersea just over
20 years ago. Battersea and Camden have both been
revamped but Camden is the smartest operation,
rolling out a mix of decent fast food, jugs of beer and
laughs aplenty. Established comics – such as Sean
Meo, Adam Hills and Gina Yashere – are regulars.

Hampstead Theatre *fresh new plays*
Eton Avenue, NW3 • 020 7722 9301 • ⊖ Swiss Cottage
>> www.hampsteadtheatre.com

Ensconced in a brand new light and airy home, the
Hampstead Theatre now has a larger auditorium, with
about 300 seats, and an extra studio space for its
most experimental work. Its ethos, however, remains
unchanged, and so it will continue to develop and
promote new writing and young actors.

Everyman *superior cinema*
`1 A5`

5 Holly Bush Vale, NW3 • 0870 066 4777
>> www.everymancinema.com

This is cinema-going at its most sophisticated. The
auditorium has an upper balcony of leather seats and
cushions, plenty of leg room and excellent sight lines –
so no having to stare at the silhouette of someone's
coiffured hair instead of the action on screen. Indeed,
the Everyman has the feel of a private club, with two
comfortable lounges and a bar offering a good
selection of whiskies, beers and wines, and a little
tapas menu, in addition to the two screening rooms.

You could easily idle away an afternoon or evening
here without even seeing a film, instead playing rounds
of backgammon, chess, jenga or mikado – a selection
of games available from the reception desk. However,
it would be a shame to forego the pleasures of an
excellent cinema programme, which takes the pick
of new films and a second look at recent releases,
and also offers classics and themed seasons.

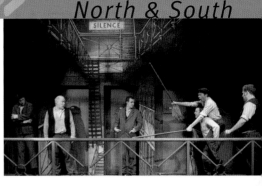

Tricycle *experimental drama*
269 Kilburn High Rd, NW6 • 020 7328 1000 • ⊖ Kilburn
>> www.tricycle.co.uk

Comprising a theatre, cinema, gallery and café-bar, the Tricycle is best known for its political and sometimes satirical plays. Musapha Matura's *Playboy of the West Indies* and Irish comedy *Stones in His Pockets* are among the productions that had their first London runs at the Tricycle.

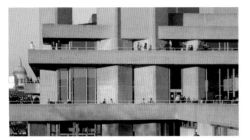

National Theatre `9 H4`
South Bank, SE1 • 020 7452 3400; bookings 020 7452 3000
>> www.nationaltheatre.org.uk

Behind foyer areas arranged on several levels are three auditoria: the fan-shaped Olivier Theatre; the smaller Lyttelton; and the Cottesloe, an experimental studio space. The programme accommodates classical and popular theatre – from big productions to experimental drama – and spectacular musicals.

South Bank Centre *music, music, music* `9 H4`
Belvedere Road & South Bank, SE1 • 0870 401 8181
>> www.rfh.org.uk

The South Bank Centre comprises three contrasting music venues: the **Festival Hall** for symphonies, the **Queen Elizabeth Hall** for chamber music and the **Purcell Room**, which specializes in solo and small ensemble performances. Rock/pop and jazz events are also hosted, including the annual Meltdown Festival each June/July. Two symphony orchestras are resident: the world-renowned Philharmonia and the highly praised London Philharmonic. The smaller London Sinfonietta also plays regularly.

The South Bank Centre is superb at putting on free entertainment too, most events taking place in the foyer/bar area and ballroom of the Festival Hall.

As part of a renovation of the Festival Hall, a row of shops (books and music) and restaurants such as Giraffe and Wagamama *(see p47)* has opened on the river front. The auditorium is due to reopen in 2007.

>> *For more information about the South Bank,* see p170

NFT (National Film Theatre) `9 H4`
South Bank, SE1 • 020 7928 3232
>> www.bfi.org.uk

This repertory cinema excels in themed seasons and serene conditions for film viewing. It's also the main venue for the London Film Festival *(see p19)*. A new extension has provided space for a gallery, a 30-seat drop-in studio cinema and a media-tech, where individuals can watch archive films for free.

Old Vic *theatrical transatlantic crossover* `10 A5`
The Cut, SE1 • Box office 0870 0606628
>> www.oldvictheatre.com

Built in 1818, the Old Vic is one of London's oldest theatres still in use and can list Laurence Olivier, John Gielgud, Vivien Leigh and Alec Guinness among its thespian credentials. With Kevin Spacey at the helm as artistic director, the Old Vic has attracted much media scrutiny as well as big-name stars.

Shakespeare's Globe *Tudor revival* `10 C4`
New Globe Walk, SE1 • 020 7401 9919
>> www.shakespeares-globe.org Theatre season: May–Sep

Recreating the ambience of Shakespearean theatre, the Globe is largely roofless, hence the summer-only season of the Bard's plays. There's bench seating in the middle and upper galleries; otherwise you have to stand, and will be encouraged to chip in with earthy comments rather than just polite applause.

Laban *dance for the 21st century* `16 A3`
Creekside, SE8 • Box office 020 8691 8600
>> www.laban.org

Housed in a prestigious building by Herzog & de Meuron (architects of Tate Modern), Laban is a centre for dance education and performance. Two venues, the Bonnie Bird and Studio theatres, offer contemporary dance and physical theatre, sometimes mixed with electronic media, such as video projections.

Ritzy *Brixton's picture palace*
Coldharbour Lane, SW2 • 0870 7550 062 • ⊖ Brixton
>> www.picturehouses.co.uk

Hugely popular with Brixtonians, the Ritzy is as much a place to meet up and hang out as a cinema per se; its upstairs café-bar is great for lounging to easygoing tracks laid down by the DJs. But with five screens, the Ritzy also has a diverse programme, mixing popular new releases with highlights from world cinema.

Battersea Arts Centre *in the studio*
Lavender Hill, SW11 • 020 7223 2223 • Train to Clapham Junction (from Victoria or Waterloo)
>> www.bac.org.uk

A centre for experimental performance, BAC favours interdisciplinary productions. With studio spaces, a main theatre and a café-bar that's an occasional venue for poetry events, BAC ensures that there's never a dull moment in leafy southwest London.

Rivoli Ballroom *a swirling time warp*
350 Brockley Rd, SE4 • 020 8692 5130
Train to Crofton Park (from Blackfriars)

This wonderful Edwardian dance hall has an arched ceiling, chandeliers and old-fashioned side-room bars. It has hosted the faux sophistication of Club Montepulciano (nights of crooning cabaret acts and light gambling), as well as salsa evenings, tea dancing, ballroom dancing, jive nights and trad jazz.

Tickets for Sporting Events
If you want to see the big football clubs, such as Arsenal and Chelsea, try official **club websites** first, then agencies such as www.footballtickets.eu.com or **www.frontrowpromotions.com**. Individuals post tickets for sale on **www.thegumtree.com**. You can also use web agencies for international rugby matches played at Twickenham (**www.rfu.com**).

London has two major cricket grounds: the Oval and Lord's *(see p113)*. Getting tickets for international Tests usually requires booking a month in advance or handing over vast sums (£200 or more) to an agency such as **www.londonticketshop.co.uk**. To catch the tennis action at Wimbledon, you need to queue in the morning or pay the exorbitant prices commanded by agencies for Centre Court matches.

pubs, bars & clubs

Pubs remain the city's main drinking institutions, but swish cocktail lounges and funky DJ bars are stealing more and more of the limelight. Meanwhile, the dance scene maintains a blistering pace, its focus now moving from mega-clubs such as Ministry of Sound to more esoteric venues such as 93 Feet East and Herbal in Shoreditch. From creaking old taverns to style bars, London's got it covered.

PUBS, BARS & CLUBS

Pubs are social hubs, where Londoners drink and chat, but the nature of the pub is changing fast. The beer served is as likely to be Japanese or Belgian as British, wine lists are expanding, and fancy foods are replacing the traditional bar snacks of salted nuts, pork scratchings and crisps. Out also goes the jukebox and in come the DJ decks, and in so doing the distinction between bars and clubs becomes ever thinner. Indeed it is the DJ bars and smaller clubs that are the best places for dance music these days.

Andrew Humphreys

Historic Pubs

Debate rages about which is London's oldest pub, and the **Prospect of Whitby** *(see p155)* – which dates back to the 16th century and was frequented by Samuel Pepys – is certainly a contender. The nearby **Grapes** *(see p155)* was a favourite of Charles Dickens, while Covent Garden's **Lamb & Flag** *(see p143)* was a 17th-century venue for boxing.

Hotel Bars

As London's hotel scene has undergone a makeover, so have the bars, and some of the most stylish drinking venues are in the city's hotels. Check out the Rococo-styled **Blue Bar** *(see p148)* at the Berkeley, the **Zeta Bar** *(see p146)* at the Mayfair Hilton and the **Lobby Bar** *(see p142)*, which exudes the same effortless style as parent hotel One Aldwych.

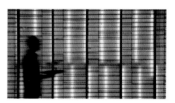

Top Clubs

New clubs open every week, but long-standing **Fabric** *(see p151)* remains one of the best. Hoxton's **Herbal** *(see p153)* may be modest in size but it still puts out guaranteed quality and variety all week long. Meanwhile, despite lacking a late licence, **93 Feet East** *(see p154)* has an enthusiastic following for its mix of cinema, gigs and club nights.

choice nightlife

Gay Bars and Clubs

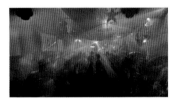

Old Compton Street is gay central but there's a pink streak running right across the capital from Brixton's **Fridge** *(see p159)*, which hosts Fusion, a gay night on the 2nd and 4th Fridays of the month, to Trade at **Turnmills** *(see p152)* and its late-night hedonism. Elsewhere, high campery is offered at the **Vauxhall Tavern** *(see p159)* on Saturday nights.

DJ Bars

Offering beats, grooves and intimate surroundings, the archtypal DJ bar is the **Embassy Bar** *(see p156)*. Similar in style are **The Social** *(see p146)*, which is owned by Heavenly Records, and **Cherry Jam** *(see p147)*, which mixes poetry jams with record decks. Opulent **Loungelover** *(see p155)* is the new darling of the scene.

Pubs Plus

As if the attractions of a pint weren't enough, London's pubs offer a wealth of further distractions. At the **Lamb & Flag** *(see p143)* there's free jazz every Sunday evening; **Café Kick** *(see p151)* has table football; the **Vauxhall Tavern** *(see p159)* has cabaret; and **Bread & Roses** *(see p161)* has stand-up comedy, board games and a Monday night quiz.

Lobby Bar *sophisticated cocktails* `9 H3`
1 Aldwych, WC2 • 020 7300 1000
≫ www.onealdwych.com Open 8am–11:30pm (8am–11pm Sun)

Located within the high-ceilinged lobby of a contemporary luxury hotel is this ultra-stylish cocktail bar. Sofas and high-backed chairs are arranged around an oversized wooden boatman. Uniformed staff mix magnificent Martinis, Bellinis and Collins, and deliver superior satay and sushi to a well-heeled clientele.

Heaven *gay nirvana* `9 G4`
Under the Arches, Villiers Street, WC2 • 020 7930 2020
≫ www.heaven-london.com Open from 10pm Mon, Wed & Sat

Set deep in the vaults of a railway bridge, Heaven is a gay clubbing institution. The regular slots are a dress-up-and-play Popcorn night on Mondays; Fruit Machine on Wednesdays (house, R&B and "pure pop") and Bang on Fridays. Saturday is party night. Men, women, gays, straights – all are welcome.

Gordon's Wine Bar *atmospheric cellar* `9 G4`
47 Villiers Street, WC2 • 020 7930 1408
Open 11am–11pm (noon–10:30pm Sun)

Tatty, candlelit and clandestinely romantic, Gordon's is an old favourite with Londoners. You'll rarely find a free table in this dusty former wine cellar between Charing Cross and Embankment stations, but the ambience makes up for the lack of comfort. With all the vintage publicity posters, smoky alcoves and rickety furniture, it feels like a relic from the 1940s.

A small bar dispenses an excellent range of reasonably priced wines, plus port, Madeira and a few sherries (there are no beers or spirits). Most customers part with £10 for a bottle of acceptable house red, but there's enough choice higher up the price scale to attract the connoisseur. A separate food counter offers a selection of cheeses and salads. The basement gives access to a row of terrace tables along Watergate Walk, a spot that's always busy on summer evenings.

The American Bar *Art Deco relic* `9 G4`
Savoy Hotel, Strand, WC2 • 020 7836 4343
» www.the-savoy.co.uk
Open noon–1am Mon–Sat, noon–10:30pm Sun

Authentic Art Deco details and the bar's classy location on the first floor of the Savoy Hotel have helped to attract decades of celebrity custom. It first gained global renown during American Prohibition, when wealthy folk from across the Atlantic demanded a higher standard of drink than was common in London at the time. Britain's first Martini was mixed here, and an entire Savoy cocktail book was compiled in 1930. Its most successful era was after World War II, when head bartender Peter Dorelli would concoct cocktail masterpieces. Ernest Hemingway and Ira Gershwin were among the rich and famous patrons.

Today's drinks list is extensive, if within traditional limitations, and pricey – all cocktails are £13 or more. There's also a selection of malt whiskies. Smart dress (including jacket and tie) is required.

Astor Bar & Grill *cocktail bar* `9 E4`
20 Glasshouse Street, W1 • 020 7734 4888
» www.astorbarandgrill.com
Open 5pm–1am Mon–Wed, 5pm–3am Thu–Sat

Previously known as – and little changed from – the Atlantic Bar & Grill, the Astor occupies the Art Deco ballroom of the former Regent Palace Hotel. Mixing master Dick Bradsell created the cocktail list; he is honoured with a private bar in his name next door.

Lamb & Flag *historic public house* `9 G3`
33 Rose Street, WC2 • 020 7497 9504
Open 11am–11pm (noon–10:30pm Sun)

In the 17th century, bare-knuckle fights were staged in the backroom of this Covent Garden old-timer – hence the pub's former name, the Bucket of Blood. Its old beams and panelling, creaky stairs and quirky signs attract quite a few tourists, but locals are also drawn by the selection of quality cask ales.

Bar Rumba *basement DJ bar*

9 F3

36 Shaftesbury Avenue, W1 • 020 7287 2715
>> www.barrumba.co.uk Open 5pm–3:30am Mon–Fri,
7pm–6am Sat, 8pm–1am Sun. Adm fee after 11pm

A well-established late-opening fixture of Soho
nightlife, this is not a glamorous place, but the
musical pedigree is impressive. Many of the world's
top DJs have spun here for a cosmopolitan crowd.
Drinks are reasonably priced.

The Endurance *Soho pub*

9 E3

90 Berwick Street, W1 • 020 7437 2944
Open noon–11pm daily

Sandwiched between second-hand record shops by
Berwick Street Market, the Endurance has a fine
range of beers and wines, and superb food at
lunchtimes. The mixed, music-oriented clientele
creates a lively ambience around a simple, one-bar
interior. Classic punk and indie are on the jukebox.

Madame Jo-Jos *Soho cabaret club*

9 E3

8–10 Brewer Street, W1 • 020 7734 3040
>> www.madamejojos.com Open Tue–Sat evening

This plush old theatre has been used as a location in
various films, including Stanley Kubrick's *Eyes Wide
Shut* (the scene where Tom Cruise meets the pianist
and tries to elicit the code word for an orgy). Club
nights include a regular Friday slot for Keb Darge's
Legendary Deep Funk, in which you'll encounter some
rare 45s and, usually, some acrobatic jazz- and break-
dancers shaking to the beats. On Saturday, Life and
Soul offers nu jazz, Latin, deep house and soul.

Madame Jo-Jos is best known for drag cabaret, and
on Saturday evenings the Kitsch Cabaret takes place
from 7 to 10pm. The excellent Kitty Cartier indulges
in sharp-tongued repartee with the audience, then
carouses them with show tunes and hits from the
1960s on. It's a big party, with raucous hen night
groups, jocular banter and the odd flash of old Soho
flesh from hired strippers.

French House *literary, gallic pub* `9 F3`
49 Dean Street, W1 • 020 7437 2799
Open noon–11pm daily (to 10:30 Sun)

This one-room cabin has a legendary past. Owned by the Belgian Berlemont family before World War I, The York Minster, as it was then known, enjoyed three golden eras. First came the cabaret days, when the great musical stars of Parisian *chanson* relaxed here between shows. Then the French Resistance used it as a London base for its clandestine operations. (De Gaulle and his Free French schemed in a room above the bar.) It became known as the French House at this time. In the 1950s, writers Dylan Thomas and Brendan Behan were among the celebrated regulars.

The Berlemonts and the bohemians have gone, but a hangover from those boozy, literary days remains. Beer is not served in pints, but in glasses. Wine, cider from Brittany, pastis and champagne are all popular; classic French labels are also sold by the half-bottle. A framed photo of De Gaulle still has pride of place.

The Player *sexy basement bar* `9 E3`
8 Broadwick Street, W1 • 020 7494 9125
Open 5:30pm–midnight (to 1am Fri & Sat)
Adm fee after 9pm Thu, Fri & Sat

This small bar is now part of the excellent Match chain, renowned for its cocktail expertise. You can expect high-volume music, slick service (many punters tip the waiters) and professional Martinis. Pre-booking a table is usually necessary.

Jerusalem *cheap eats & quality lagers* `9 E2`
33–4 Rathbone Place, W1 • 020 7255 1120
>> www.thebreakfastgroup.co.uk
Open all day from noon Mon–Fri (to 1am Thu & Fri),
7pm–1am Sat. Adm fee after 9pm (10pm Fri & Sat)

At lunchtime the long wooden tables of this basement bar/restaurant heave with media folk from Soho. By night, it vibrates with a thriving club scene; in between, a trendy, post-work crowd dives into pitchers of beer.

Market Place *Continental terrace scene* `9 E2`
1 Market Place, W1 • 020 7079 2020
Open noon–midnight Mon–Wed, noon–1am Thu–Sat,
noon–11:30pm Sun

The Market Place prides itself on a roster of great
DJs. It's part of the highly regarded Cantaloupe group
(see p51), which ensures a creative array of food and
cocktails, and unusual international beers. Having to
queue for entry is the only drawback.

Mash *bar-diner with long opening hours* `8 D2`
19–21 Great Portland Street, W1 • 020 7637 5555
Open 10am–2am Mon–Fri, 11am–2am Sat

Tongue-in-cheek retro chic defines the look. The
bar's back wall exposes huge vats of the Mash range
of house beers (draught pilsner, wheat, fruit or stout
varieties). There are cocktails on offer, too, and
sophisticated snacks, because the kitchen also
caters for a high-standard restaurant upstairs.

Zeta Bar *swish hotel lounge bar* `8 C5`
Mayfair Hilton Hotel, 35 Hertford Street, W1 • 020 7208 4067
›› www.zeta-bar.com Open from 5pm Mon–Sat (to 1am Mon &
Tue, to 3am Wed–Sat), 8pm–1am Sun. Adm fee after 11pm

Foxy decor, innovative cocktails and clubby music at
conversational volume help make the Hilton's bar a
destination in its own right. Better still, bar prices,
for Mayfair, are far from outrageous. The polished
clientele can enjoy oysters and Thai fish cakes too.

The Social *diner by day, club bar by night* `8 D2`
5 Little Portland Street, W1 • 020 7636 4992
›› www.thesocial.com
Open noon–midnight Mon–Fri, 1pm–midnight Sat

Daytime sees this street-level cabin café serve honest
fodder (burgers, pies etc), as well as beer, hot drinks
and the occasional cocktail. After dark, the area
downstairs becomes a DJ bar of renown. Live acts
have included Primal Scream and Badly Drawn Boy.

Cherry Jam *DJ bar* `7 F2`
58 Porchester Road, W2 • 020 7727 9950
>> www.cherryjam.net Open 6pm–2am Mon–Sat;
4pm–midnight Sun. Adm fee after 8pm

This is co-owned by Ben Watt of Everything But The
Girl fame. In the early evening the place is fairly quiet
and acts as a modest hangout for local hipsters.
Bands or record decks start playing after about 9pm.
Drinks include bottled beers, cocktails and coffee.

Lamb *characterful old pub* `9 H1`
94 Lamb's Conduit Street, WC1 • 020 7405 0713
Open 11am–11pm Mon–Sat, noon–4pm & 7–10:30pm Sun

A curio between Clerkenwell and Bloomsbury, the
Lamb is approaching its 300th anniversary, though
what is preserved is a masterpiece from the Victorian
era. Details include framed caricatures, etched glass
and delicate screens giving customers privacy. The
antique Polyphone music box is still in working order.

The End *steely cool club* `9 G2`
18 West Central St, WC1 • 020 7419 9199
>> www.endclub.com Open from 10pm; to 3am Mon & Wed,
to 4am Thu, to 6am Fri & Sat

Down in the vaults of a former post office, The End is
stylish in a minimalist way, with a kicking main room
and a slightly more laid-back lounge, where Rob
Mello and guests provide a mesmerizing concoction
of electronic funk and house. Great sound system.

Nag's Head *London's most eccentric pub* `14 B1`
53 Kinnerton Street, SW1 • 020 7235 1135
Open 11am–11pm Mon–Sat, noon–10:30pm Sun

The intimate layout and interior oddities of this neighbourhood pub, set in a cobbled cul-de-sac, hark back
to the early 1800s, when the place provided lodgings
for stablehands. An excellent choice of traditional ales,
fine food, a jazzy soundtrack and civilized atmosphere help ensure a solid core of amiable regulars.

>> *Many pubs do not serve food in the afternoons, after 2pm or 3pm*

Pubs, Bars & Clubs

Blue Bar *hotel bar of the highest standard* `14 B1`
Berkeley Hotel, Wilton Place, SW1 • 020 7235 6000
>> www.the-berkeley.co.uk
Open 4pm–1am Mon–Sat, 3pm–midnight Sun

The Blue Bar at the Berkeley Hotel is a triumph of detail. Touches of Rococo and Art Deco blend into an eye-pleasing backdrop of stucco and Wedgwood blue in an interior of restrained style. An equally polished bar staff quietly dispenses bowls of warmed nuts and large, spicy olives as guests peruse an extensive list of cocktails, champagnes, Highland and Island malt whiskies and fine wines. Cocktails such as a classic Martini or champagne-based drinks are perfect in mix and presentation.

American customers often opt for a classic malt and a cigar from the bar-side cabinet. The snack menu offers modern tapas dishes, which are as delicately presented as everything else here. On leaving, customers receive the same impeccably discreet nod that greeted them on the way in.

Townhouse *easy-going style bar* `14 A1`
31 Beauchamp Place, SW3 • 0870 242 1428
>> www.lab-townhouse.com Open 4pm–midnight Mon–Fri, noon–midnight Sat, 4–11:30pm Sun

This chic bar, set in a three-storey Georgian townhouse, serves cocktails created by famed mixologist Douglas Ankrah. There are more than 100 to consider, making for a tricky choice if your attention is further distracted by the classic movies projected silently on to a wall.

Apartment 195 *upmarket lounge bar* `14 A4`
195 King's Road, SW3 • 020 7351 5195
>> www.apartment195.co.uk Open from 4pm Mon–Sun

This exclusive style bar has created a much-needed buzz down the King's Road. Members and stylish guests mingle in the cocktail lounge, salon and TV room, sipping professionally mixed classic cocktails (moderately priced), fine wines and classy beers. Phone to reserve a table on Fridays and Saturdays.

Lonsdale *concept bar of renown* `6 D3`
44–8 Lonsdale Road, W11 • 020 7727 4080
»» www.thelonsdale.co.uk
Open 6pm–midnight daily (to 11:30 Sun)

A recipient of many Best Bar awards, the Lonsdale scores top marks for its decor, superior drinks and tapas-style snacks. Beyond the starchy doormen, the atmosphere is loungy and laidback – even though you know that the "just got out of bed" look sported by all present took hours to create. The interior, designed by leading bar architects Fusion, features futuristic, aged-bronze hemispheres on the walls, and steel bobbles in the smaller upstairs bar.

The famous cocktail list has been designed by London mixologists Dick Bradsell and Henry Besant. Martinis (choose from elderflower, rose petal, marmalade and other variants) are joined by fresh Raspberry Mules, Earl Grey Fizzes (delicate tea, mixed with bisongrass vodka and prosecco), Diane Von Furstenbergs (vodka, fruit, vanilla) and 60 others.

Trailer H *modest basement bar* `6 C2`
177 Portobello Road, W11 • 020 7727 2700
Open 5pm–late Tue–Fri, 6pm–late Sat

The H stands for "happiness"; indeed, the drinks list here is as good as it gets. House specials are lurid-coloured *tiki* cocktails, which look as innocuous as fruit smoothies but, boy, do they kick. Zombies are limited to two per person. It's the ideal venue for an apéritif before going to the Electric Cinema *(see p129)*.

Golborne Grove *pub/bar/restaurant* `6 C1`
36 Golborne Road, W10 • 020 8960 6260
»» www.groverestaurants.co.uk Open 11am–midnight daily

Golborne Road is London's "Little Casablanca", busy with Moroccan eateries and shops. The landscape is less colourful at its western end, but relief is offered by this popular establishment, which offers excellent food (international) from a daily changing menu, a fine wine list and all the usual beers and spirits.

»» *Smoking is still permissable in most pubs, though there are frequently no-smoking areas*

Pubs, Bars & Clubs ⟫⟫⟫

Notting Hill Arts Club *acoustic pioneer* `7 E4`
21 Notting Hill Gate, W11 • 020 7598 5226
⟫ www.nottinghillartsclub.com Open 6pm–1am Mon–Wed,
6pm–2am Thu & Fri, 4pm–2am Sat, 4pm–1am Sun

NHAC is always searching for new and exciting music
and art, and programmes a diverse range of club
nights, film screenings and live bands. Wednesdays
are for nostalgics, though, as Death Disco crashes
through some punk and indie rock.

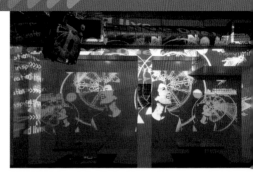

Windsor Castle *alfresco pints* `7 E5`
114 Campden Hill Road, W8 • 020 7243 9551
Open noon–11pm Mon–Sat, noon–10:30pm Sun

This characterful and friendly old pub is a prime
summer destination, thanks to its leafy beer garden
at the back. Fish and chips and traditional pub grub
always seem to taste that much better in the open
air. At less clement times of the year, drinkers cosy
up in a warren of oak-panelled rooms.

Black Friar *extraordinary interior* `10 B3`
174 Queen Victoria Street, EC4 • 020 7236 5474
Open 11:30am–11pm Mon–Fri, noon–10:30pm Sat

An unusual and much-loved landmark, the Black Friar
was built in Victorian style on the site of a former
Dominican monastery. An extravagant early-20th-
century Art Nouveau makeover left an interior with
marble surfaces, mirrored alcoves and decorative
monks. Grab a seat before the after-work crowd arrives.

Notorious Pubs & Literary Haunts
In the first half of the 20th century, the **Fitzroy
Tavern** was a shrine of London bohemia, frequented
at one time or another by writers Dylan Thomas and
George Orwell, magician Aleister Crowley and chief
hangman Albert Pierrepoint. South of Oxford Street
is the **Pillars of Hercules**, which is found in Dickens'
A Tale of Two Cities (1859) and was a favourite
meeting point in the 1980s for authors such as Ian
McEwan. On the same street is the **Coach & Horses**,
with the self-proclaimed "rudest landlord in Soho".
Hard-drinking journalist Jeffrey Bernard was a
regular here. The nearby **French House** *(see p145)*
has also been favoured by literary hellraisers and
troubled souls, including poet and novelist Sylvia
Plath. For individual pub details, *see p232.*

For the very latest on London go to ⟫ www.realcity.dk.com

Vertigo *London's highest bar* `10 D2`
Level 42, Tower 42, 25 Old Broad Street, EC2 • 020 7877 7842
>> www.vertigo42.co.uk Open by reservation only

Book in advance and dress smartly, and join City executives at the top of the former NatWest Tower for an unparalleled view of the capital. A choice of 30 brands of champagne, 10 fine wines and a range of classy, seafood-based dishes help to heighten the experience even further.

Café Kick *homage to the beautiful game* `4 A5`
43 Exmouth Market, EC1 • 020 7837 8077
>> www.cafekick.co.uk
Open noon–11pm Mon–Sat, noon–10:30pm Sun

A continental-style café-bar where twentysomethings are lured by the classic Rene Pierre table football, creating a vibe of friendly rivalry. European football memorabilia, bottled beers, wines and snacks from southern Europe add to the cosmopolitan mix.

Fabric *hedonistic clubbing at its finest* `10 B1`
77a Charterhouse St, EC1 • 020 7336 8898
>> www.fabriclondon.com Open 9:30pm–5am Fri, 10pm–7am Sat; check website for details

With three great rooms and sound systems that make your legs shake, Fabric is quite possibly the best club in London – at least, that's how it feels when you're in it. Club nights aren't all about big name DJs, but it's hard not to be impressed by a line-up of turntablists and musicians which might include James Lavelle, Craig Richards, DJ Hype, Peter Kruder or Grooverider. When he's not over at Herbal *(see p153)*, Goldie sometimes makes an appearance with his Metalheadz crew for an onslaught of junglist drum 'n' bass. Fabric's musical focus is house and techno on Saturdays and breakbeat, hip-hop and drum 'n' bass for Friday's FabricLive session, but you'll also hear electro and nu jazz. FabricLive has also been instrumental in bringing to London's attention live acts such as Norway's Röyksopp.

Fluid *the perfect start to an all-nighter* `10 B1`

40 Charterhouse Street, EC1 • 020 7253 3444
⟩⟩ www.fluidbar.com Open noon–midnight Mon–Wed,
noon–2am Thu & Fri, 7pm–2am Sat. Adm fee Fri & Sat

Fluid is a delightfully kitsch DJ bar with Japanese
details – screen prints, Asahi beer, rice-wine cocktails,
even a photo-sticker booth. With its retro video games
and superb soundtrack (leftfield beats, jazz dub,
chunky house), it's the ideal pre-club bar.

Jerusalem Tavern *old English pub* `10 B1`

55 Britton Street, EC1 • 020 7490 4281
Open 11am–11pm Mon–Fri

A simple, small wooden coffee house dating from
the early 18th century is now the flagship outlet for
North Suffolk's excellent St Peter's Brewery. Unusual
fruit beers and classic ales are served, while fine
pub lunches are provided for habitués of Clerkenwell
looking for a little respite from the area's DJ bars.

Turnmills *dance club* `10 B1`

63b Clerkenwell Rd, EC1 • 020 7250 3409
⟩⟩ www.turnmills.co.uk Open 6:30pm–midnight Tue,
10pm–4am Thu, 10:30pm–7:30am Fri, 10pm–6am Sat

An industrial-gothic interior with low ceilings gives
Turnmills a deep, dark and sweaty feel once the up-
for-it crowd gets into the groove. The club's rooms
include two main dance floors and some chill-out
areas; the music tips towards house and clubby R&B.

Cargo *live music & all-day drinking* `5 E5`

83 Rivington St, EC2 • 020 7739 3440
⟩⟩ www.cargo-london.com Open 6pm–1am Mon, noon–1am
Tue–Thu, noon–3am Fri, 6pm–3am Sat, 1pm–midnight Sun

Under the railway arches of Shoreditch, Cargo is a
daytime bar-café, a live music venue and a dance
club all in one. International sounds get an airing at
Champions of Sound (Fridays), and Cargo's occasional
mini festivals also promote diverse, global music.

Herbal *mixed bag of music* `5 E4`
10–14 Kingsland Rd, Shoreditch, E2 • 020 7613 4462
» www.herbaluk.com Open 9pm–2am Mon, Wed & Thu,
8pm–1am Tue, 9pm–3am Fri & Sat, 9pm–2am Sun

This is a club that's got all its priorities right: an old
warehouse building that's left largely untouched;
comfy bar with wooden floors and windows
overlooking the street; a superior sound system;
and, best of all, a menu of musical flavours that
pulls the initiated back again and again.

One of the best (irregular) nights is Eastern Drum
and Breaks: in the main dance area you can lose
yourself in some intense London-style tabla breaks,
while upstairs in the bar the mood is mellower, for
more Anglo-Asian experiments in sound. Other great
nights include the monthly Hospitality, for a less-
abrasive form of drum 'n' bass, Starf*cker for funky
house, and DJ Livewire's Sunday Service on the first
Sunday of the month. Herbal's guest DJs have
included Grooverider, Gilles Peterson and Goldie.

Hoxton Square Bar & `5 E5`
Kitchen *groundbreaking style bar*
2–4 Hoxton Square, N1 • 020 7613 0709 Open 10am–midnight
Mon–Thu, 10am–2am Fri & Sat, 10am–12:30am Sun

Formerly the Lux Bar (when it kick-started London's
style-bar revolution), HSB&K now has even more bare
concrete space and battered old sofas to lounge on.
Decent, simple bar food and good European lagers are
served. Grab a window seat before the evening rush.

Mother/333 *DJ bar and club* `5 E5`
333 Old Street, EC1 • 020 7739 5949
» www.333mother.com Open 8pm to 3 or 4am nightly

The first-floor Mother bar opens at 8pm nightly;
closing time depends on what's on. Club 333
downstairs joins up with Mother on weekend nights
for sweaty fun and a real mix of music. Top-notch DJs
such as Andrew Weatherall, DJ Pilly, DJ Blakey and
Smilex keep the mood upbeat.

Pubs, Bars & Clubs ❯❯❯

Vibe Bar *bohemian DJ bar* `11 F1`
Old Truman Brewery, 91–5 Brick Lane, E1 • 020 7377 2899
❯❯ www.vibe-bar.co.uk Open 11am–11:30pm Mon–Thu & Sun,
11am–1am Fri–Sat. Adm fee after 8pm Fri & Sat

Spread around various poky spaces in a former
brewery, this arty venue doubles up as a successful
DJ bar and live music outlet, and has helped to
regenerate the cultural life of the Brick Lane area *(see
p166)*. The main room may look makeshift – haphazard
furniture, murals, an old piano and a DJ shack – but
the Vibe is a well-run, multidisciplined organization
attracting customers from all income brackets.

A menu of curries, kebabs, pies and salads helps
wash down standard beers and strong cocktails. One
side room is sometimes given over to obscure board
games from the Indian Subcontinent; there's
Internet access, too. The best space is a cobbled
courtyard (covered and heated in winter), which
lends an al fresco, continental air to this otherwise
truly cross-cultural London experience.

Pride of Spitalfields *East End boozer* `11 F1`
3 Heneage Street, E1 • 020 7247 8933
Open 11am–11pm Mon–Sat, noon–10:30pm Sun

A solid, honest-to-goodness pub, located on a side
road off Brick Lane. Many come here for a swift drink
before visiting a nearby curry house. Traditional ales
include Crouch Vale Best, Fuller's ESB and London
Pride, plus obscure guest ales. Authentic jellied eels
come free on Sunday lunchtimes.

93 Feet East *bar & evening club* `11 F1`
150 Brick Lane, E1 • 020 7247 3293
❯❯ www.93feeteast.co.uk Open 5–11pm Mon–Thu, 5pm–1am
Fri, noon–1am Sat, noon–10:30pm Sun

You know this place must be a bit special, because
it manages to draw in a regular crowd despite
restricted opening hours. Success is due to a
searching music policy, mixing live acts, visuals and
great DJs, plus cool bar areas and a courtyard too.

Golden Hart *artists' haunt* `11 F1`
110 Commercial Street, E1 • 020 7247 2158
Open 11am–11pm Mon–Sat, noon–10:30pm Sun

Popularized by the 1990s crop of young British artists, this smoky Victorian institution of dark-wood panelling and traditional ales is also a favourite of workers from Shoreditch market. This gives the pub the feel of a genuine "local". In summer, there is outside seating. Be warned: the bar staff are notoriously abrupt.

Loungelover *hedonistic bar* `5 F5`
1 Whitby Street, E1 • 020 7012 1234
➤➤ www.loungelover.co.uk Open 6pm–midnight Tue–Thu, 6pm–1am Fri, 7pm–1am Sat, 4pm–10:30pm Sun

Next door to Les Trois Garçons *(see p51)*, Loungelover offers a camp interior of chandeliers and bizarre bric-a-brac, complemented by Lover-themed cocktails and champagne frosts, delivered by a studiously trendy bar staff. Book a table in advance at weekends.

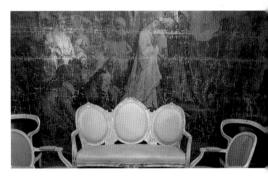

Prospect of Whitby *ancient inn on the Thames*
57 Wapping Wall, E1 • 020 7481 1095 • ☺ Wapping
Open 11:30am–11pm Mon–Sat, noon–10:30pm Sun

London's oldest riverside pub, still with its flagstone floor and pewter-covered bar counter, was a smugglers' inn in the 16th century, and later served liquid refreshment to Samuel Pepys and Charles Dickens. Today, it is enjoyed by locals and visitors alike, lured by real ales and views from the terrace.

The Grapes *another historic riverside boozer*
76 Narrow Street, E14 • 020 7987 4396 • Limehouse DLR
Open noon–3 & 5:30–11 Mon–Fri, noon–11 Sat, noon–10:30 Sun

As wonky and haphazard as when Charles Dickens described it in *Our Mutual Friend* (1864), this creaking wooden pub still boasts its riverside platform terrace. Today, it also has a first-class fish restaurant upstairs, and excellent seafood-oriented bar snacks. Real ales are on offer, too.

Pubs, Bars & Clubs

Medicine Bar *very popular DJ bar* `4 B2`

181 Upper Street, N1 • 020 7704 9536
Also at 89 Great Eastern Street, EC2
>> www.medicinebar.net

Open 5pm–midnight Mon–Thu, 5pm–2am Fri, noon–2am Sat,
noon–midnight Sun. Adm fee after 9pm Fri & Sat; DJs Thu–Sun

This enormously successful clubby bar on Islington's main street has now spawned a branch in hipper Shoreditch, but the original venue cannot be beaten. The formula is quite simple: take an ornate bar of the traditional pub variety; around it, create a laid-back interior of subtle lighting, tatty sofas and greenery; make sure you keep dispensing spot-on cocktails and standard beers at very reasonable prices; and, finally, hire a DJ to mix up a storm.

The sounds encompass jazz funk, soul, hip-hop, jazzy drum 'n' bass and house. There's a modest chill-out room, and on summer evenings the adjoining passage is filled with tables. The atmosphere is sexy and slightly bohemian; the clientele second-generation clubbers, who've sampled all kinds of nightlife and feel at home with something less full-on than a proper club night.

Admirably unpretentious, the Medicine Bar's only snag is its very popularity and infectious spirit. Two hundred people jigging around the narrow main bar on a busy night leaves little room for manoeuvre. Those people swanning to the head of the queue and enjoying discounts have gone to the trouble of obtaining a membership card – check the venue's funky website for details of this and forthcoming DJs.

Embassy Bar *very cool bar* `4 B2`

119 Essex Road, N1 • 020 7226 7901
>> www.embassybar.com
Open 5pm–midnight Mon–Fri, 5pm–2am Fri & Sat

While nearby Upper Street is big with party crowds, this bar draws the discerning. Behind an all-black exterior is a small bar room with a central, semi-circular counter and an outer ring of black leather furniture for lounging. Downstairs is the dance floor.

The Crown *friendly gastropub* `4 A3`
116 Cloudesley Road, N1 • 020 7837 7107
Open noon–11pm Mon–Sat, noon–10:30pm Sun

Fuller's Brewery made a wise choice when they decided to give this standard local a serious upgrade in the late 1990s. Set in a tranquil street surrounded by grand townhouses, The Crown's catchment area was undergoing a serious demographic shift. Soon the newly rusticated interior was filled with discerning high-income professional couples, ably catered to by an open kitchen *au fait* with chargrilled meats and continental sauces. The quality of wine on offer has improved beyond recognition, and cocktails, too, are of a standard (and a price) expected in the West End. The character of the original pub has been kept, with the etched-glass panels and a beautifully carved oak bar. The menu, chalked up on a board, invariably features a couple of safe standards, not least a superb Sunday roast. A patio comes into good use in summer, and children are welcome all year round.

Island Queen *elegant old pub* `4 B3`
87 Noel Road, N1 • 020 7704 7631
Open noon–11pm Mon–Sat, noon–10:30pm Sun

A haunt of actors and canal-side residents, the Island Queen is a study in decorum and good taste. Ships' figureheads set against dark wood and etched glass are attractive features of this venerable establishment. It is also appreciated for its fine ales (such as London Pride) and no-smoking section in the snug.

Pineapple *a locals' local*
51 Leverton Street, NW5 • 020 7284 4631 • ⊖ Kentish Town
Open 11am–11pm Mon–Sat, 11am–10:30pm Sun

The Pineapple is a gem of a pub, hidden away in the backstreets of Kentish Town. A cool, arty crowd served by cool, arty barstaff in cool, arty surroundings are the key elements. It also has real ales (including the sought-after Marston's Pedigree), good music and a conservatory.

Lock Tavern *DJ-run Brit pub* `2 D2`
35 Chalk Farm Road, NW1 • 020 7482 7163
»» www.lock-tavern.co.uk
Open noon–11pm Mon–Sat, noon–10:30pm Sun

This landmark venue in Camden (not by the Lock,
ironically) offers a textbook lesson in how to run a
modern, urban public house. Once a grimy Victorian
city pub, it has been renovated by a music-minded
team keen to appeal to discerning punters. The Lock
retains the comforts of a local pub – leather furniture in
the main downstairs bar, armchairs around the fireside
in the upstairs one – and runs an excellent kitchen,
providing what is best described as British tapas,
reasonably priced and catering to vegetarians.

   Fine ales are poured alongside standard lagers,
and sunk with abandon at weekends. The beer
garden (covered and heated in winter) and roof
terrace overlooking Camden Market buzz with savvy
young urbanites, happy to waste entire Sundays
here, when DJs play throughout the day.

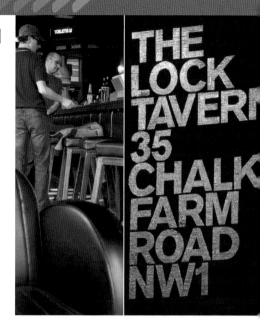

Peachy Keen *chilled cocktails* `2 D2`
112 Kentish Town Road, NW1 • 020 7432 2300
»» www.peachy-keen.com
Open 5–11:30pm Mon–Thu, 5pm–midnight Fri & Sat

The name comes from a line delivered by the Rizzo
character in *Grease*, but this is no dreaded theme
bar. Rather it's a classy two-floored venue of white
walls and low-slung seating in which to sip cocktails
– Martinis, Daiquiris, Sours and Mojitos.

Lockside Lounge *hip DJ hangout* `3 E2`
75–89 West Yard, Camden Lock, NW1 • 020 7284 0007
Open noon–11 Sun–Thu, noon–1am Fri & Sat

Super-stylish decor and fresh DJ sounds make this
Camden bar a local favourite of NW1 residents and the
throngs who've come to visit the market *(see p169)*. In
addition to an eclectic choice of beers and cocktails,
the Lockside Lounge serves delicious food in a long
thin room that's reminiscent of a barge interior.

Anchor Bankside *historic riverside pub* `10 C4`
34 Park Street, SE1 • 020 7407 1577
Open 11am–11pm Mon–Sat, noon–10:30pm Sun

Its heavy beams and bare stonework bore witness to
such famous figures as Dr Samuel Johnson in the 18th
century. Today, the Anchor's proximity to the Globe
and Tate Modern makes it popular with visitors and
it can feel overrun. But the riverside terrace offering
a City panorama is an undeniable draw in summer.

Vauxhall Tavern *high camp fun & laughs* `15 H4`
372 Kennington Lane, SE11 • 020 7737 4043
Open 9pm–2am Sat, noon–midnight Sun

Saturday is the big night here, when Duckie – a gay
London institution – features cabaret, punk, post-
punk and electro spun on the decks by London
Readers Wifes (sic). Between the main acts, hostess
Amy Lamé *(right)* orchestrates a quiz or two.
Sundays are for lounging with Slags Chillout DJ set.

Ministry of Sound *branded superclub*
103 Gaunt Street, SE1 • 0870 0600010 • ⊖ Elephant & Castle
» www.ministryofsound.com Open 10:30pm–5am Fri,
11pm–7am Sat; check website for other club nights

Many die-hard clubbers now shun the Ministry (in
part for its megalomaniacal branding), but you'd be a
fool to ignore one of its big nights, when the likes of
Little Louie Vega from Masters At Work or London's
very own Norman Jay take to the decks – bliss.

Fridge/Fridge Bar *Brixton institutions*
1 Town Hall Parade, SW2 • 020 7326 5100 • ⊖ Brixton
» www.fridgelondon.com Fridge open 10pm–6am Fri & Sat;
Fridge Bar open 11am–midnight daily (to 3am Fri & Sat)

Saturday's Love Muscle is the regular, pumped-up gay
night. On every other Friday, Fusion keeps things fast
and sweaty for clubbers of all persuasions until dawn.
The Fridge Bar has its own club – try the occasional
'Til Shiloh night, for dub, and roots and culture.

Beer Gardens
Few city-centre pubs have beer gardens, but there
are plenty further afield where Londoners revel in
a combination of beer and sun at the first warming
of the weather. One of the largest gardens belongs
to the **Freemason's Arms** just off Hampstead
Heath, and there's a smaller, prettier garden
attached to the nearby historic **Spaniards Inn**.

Islington residents drink under open skies at the
countryfied **Albion**; while over in Camden, the
defiantly urban **Lock Tavern** *(see opposite)* boasts
a roof terrace. Pick of the South London pubs for
alfresco boozing is the **Windmill**, which has
Clapham Common as its garden. The **Royal Inn on
the Park** is a fine East London pub on the edge of
Victoria Park. For individual pub details, *see p232.*

Pubs, Bars & Clubs

Babalou *DJs in the crypt*
The Crypt, Brixton Hill, SW2 • 020 7738 3366 • ⊖ Brixton
» www.babalou.net
Open 5pm–midnight Wed, Thu & Sun, 5pm–5am Fri & Sat

This destination DJ bar, club and restaurant, located in a spacious stone crypt beneath Brixton's St Matthew's Church, has recently been refurbished and renamed. It has a lounge feel, with stylish leather seats and benches, low tables and Moroccan lights that give the place a warm, mellow glow – a vibe completed by large church candles on every table.

Club nights are Fridays and Saturdays, with Friday nights devoted to arty classics, pop, house, R&B, funk and soul. Saturdays are concentrated on pure house. Resident DJs include Normski, Neil Fearnely and Danny Foster, backed up by an ever-changing roster of guest DJs. Reasonably priced cocktails and a loyal core of regulars – plus a surprising number happy to travel across the river for a night here – ensure that Babalou is in no danger of succumbing to over-gentrification.

Dogstar *DJ bar with attitude*
389 Coldharbour Lane, SW9 • 020 7733 7515 • ⊖ Brixton
» www.thedogstar.com
Open noon–2am Sun–Thu (to 4am Fri & Sat)

Dogstar is a large, loud dance bar, revered for having kick-started the Brixton nightlife revolution in the mid-1990s. A younger generation now meets under the overhead projectors, but the formula is pretty much the same: late, late nights, and serious partying.

Riverside Pubs

The **Founders Arms**, a modern brick bunker near Tate Modern, is the most central Thames-side pub. For more atmosphere and a riverside terrace, try **Anchor Bankside** *(see p158)*, which dates from 1775. Further east, other historic riverside pubs include the **Prospect of Whitby**, **The Grapes** *(both p155)* and, in Greenwich, the **Trafalgar Tavern** *(see opposite)*.

Hammersmith boasts a string of pubs linked by a riverside walkway. Best of the bunch is **The Dove**, which began life in the 18th century as a coffee-house and has Britain's smallest bar. The nearby **Blue Anchor** is where Gwyneth Paltrow engaged in silly drinking games in *Sliding Doors*. Richmond has perhaps the finest riverside pubs, notably the **White Cross**. For individual pub details, *see pp232–3*.

"Our lives shall not be swe
Hearts starve as well as bodi

Bread & Roses *family-oriented pub*
68 Clapham Manor St, SW4 • 020 7498 1779 • ⊖ Clapham North
>> www.breadandrosespub.com
Open noon–11pm Mon–Sat, noon–10:30pm Sun

This pub is run by the Workers' Beer Company, which lines up its own house ale alongside other quality varieties, and names its potent cocktails after famous revolutionaries. The pub food is wholesome, and children are unusually well catered for.

Prince of Wales *a pub with character*
38 Old Town, SW4 • 020 7622 3530 • ⊖ Clapham Common
Open 5–11pm Mon–Fri, 1–11pm Sat, 1–10:30pm Sun

The Prince of Wales is an eccentric pub, full of curios accumulated by the present landlord after a lifetime at sea. Superb ales feature strongly, although finding the space to enjoy them amid all the junk can be a problem. The pub attracts South London's bohemian dreamers, and serenades them with alternative music.

Greenwich Union *own-brew places*   `16 B3`
56 Royal Hill, SE10 • 020 8692 6258
Open 11am–11pm Mon–Fri, 10am–11pm Sat (to 10:30pm Sun)

Interesting house beers are available at this establishment, run by the Meantime Brewing Company. They include the company's Union brand, alongside raspberry and chocolate varieties and traditional Central European brews. There's excellent food, regular live jazz, a front terrace and a back garden.

Trafalgar Tavern *historic ale house*   `16 C1`
Park Row, SE10 • 020 8858 2909
>> www.trafalgartavern.co.uk
Open 11:30am–11pm Mon–Sat, noon–10:30pm Sun

This has been a Greenwich institution for over 150 years, its sturdy walls lapped by the Thames and its grand, high-ceilinged rooms dotted with maritime memorabilia. Real ales and wine are served in the three bars, and whitebait is a fixture of the menu.

streetlife

Markets are the pulse of local neighbourhoods such as Notting Hill, Spitalfields and Borough. Elsewhere, it is the bars, shops, galleries and cafés that provide the spark – as in Hoxton, where locals spill out of the pubs and onto the pavements at the first glimmer of sunshine. Other areas, notably Brixton and Soho, come into their own after nightfall.

Soho *24-hour party people* `9 F3`

The densely packed district between Oxford Street to the north and Chinatown to the south is a hive of activity day and night. **Old Compton Street**, Soho's main thoroughfare, represents London at its most sexually relaxed – almost every bar and café along the road (from **G-A-Y** to **Comptons**) has a predominantly gay clientele. There is a wider, international appeal to adjoining streets, where you find the **French House** *(see p145)*, the **Gay Hussar** (No. 2 Greek St) and the non-stop, caffeine-fuelled **Bar Italia** (Frith Street), in which Italian football plays on the screen whenever games are broadcast.

Wardour Street is busier, with some good food stops, such as **Satsuma, Meza** and **Spiga**, but the grittiest and most varied part of Soho lies between **Brewer** and **Broadwick** streets. Brewer is home to **Madame Jo-Jos** *(see p144)* and **The Escape Bar** (gay dance acts); style books (**Soho's Original Book Shop**) and gay erotica (**Prowler Soho**); **Randall & Aubin** for seafood and champagne; and **Lina Stores** *(see p71)*, one of the few remaining Italian delis in Soho (along with **Camisa** at No. 61 Old Compton Street).

Walker's Court leads through to **Berwick Street**, passing a concentration of sex shops and peep shows. Berwick Street retains a lively street market and is renowned for its record shops. **Vinyl Junkies** offers the latest in good dance music, and **Sister Ray** and **Selectadisc** offer a mixed bag of music styles, old and new. There is also a great selection of fabric shops, selling everything from silk to PVC.

Rainy nights and Soho go hand in hand, but if you find yourself here on a bright summer's day, pick up something sweet at **Patisserie Valerie** *(see p30)* and head for prim **Soho Square** or the spruced up **St Anne's Churchyard**. Here you can laze the afternoon away, until the lure of sweaty bars and loud music drags you back into the melee.

Portobello Road *shops, stalls & cafés* `6 D3`

Antiques market open 7:30am–5:30pm Sat;
general market & shops 9am–5pm Mon–Sat (to 1pm Thu)

This is one of the most characterful streets in London. A mile-long walk along its north-south axis takes you from pastel-hued Notting Hill cottages and quaint little antiques shops to a blankets-on-the-floor street market in the shadows of the Westway flyover. The area was lowly in the 1950s, and bohemian in the 1960s and 1970s. Today it remains – despite the influence of well-heeled local celebrities and films such as *Notting Hill* – eclectic, vibrant and fun.

The southern end of the road is at its busiest best on Saturdays, when the antiques market holds sway. The quaint shops have a preponderance of well-oiled cricket bats, ancient golf clubs, tanned leather foot-balls and old curling stones destined for re-use as doorstops. A clutter of Victoriana – enamel signs, painted buckets and faded flags – can be trawled through at **Alice's** (No. 86). Close by, refreshment is

readily available at the **Earl of Londsdale** on the corner of Westbourne Grove or the **Fluid Juice Bar** on Elgin Crescent. Just beyond the **Electric Cinema** *(see p129)* and its brasserie, Blenheim Crescent cuts across Portobello. Situated here are two excellent bookshops, **Blenheim Books** and the **Travel Bookshop**, which has a good selection on London.

The **general market** (with a nice stall for olives and breads) takes place below the flyover. Here, the **Market Bar** is always good for a lager or cocktail. **Café Grove** opposite has a first-floor terrace.

North of the Westway is **Portobello Green** *(see p87)* and a rambling Saturday market that peters out as it reaches the Golborne Road. Here funky clothes shops *(see p89)* and antique furniture shops spill out onto the pavements, and there are some good bars and eateries: **Bed** for drinks from early evening, **Galicia** for tapas; **Golborne Grove** *(see p149)* as the requisite gastropub; **Lisboa Patisserie** *(see p46)*; and **George's Portobello Fish Bar** for takeaways.

Streetlife

Westbourne Park *upmarket Notting Hill* `6 D3`

The joys of this characterful West London enclave are split between the leisurely shops of **Westbourne Grove**, and the eateries on **Westbourne Park Road**.

The Grove is a place for boutique-browsing on sunny days. Its focal point, strangely, is a Piers Gough-designed turquoise-brick public toilet building, reminiscent of the Art Nouveau Métro entrances of Paris. A flower kiosk, **Wild at Heart**, is built into the structure. Nearby shops include **Joseph** (No. 236), **Agnès B** (No. 235), **Camper** (No. 214), **Jigsaw** (No. 192) and **Anne Wiberg's** "trash couture" (No. 170). A 5-minute stroll up Chepstow Road – passing or otherwise the **Prince Bonaparte** – takes you to Westbourne Park Road. To your left are **The Oak** gastropub and **Lucky 7**, a groovy diner-type place for soups, sandwiches, hot dogs, beers and shakes. And to your right, the wonderful **Cow** and its friendly rival **The Westbourne**, both gastropubs of renown. For a quieter meal, there's **Rosa's**, a simple, almost rustic dining room at No. 69.

Brick Lane *curry houses & style shops* `11 F1`

Once synonymous with fantastic cheap curry houses, Brick Lane in London's East End has a more diverse character these days. The restaurants are still there – **Preethi, Le Taj, Café Naz, Bengal Cuisine, Meraz Café** on Hanbury Street, to name a few – though price rises and touting have tainted their image. North of the **Truman's Brewery** there is now a cluster of fashion outlets, stylish furniture shops and hip cafés and bars. The most interesting clothes shops are in Dray Walk on the old brewery site – **Junky, Public Beware** and **Gloria's Super Deluxe**. Nearby, **93 Feet East** and the **Vibe Bar** *(see p154)* soak up the evening crowds.

A daytime visit is best on Sundays, when the trashy morning market brings throngs of people to the streets here, but any evening is good for wandering between the neon-signed curry houses and maybe stopping in for a pint at the old-fashioned **Pride of Spitalfields** *(see p154)*. For more about shopping in Brick Lane and nearby **Cheshire Street**, *see p92*.

Spitalfields Market *fashion & furniture* `11 F1`

020 7247 8556

Open 10:30–4:30 Mon–Fri, 10–5 Sun

Currently London's most exciting market, Spitalfields – set in a historic building just east of the City – is jam-packed on Sundays with stalls selling everything from organic vegetables to retro furniture. Fashion has become its greatest strength, though – look out for the Vivienne Westwood-inspired **Grunge Vogue** and a young designer called **Kim**. Flower stalls, such as **Chayapa Flowers**, add to the fun, and permanent stalls such as **Arkansas Café** (barbecued steaks and roast poultry) provide tasty nourishment.

Weekdays are much quieter, but the market continues and on Thursdays trades almost exclusively in fashion. Lamb Street to the north and Brushfield Street to the south are home to interesting vintage furniture outlets, quality poster shops and traditional British food shop **A Gold** *(see p91)*. The **Market Coffee House** is perfect for a moment of repose.

Columbia Road *East End flower market* `5 F4`

From the break of dawn on Sunday mornings, this short stretch of narrow East London road rouses itself into a vibrant flower- and foliage-filled market. Stall traders shout about their bargain trays of bedding plants and wait for the late-rising urbanites to turn up for exotica in the form of banana plants and tree ferns. Snack stalls and cafés offer breakfasts, brunches and early lunches and, when that's done, the **Birdcage** pub on the corner of Columbia Road and Cosset Road is on hand to slake mid-morning thirsts. If that doesn't take your fancy, there's **Laxeiro** tapas bar at the other end of the market, **Stingray Global Café** for oversize pizzas or the more secretive **Nelson's Head** pub, tucked away on Horatio Street.

Alongside the horticulture, Columbia Road's shops offer a nice line in furniture (old, retro and new) as well as ceramics and funky light shades. By early afternoon, the crowds disperse, most carrying a pet-sized piece of the great natural world back to their city flats.

>> *For information about all Brick Lane's curry houses, see www.bricklanerestaurants.com*

Hoxton *bohemian Shoreditch* `5 E5`

It's indisputably London's coolest area for an artsy crowd – and Hoxton's bubble is far from bursting. Designers, artists and other creative types saw the potential in this down-at-heel district in the mid-90s, converting derelict buildings into studios and live-work lofts. A smattering of bars followed. Now the streets around Hoxton Square and Charlotte Road are lined with hip restaurants, clubs, design shops and galleries.

Hoxton wakes up late, and the daytime streets can feel quite lazy, especially at weekends when people saunter between the galleries. Jay Jopling's **White Cube**, situated on the square, is the biggest gallery; **The Agency** (ring the buzzer at 18 Charlotte Road) is one of the longest established. There's also a great contemporary arts bookshop, **ARTWORDS**, at 65 Rivington Street. Arrive late in the afternoon, take up a seat at one of the bars and watch the throngs gather as the sky darkens. **The Bricklayer's Arms** on Charlotte Road is an old stalwart, while **Zigfrid** has Chesterfield sofas and large windows framing the square.

Ktchn (35 Charlotte Rd) does excellent European/Middle Eastern salads to take-away. Many of the bars serve decent food (**Cantaloupe**, *see p51*, and the **Great Eastern Dining Room**, *see p52*), **Hoxton Square Bar & Kitchen**, *see p153*, and again, Zigfrid). For a little more formality, head for the **Hoxton Apprentice** (on the square at No. 16), **Rivington Bar and Grill** (Rivington St) or **The Eyre Brothers** (Leonard St).

On Curtain Road and Shoreditch High Street, the bars have more of a boyish feel to them, with much evidence of pool tables (**Elbow Room** and **Pool**, opposite each other on Curtain Road). **Bar Kick** on Shoreditch High Street has table football. **Juno**, next door, has a variety of nostalgic games for those who grew up in the age of *Space Invaders* and *Pac Man*.

Round the corner on Kingsland Road is a bar called **Dream Bags/Jaguar Shoes**. The name was left over from a shop that used to occupy the site – a ruse that befits the bar's laid-back, arty style. For the late-night, early-morning crowd, there are the clubs **Herbal**, **Cargo** and **Mother/333** *(see pp152–3)*.

Camden Lock *Camden Market's best spot* **2 D2**

The roadway from Camden Tube to Chalk Farm Road Tube is awash with stalls dishing out T-shirts, cheap fashionwear and all manner of smoking paraphernalia. The nicest part of **Camden Market**, though, is at its furthest reaches, in and around the railway arches of **Stables Market**. Here, you'll find a good mix of retro-style clothes, furniture and curios. There's also "goth" gear and techno clubwear – the latter in the clublike space of **Cyberdog**, where a bar serves guarana drinks and fruity "detox" concoctions. The music gets evermore manic, and the whiff of incense and cooking hangs everywhere.

The snacks served by the market food stalls are just belly-fillers, though. If you want a more carefully prepared meal and a drink, head across Chalk Farm Road to the **Lock Tavern** *(see p158)*, or to its near neighbour the **Loch Fyne Oyster Bar**. **The Enterprise**, a free house (pub) right outside Chalk Farm Road station, serves up a good pint.

Borough *London's larder by the river* **10 D4**

With the rumble and clatter of trains passing overhead, **Borough Market** (open noon–6pm Fri and 9am–4pm Sat; some stalls Thu) on the South Bank brightens the shadows of Southwark's railway arches with bright red and yellow awnings spread above stalls selling Spanish hams, local breads, French cheeses, and wild game from the Highlands of Scotland. This is the belly of modern London, a neighbourhood crammed with the warehouses of food importers. As well as buying food to take away, market regulars can munch on juicy venison burgers, washed down with a pint at the **Market Porter**, **The Wheatsheaf** or the **Globe Tavern**. Day-trippers tend to take a more leisurely lunch, with a meal at **Fish!** or **Cantina Vinopolis**.

Though the attractions of the riverbank are great, it's worth exploring a few of Borough's inland streets, which yield up great pubs, such as the **Old King's Head** and the historic **George Inn**, both situated in yards just off Borough High Street.

The South Bank *riverside culture* `10 A4`

At the heart of an arching, river-hugging cultural quarter, the South Bank Complex includes the **South Bank Centre** *(see p135)*, **Hayward Gallery** *(see p115)* and the **National Theatre** *(see p135)*. Tucked under Waterloo Bridge are the **NFT** *(see p136)*, its lively **Film Café** and some second-hand bookstalls.

Few people are indifferent to the Brutalist/International Style architecture of these buildings, and the National Theatre in particular is often vilified – unjustly so, given the fantastic interior spaces, which include many café, bar and foyer areas for socializing and free entertainment. The Long Bar at the National, for example, hosts an excellent pre-theatre programme of World Music in the early evening.

To the west of this complex is the touristy area around the **London Eye** *(see p13)*. To the east, along the riverbank, is the quieter, prettier area of **Gabriel's**

Wharf – a kind of middle-class shanty town, with pizzerias and crafts shops, a place to hire bicycles (**London Bicycle Tour Co**) and **Riverside Therapies** for a shiatsu or Swedish back rub. Further east, crafts continue at the **Oxo Tower Wharf** *(see p95)*, also home to its namesake restaurant *(see p58)*.

Tate Modern *(see p117)* brings thousands to Bankside daily, along the riverside walk, across the **Millennium Bridge** from the direction of St Paul's, or by riverboat *(see p102)*. Visitors to **Shakespeare's Globe** *(see p14)* and to **Vinopolis** (a wine museum with a good bistro) swell the numbers further. Two pubs on hand, the **Anchor** *(see p158)* and the **Founders Arms** *(see p160)*, get very busy in summer. Venture a little further along the river to the freshly scrubbed **Southwark Cathedral** *(see p115)*, and you will find plenty of great pubs and cafés, and the superb food market at **Borough** *(see p169)*.

Northcote Road *neighbourhood food market*
Train to Clapham Junction (from Waterloo or Victoria)
Market open 9–5 Thu, Fri & Sat

Clapham's market road is at its jolliest on Saturdays. London's foodies are well served by delicatessens, shops and stalls selling designer kitchenware, cheeses, artisan breads, meats and fresh fish. Make up a picnic to take to nearby Clapham Common or eat at the superb **Gourmet Burger Bar Kitchen** (No. 44). For a drink, it has to be **The Eagle** on Chatham Road.

Brixton *lively days & even livelier nights*
At the southern end of the Victoria Tube line, Brixton is home to a mix of cultures and social groups. This diversity is reflected in the shops, cafés, restaurants, bars and clubs. Busy with a lively market by day, it is, however, at night that Brixton comes into its own, when it draws in a youthful, partying crowd.

The **Dogstar** *(see p160)*, **Living** and the **Fridge Bar** *(see p159)* all get going early, as do the local eateries – **Ichiban** for sushi, **Fujiyama** and the **Satay Bar** for noodles and rice dishes, and **Bamboula** for Caribbean food. For an unusual dining experience, try the atmospheric **Babalou** *(see p160)*, which sits in the crypt of St Matthew's Church, or opt for **66 Atlantic** if you want a cool, street-side setting on Atlantic Road.

As the night draws on, the streets are criss-crossed with people heading in different directions: the **Brixton Academy** for live bands; the **Ritzy** *(see p137)* for films; **Tongue & Groove** and **Neon** for cocktails in a clubby vibe; or the pulsating **George IV** and **White Horse** DJ bars on Brixton Hill. **Mass, Substation South** (gay) and the **Fridge** (mixed, *see p159*) are the big clubs with all-nighters on Fridays and Saturdays. Adding a new note to these long-established dance venues is **Plan B**, a bar/club on Brixton Road.

Throughout the night, buses head back into central London from outside the Fridge, and there's a black cab rank outside the cinema. But many revellers stay until 6am, spilling out onto Brixton's green by the church in the early morning sunlight.

havens

Sometimes you just need to steal away from the accelerated pace of city life. A wealth of parks makes London one of the world's greenest cities. But, even in the centre of town, there are many other places that offer solace and respite. Health spas and massages provide deep relaxation, while secret courtyards, old stone churches and tranquil woodland cemeteries afford the opportunity for a quiet stroll and contemplation.

Havens

Temple *serene courtyards of the judiciary* 10 A3
Off Fleet Street, EC4 • Tours 020 7797 8241 (minimum of 5)
>> www.innertemple.org.uk or www.middletemple.org.uk

Background noise drops to the level of polished shoes clipping across worn flagstones as soon as you venture through the small archway of Inner Temple Lane. Take a slow stroll around the interconnected courtyards of the Inner and Middle Temples, surrounded by the chambers of law firms established here since the mid-14th century. Before that time, the area belonged to the Knights Templar; the statue by Temple Church *(see p104)*, which depicts two knights sharing a horse, recalls the vows of poverty made by that military brotherhood when it was formed in 1117.

By the side of Middle Temple's Elizabethan Banqueting Hall is the perfect oasis of Fountain Court, its gnarled trees propped up by posts around a small pool and fountain, with plane trees towering overhead. Beyond here, lawns (usually open 12:30–3pm Mon–Fri) stretch down towards the Thames.

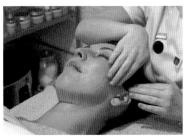

Indian Head Massage *free your mind* 8 C3
Farmacia, Selfridges, 400 Oxford Street, W1 • 020 7318 2365
>> www.farmacia123.com Head massage on Tue, Thu & every other Sat

The Indian head massage technique uses pressure, finger taps and light flicks to release tension. The masseuse will concentrate on your head and neck, but may work all the way down to the tips of your toes in order to find the source of tension. You may experience some discomfort here and there, but, by the end of the half-hour session, you should feel a deep sense of relaxation.

Victoria Embankment Gardens *breathing space* 9 G4

Though small, these gardens are a treasure for anyone wishing to steal away from the hurly-burly of the city. A small café rustles up all-day breakfasts, and music plays from the bandstand in summer, while workers on their lunch break soak up the sunshine. Look for the implausibly placed watergate – the land around here was claimed from the Thames in 1862.

For the very latest on London go to >> www.realcity.dk.com

Elemis Day Spa *queenly pampering* `8 D3`
2–3 Lancashire Court, W1 • 020 7499 5095
>> www.elemis.com Open from 9am daily

Both men and women are welcome at this spa, which is renowned for discreet ocean wraps, Japanese silk facials, stone therapies, Balinese borehs and dozens of other exotic rituals. A "rasul" with mud in a steam room is the cheapest option, but you must book several weeks in advance or hope for a cancellation.

Bunhill Fields Burial Ground *Blake's resting place* `10 D1`
City Road & Bunhill Row, EC1 • 020 7374 4127
Open 7:30am–7pm Mon–Fri, 9:30–sunset Sat & Sun (Oct–Mar: closes 4pm)

Close to the Barbican and a short walk from the buzz of Hoxton, Bunhill Fields is a remarkably quiet and shady spot. A pathway cuts through its little wooded burial ground, where the tombs of writers William Blake, Daniel Defoe and John Bunyan take pride of place. To the side of the graves is a glade-like lawn – a magical place to stretch out on a summer's day and listen to the birdsong.

St Olave's Recitals *a melodious hour* `11 E3`
Hart Street, EC3 • 020 7488 4318
Recitals Wed & Thu 1–2pm; donations welcome

Sitting in the cool of a stone church and listening to one of St Olave's free lunchtime recitals is a splendid way to relax into a contemplative mood. London's 17th-century diarist Samuel Pepys cherished St Olave's, though he often slept through sermons. There's a pretty little churchyard at the Seething Lane entrance.

The Royal Parks

There are nine Royal Parks in all, some of them far from the city centre, in places such as Richmond and Greenwich *(p180)*. Of the central parks **St James's** is the oldest, and is considered by many to be the most elegant. It separates Crown (Buckingham Palace) and State (the Houses of Parliament) with a swathe of grassland and a lake fringed by languid willows. The biggest is **Hyde Park,** though technically its western end – where you'll find the Serpentine Gallery *(see p107)* and the Orangery *(see p176)* – is **Kensington Gardens. Regent's Park** has attractive formal gardens as well as wide open spaces, which host open-air theatre and concerts. Both Hyde Park and Regent's Park offer guided nature walks. For details, visit www.royalparks.gov.uk.

Havens

Holland Park *genteel charm*   6 D5

The former grounds of a Jacobean country house, Holland Park holds a variety of delights, including woodland walks, formal English gardens and a splendid French restaurant. The house itself stands at the centre of the park, but, never having recovered from bomb damage in World War II, it now serves mainly as a backdrop to outdoor performances on summer evenings.

The outbuildings have fared better, with the Garden Ballroom now home to Marco Pierre White's Belvedere restaurant (modestly priced for a set lunch). If your appetite or wallet are not up to that, look for the pleasant café offering simpler fare that has taken root next to one of the garden walls.

The Rose Garden is perhaps the greatest sensorial delight of the formal gardens, while the Kyoto Garden, severe when laid out in 1991, has mellowed into a serene corner. The call of peacocks as they strut around their domain adds to the charm of the park.

Porchester Spa *Art Deco retreat*   7 F3
Queensway, W2 • 020 7792 3980
Open 10–10 daily; call for details of men-only, women-only & mixed sessions

This beautiful Art Deco day spa of the 1920s is great value and attracts a diverse mix of people. Enjoy a Swedish massage or Moroccan glove body scrub, along with unlimited access to Turkish baths, Russian steam rooms and an icy plunge pool. Snacks are served in the frigidarium (cool room) upstairs.

Orangery *antidote to museum fatigue*   7 F5
Kensington Gardens, W8 • 020 7938 1406
Open Mar–Oct 10–6; Nov–Feb 10–5; tea served from 3pm

Set next to Kensington Palace, the graceful Orangery, dating from 1704, is a light-filled, yet cool retreat. Add to this the glorious gardens and the chance to enjoy a leisurely summer lunch or afternoon tea at this superior café, and you have ample reward for a morning spent shopping or in the museums of Kensington.

Chelsea Physic Garden *herbal cures* `14 B4`

Swan Walk, SW3 • 020 7352 5646
➤➤ www.chelseaphysicgarden.co.uk
Open Apr–Oct: noon–5 Wed, 2–6 Sun & special events

A gateway bristling with knotted vegetation leads you into the secluded world of a garden in which the beauty and fragrance of the plants are matched by their restorative qualities. Established by the Society of Apothecaries in 1673, this was the herbal medicine cabinet of its day, and still operates as a research centre. Though dripping with blooms and bursting with verdant foliage, the World Medicine Garden and other areas retain a scientific orderliness, with small cards indicating the curative properties of each specimen. The pomegranate turns out to be quite a fruit – not only has it been used to purge envy, but it is also thought to be a reasonable cure for worms.

Sit in one of the tranquil spots where chairs have been set, and you'll soon appreciate the simpler restorative qualities of this unique English garden.

Little Venice *canal boats, cafés and bars* `7 G1`

Blomfield Road & Warwick Crescent, W2
Boat trips: London Waterbus Company, 020 7482 2660

Little Venice centres on the junction of two canals: Regent's Canal, which links to the Thames, and the Grand Union, which extends all the way to Birmingham. Until relatively recently, this area was known as Browning's Pool, in honour of the 19th-century poet Robert Browning, who lived nearby. The tranquil waterways are a delightful city oasis, overlooked by Rembrandt Gardens, and dotted with colourful houseboats, barges and pleasure craft. Locals sit and gaze at the scene, while boat owners potter about their cheerily decorated vessels.

The neighbourhood has several nice eateries. One of the best is **The Bridge House Canal Theatre Café** on Delamere Terrace. This serves tasty food, and there's also live comedy, music and theatre upstairs. You can also board a ferry at Little Venice, and take a 50-minute trip through Regent's Park to Camden.

Havens

Hampstead Heath *ancient heathland* `1 C2`

This vast, elevated expanse of grassy slopes and woodlands, bordered on all sides by North London's wealthiest residential districts, is a magnificent remnant of real countryside within walking distance of the Tube. Londoners travel up here – in droves on Sundays – to gaze down upon their city, breathe deep and shake off urban stresses.

For a satisfying exploration of the Heath, try a circular walk from Hampstead village. Starting at the Tube station, wander through the quiet back roads past historic houses where luminaries such as John Keats *(see p114)*, George Orwell and H G Wells once lived. Crossing East Heath Road, you then step into the wilds, initially following a wide track through the woods. The destinations of the many crisscrossing paths are not easy to fathom, and it's best to

meander in a vaguely northeasterly direction, through woodlands up to **Kenwood House** *(see p114)*, home to the Iveagh Bequest, with a café in the old coach house. Just beyond the house, in the direction of Highgate, are fantastic views. From these lofty heights, central London unfolds in a smoky blue haze along the shallow valley of the Thames, the distant towers and construction cranes of the City and Docklands contrasting with the slope of long grass at your feet.

Follow the path down the open slope and turn right at the bottom of South Wood, which forms the boundary of the Kenwood estate. From here, the path will take you back to Hampstead, past playing fields and old duelling grounds. Return to the welcoming pubs of Hampstead – **The Freemason's Arms** (Downshire Hill), **The Flask** (Flask Lane), **Ye Olde White Bear** (Well Road) and the **Holly Bush** (Holly Bush Steps).

Highgate Woods *woodland ramble*

A short walk up Muswell Hill Road from Highgate Tube station brings the woods into view: to your left, **Highgate Wood** proper; to your right, the dell of **Queen's Wood**. Both are rich in oak and hornbeam and the sound of birdsong – about 70 species of birds have been spotted here. Either wood is blissful for an hour or so of rambling on footpaths. Highgate Wood is more open, the wide paths eventually giving way to a playing field and the pleasant **Oshobasho Café** (open 8:30am–6pm or dusk if earlier). The more densely forested Queen's Wood has a **Weekend Café** (10–6 Sat & Sun), charmingly set amid the trees in a cottage with a verandah.

Having cleared mind and lungs, reintroduce yourself to city life gradually by way of **Highgate Village**. Drop by the **Flask** (corner of The Grove and Highgate West Hill), which serves English ales and Belgian monastery brews, and good pub food. Also pay a visit to **Highgate Cemetery** *(see p111)*, off Swain's Lane.

Abney Park Cemetery *graveyard for dissenters*

Stoke Newington Church Street, N16 • ⊖ Angel or King's Cross, then bus No. 73; or train to Stoke Newington (from Liverpool St) **≫** www.abney-park.org.uk Open daylight hours daily

Neglected for much of the 20th century, Abney Park is a gothic fantasy – gravestones broken and scattered, statues toppled and overrun with ivy, and green tendrils grasping to reclaim the ground. This natural tide has been only partially stemmed by recent interventions to clear pathways, and it remains a wild and enchanting woodland. Among the religious nonconformists buried here the most famous is William Booth, founder of the Salvation Army.

The main entrance, with its dramatic Egyptian gateway, is on Stamford Hill, but the more secretive way in is via a small gate on Church Street. The inner reaches – where you'll eventually reach a decrepit chapel – can feel very remote, and if you are visiting alone you may feel safer at the weekend, when it becomes the haunt of local families.

Havens

Greenwich Park *panoramic views*
16 C3

Greenwich, SE10 • Park Office: 020 8858 2608
>> www.royalparks.gov.uk/parks/greenwich_park
Open from 6am daily

A walk around this breezy, partly formal, partly wild park, which stretches from the historic dockyards at Greenwich up the hill to Blackheath, offers fine views of London. From the top of the park, you can see the Thames wend through the metropolis, its banks giving rise to some of the densest clusters of development at Docklands, The City and Westminster.

Between the moored **Cutty Sark** at Greenwich Pier and Wren's **Old Observatory** at the top of the hill, the park's main paths are usually thronged with visitors, but stray from them and you can soon lose the crowds. Beyond the Observatory, heading south, you'll find a cricket green, the wilds of a deer park, formal gardens and even Roman earthworks to explore. But if you don't want to lose sight of the river, head east to another promontory, One Tree Hill, on the Maze Hill side of the park. From here, there are views across to the Observatory and down to the **Old Royal Naval College** and the **Queen's House** *(see p119)*. The latter is mostly obscured by a clump of trees at the foot of the hill, while beyond looms Canary Wharf, the brown, silty Thames looping at its feet.

Walk down one of the meandering pathways, past the children's playground and then towards a gate that brings you out onto Park Row. You can either head to the Thames end of the road for a drink and a plate of whitebait at the **Trafalgar Tavern** *(see p161)* or take an immediate right for a quieter drink at **The Plume of Feathers**. Either way, it's good to finish off a walk in Greenwich with a riverside stroll back to the pier.

Kew Gardens *World Heritage beauty spot*

Kew • 020 8332 5655 • ⊕ Kew Gardens

➤➤ www.kew.org Open 9:30–6 Mon–Fri, 9:30–7 Sat & Sun

The extensive, astonishingly lovely Royal Botanical Gardens are stocked with mature specimens of rare (and ordinary) trees, plants and flowers collected over hundreds of years from the remotest corners of the world. From the Tube and train station it's a well-signed 5-minute walk along leafy residential streets to the main, Victoria Park entrance. Maps, supplied with your tickets, place everything clearly.

The scale of Kew means that it is not difficult to find private space. The gardens comprise both wild and formal areas – woodlands; formal lawns and beds overflowing with ever-changing floral displays; lakes stocked with wildfowl; elegant glasshouses; and an eclectic collection of buildings including the landmark 10-storey **Pagoda** (now open to the public).

Near the entrance, the beautiful, steamy **Palm House** (1848) is popular, but you can ascend a spiral staircase to the quieter elevated walkway. The **Princess of Wales Conservatory**, a mix of dry and moist habitats, also draws a crowd, but is worth a saunter in May during the orchid festival. **Queen Charlotte's Cottage** dates from the 18th century and was a favourite spot of this queen. She and husband King George III would picnic here. It remains a perfect idyll for a lazy afternoon munching sandwiches. If you are lucky, you may be serenaded by a blackbird from the branches of a silver birch. If you've neglected to bring a picnic, the **Orangery** is the best of several eating options, serving simple meals and cakes.

Between the Orangery and the river are the formal **Queen's Garden** and the newly reopened **Kew Palace**, a neat red-brick, Dutch-gabled house, with splendidly renovated Georgian interiors. **Adm**

hotels

In this eclectic city, your choice of accommodation sets the tone for your visit. Would you like a classy residence in Chelsea, close to the boutiques? Or is high-voltage Covent Garden, right in the centre, more your style? Perhaps you'd like to sample the edgy glamour of Notting Hill or the laid-back cool of Clerkenwell. Hotel rates are quite high, but there's memorable accommodation for all budgets.

HOTELS

Not long ago, accommodation in London broadly fell into two camps: grand hotels offering impeccable service and untold luxury; and budget hotels and B&Bs, blighted by dated decor and no-frills rooms. Thankfully, over the past few years things have improved considerably. Inexpensive guesthouses are smartening up their act and adding extras, there's a new breed of affordable design hotels, such as Malmaison and the Zetter, and it's easy to bag a deluxe room at a bargain rate online.

Lisa Ritchie

Hotels with History

Hazlitt's *(see p187)* has a distinguished literary past: Bill Bryson and J K Rowling have stayed here, and in the 18th century, when the building was a boarding house, it hosted Jonathan Swift. JFK and Freud both stayed at **The Colonnade** *(see p191)*, while **The Savoy** *(see p189)* has hosted many musical stars, from Enrico Caruso to Elton John and U2.

Sports and Spas

The state-of-the-art gym at **One Aldwych** *(see p186)* boasts one of London's largest hotel pools (18 m/60 ft), complete with underwater music. For unashamed pampering, check into the **Dorchester** *(see p189)*, where the Art Deco spa has recently had a facelift. Guests at the **Crescent** *(see p187)* have access to private tennis courts opposite.

Gastronomic Hotels

Some of the city's destination restaurants are housed in hotels, and top of the food chain is **Gordon Ramsay at Claridges** *(see p189)*. Though not part of the hotel, **Nobu** *(see p38)* sits atop **The Metropolitan** *(see p188)*, and over in the City restaurateur Terence Conran has installed spectacular dining rooms at the **Great Eastern** *(see p193)*.

choice stays

Style Statements

London's first "loft hotel", **The Zetter** *(see p194)*, features warehouse windows, vintage furniture and exposed brick. Designed by Anouska Hempel, the rooms of boutique hotel **Blakes** *(see p191)* bring glossy interiors magazines to life, while **The Metropolitan** *(see p188)* still cuts a fine figure, with its minimalist chic and understated elegance.

Best of the Bargains

Boutique-style beauty the **Mayflower** *(see p190)* manages to combine budget rates with marble bathrooms. Set within the former County Hall, **Travel Inn** *(see p195)* offers comfortable, no-frills accommodation, while if you're looking to party, backpackers' favourite **Generator** *(see p187)* has a late bar and some of the cheapest beds in town.

Hot Spots

If you want to be where the action is, you can't beat the **Covent Garden Hotel** *(see p186)*. For a more laid-back vibe with equally chic boutiques and cafés, try **The Portobello** *(see p192)* in Notting Hill. And the **Holiday Inn Express** *(see p195)* in hip Hoxton is perfect for checking out galleries and markets by day, bars and clubs by night.

One Aldwych _contemporary grand hotel_ `9 H3`
1 Aldwych, WC2 • 020 7300 1000
>> www.onealdwych.co.uk

The neo-grand design of this hotel became an instant hit with the style-conscious when it opened in the late 1990s. Occupying a former newspaper HQ on one corner of the Aldwych, it gives monumental elegance a modern edge. Staff wear lavender shirts designed by cool Savile Row tailor Richard James, and the walls are adorned with 350 original works of art. The rooms are surprisingly quiet, given the hotel's central position. Their styling is contemporary yet colourful, with silk drapes and plush upholstery. The suites at the front of the building, under a coppered cupola, are circular. Every detail has been considered: flowers are changed daily, and the terrazzo-stone bathrooms have heated floors and mini TVs. The health club surpasses most hotel gyms, with personal trainers on call and a pool with underwater music.

The **Lobby Bar** _(see p142)_, with its high ceiling, arched windows and dramatic sculptures, is always lively. There are two well-regarded restaurants, Axis and the less formal Indigo (both modern European cuisine), and a chic coffee bar. **Expensive**

Covent Garden Hotel _theatreland retreat_ `9 F3`
10 Monmouth Street, WC2 • 020 7806 1000
>> www.firmdalehotels.com

Its location in London's Theatreland makes this cosy hotel a favourite with actors and others in the film and performing arts industries. The luxurious screening room gets plenty of use. Rooms are individually decorated in updated English style, one with a vast four-poster bed. **Expensive**

Hazlitt's *authentic period hotel* `9 F3`
6 Frith Street, W1 • 020 7434 1771
>> www.hazlittshotel.com

The Soho home of 18th-century essayist William Hazlitt is true to its heritage while providing 21st-century comforts. The panelled rooms contain fireplaces, antique headboards and rolltop baths, yet there's also air conditioning and Internet access. The drawing room has books signed by literary guests. **Expensive**

Charlotte Street Hotel *artistic digs* `9 E2`
15 Charlotte Street, W1 • 020 7806 2000
>> www.charlottestreethotel.com

Set amid Charlotte Street's eclectic restaurants, this understated hotel combines original works by "Bloomsbury set" artists, reflecting the legacy of its location, with modern gadgets such as mini TVs in the luxurious granite bathrooms. The bar buzzes with media folk, and there's a swanky screening room. **Expensive**

Crescent Hotel *tidy guesthouse* `3 F5`
49–50 Cartwright Gardens, WC1 • 020 7387 1515
>> www.CrescentHotelofLondon.com

The best of several small hotels occupying a Georgian crescent near University College, the Crescent is smart and well kept. There are TVs in the bedrooms, a guests' lounge and a cheerful breakfast room with a characterful old cast-iron cooker. Guests may use the tennis courts in the garden opposite. **Cheap**

Generator *futuristic budget hotel* `3 G5`
Compton Pl, off Tavistock Pl, WC1 • 020 7388 7666
>> www.generatorhostels.com

London's biggest backpackers' hostel is decked out in stainless steel and neon. Accommodation is no-frills: bed down in a communal dorm or pay a little more for a private room. However, with a bar open until 2am, karaoke and a 24-hour Internet café, the young guests aren't here just to rest. **Cheap**

>> *Expensive: over £200 for a double room per night; moderate: £120–200; cheap: £10–120*

The Metropolitan *cool & contemporary* **8 C5**
Old Park Lane, W1 • 020 7447 1000
>> www.metropolitan.como.bz

This minimalist upstart caused a stir when it joined the luxury line-up overlooking Hyde Park in 1997; it was the first new hotel to open on Park Lane for two decades. Its understated chic hasn't dated a bit. Armani-clad staff waft around the cream lobby, with its 1930s-inspired club chairs. Rooms are contemporary yet comfortable, with blond-wood furniture, harmonious pale fabrics, and plenty of light (London weather permitting) streaming through the plate-glass windows. The Metropolitan has all the amenities you would expect from a top-class hotel – glamorous marble bathrooms, Internet access, CD players, DVDs on request – plus some fabulous "extras" that make it a bit more special. The health club offers holistic treatments using the natural COMO Shambhala products devised at the hotel's Caribbean sister resort. As a guest, you're assured entry to the tiny members-only Met Bar – a notorious celebrity hotspot in the 1990s, which still draws a cool clientele. The Michelin-starred modern Japanese restaurant **Nobu** *(see p38)* is literally on your doorstep. **Expensive**

Durrants *authentic Georgian pile* **8 B2**
George Street, W1 • 020 7935 8131
>> www.durrantshotel.co.uk

Established in 1790, Durrants, in trendy Marylebone, is appealingly old-fashioned. The hotel has a warren of rooms spread across several terraced houses. Antiques and old prints feature heavily. Bathrooms, thankfully, are comfortably modern. The restaurant and bar have the air of a gentlemen's club. **Moderate**

Dorset Square *English country chic* `8B1`
39 Dorset Square, NW1 • 020 7723 7874
» www.dorsetsquare.co.uk

Overlooking a lovely garden square – the site of the world's first cricket ground – this sprawling Regency house has a rustic feel, with distressed wood, floral fabrics and a cosy drawing room. The restaurant serves modern European cuisine. Marylebone Village and Regent's Park are a stroll away. **Expensive**

Dover Hotel *well-maintained modern B&B* `15 E3`
42–4 Belgrave Road, SW1 • 020 7821 9085
» www.dover-hotel.co.uk

Just up the road from Victoria Station and well placed for the pubs and cafés of Pimlico, this welcoming B&B in a grand stucco-fronted terrace offers an ensuite shower, WC and satellite TV in every room. It may not be fancy, but its rooms are refreshingly modern and immaculately clean. **Cheap**

Tophams Belgravia *essentially English* `14 D2`
28 Ebury Street, SW1 • 020 7730 8147
» www.zolahotels.com

This hotel (previously owned by the Topham family for over 60 years) occupies five 19th-century houses in an upmarket Belgravia street. In terms of decor, it's like staying with an elderly aunt (think chintz and china cabinets), but it's cosy and characterful, and has an elegant restaurant. **Moderate**

Grand Old Dames

Just off smart shopping strip Bond Street, **Claridge's** has long been favoured by European royalty, and now lures gourmets with Michelin-starred chef Gordon Ramsay's eponymous restaurant. Opened in 1889 to accommodate theatre-goers, **The Savoy**, on the Strand, has numerous show business connections, and its legendary American Bar *(see p143)* was the birthplace of the dry Martini. For unashamed indulgence, the grandiose **Dorchester** overlooking Hyde Park boasts an Art Deco spa and a ratio of nearly three staff for every guest room. Rooms at the **Ritz**, on Piccadilly, are sumptuous in Louis XVI style. Its 1930s Rivoli Bar has been splendidly restored. For details of all hotels, *see p233.*

» *Our price categories are based on hotel "rack" rates, but big discounts are frequently available* **189**

Hotels

City Inn Westminster *unpretentious* `15 F3`

30 John Islip Street, SW1 • 020 7630 1000
>> www.cityinn.com

Around the corner from Tate Britain and handy Millbank Pier, this slick, design-conscious newcomer is part of a small chain. It offers many of the facilities of a luxury hotel – DVD players, broadband Internet, bathrobes – without any attitude. Deals on the website make it even more of a bargain. **Moderate**

The Franklin *understated townhouse* `14 A2`

28 Egerton Gardens, SW3 • 020 7584 5533
>> www.franklinhotel.co.uk

Located in a quiet Knightsbridge street, the Franklin offers an opportunity to see how the other half lives. It's like staying in the private home of an affluent family, complete with framed portraits, antiques, fine English fabrics and secluded residents' gardens at the back. **Moderate**

Mayflower *affordable "boutique" style* `13 E3`

26–8 Trebovir Road, SW5 • 020 7370 0991
>> www.mayflowerhotel.co.uk

This affordable gem, in a grand terrace in busy Earl's Court, has recently been refurbished. Now each room has its own style, which might be contemporary, antique or slightly Oriental. Touches of luxury include marble bathrooms and balconies off some rooms. **Cheap**

Five Sumner Place *spacious & attractive* `13 H3`

5 Sumner Place, SW7 • 020 7723 4089
>> www.sumnerplace.com

Set in a white stuccoed terrace, this immaculately maintained hotel is well placed for the museums and shops of South Kensington. Although decorated in an unremarkable traditional English style, the rooms are comfortable, and large by London standards. Breakfast is served in a pretty conservatory. **Moderate**

Blakes *sumptuous designer hideaway* `13 G3`
33 Roland Gardens, SW7 • 020 7370 6701
» www.blakeshotels.com

Opened in the early 1980s by socialite designer Anouska Hempel, Blakes is London's original boutique hotel. Its effortless sense of style and discreet Kensington location have attracted the rich and famous from the beginning.

In contrast to Hempel's homage to minimalism in her eponymous hotel, The Hempel, Blakes is a riot of beautiful furniture and curios; a living textbook for designers and aficionados of interiors, packing in a wide array of styles. The lobby has a colonial air, with bamboo furniture, antique birdcages and vintage Louis Vuitton trunks. The individually designed bedrooms, with sweeping draperies and exceptional items of antique furniture and artifacts – many of which were acquired by Hempel on her travels – range in theme from opulent Oriental to Baroque Italian. The restaurant is in the basement, its cuisine a blend of East and West. Adjoining it are Blakes Bar and the Chinese Room – a dark, mysterious lounge, dressed with an elaborate screen, banquettes and cushions. **Expensive**

The Colonnade *informal grand house* `7F1`
2 Warrington Crescent, W9 • 020 7286 1052
» www.theetoncollection.com

There's an air of posh informality about this hotel, which comprises two Victorian mansions near Little Venice (*see p177*). Open since the 1930s, it's been extensively refurbished. Most rooms are comfortably opulent, some with four-poster beds. The sea-themed "Cabin" has a bunk bed and portholes. **Moderate**

The Portobello · *divinely decadent* · `6 D3`
22 Stanley Gardens, W11 • 020 7727 2777
>> www.portobello-hotel.co.uk

Join the list of rock and film stars who have stayed at this over-the-top Notting Hill townhouse. Many rooms are themed – Moroccan, Japanese, Colonial – with exciting features such as round or four-poster beds and Victorian bathtubs (Alice Cooper kept his boa constrictor in one). **Moderate**

Miller's Residence · *unusual guesthouse* · `7 E3`
111a Westbourne Grove, W2 • 020 7243 1024
>> www.millersuk.com

A discreet entrance off busy Westbourne Grove leads to one of London's most atmospheric hotels. Owned by antiques expert Martin Miller, it's crammed with bric-a-brac and unusual pieces. There's a free bar and snacks are available in the cluttered drawing room, which is candlelit at night. **Moderate**

Abbey House · *superior B&B* · `7 E5`
11 Vicarage Gate, W8 • 020 7727 2594
>> www.abbeyhousekensington.com

This friendly B&B in a grand Victorian house near Kensington High Street has been owned by the same family for 25 years. It is refurbished annually and offers spotlessly clean, comfortable accommodation with shared facilities. All rooms have orthopaedic mattresses and colour TVs. **Cheap**

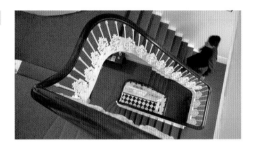

Booking a Hotel

Book as far as possible in advance for the best rates and widest choice. Special deals often feature on hotel websites and sites of the many Internet-based agencies. Try **www.visitlondon.com** – the website of the official tourist board – which has reviews, discounted rates and links to dozens of London hotels. **The British Hotel Reservation Centre** operates a 24-hour booking service by phone (020 7340 1616) and online at **www.bhrc.co.uk**. The agency **www.pinkhotels.com** specializes in finding rooms at gay- and lesbian-friendly hotels. Always check the booking details. Many hotels do not include VAT (17.5%) in the quotation, but add it to the final bill. Some quotes are per person, others are per room. Check, too, whether breakfast is included.

Great Eastern *Conran-styled grand hotel* `11 E2`
Liverpool Street, EC2 • 020 7618 5000
>> www.great-eastern-hotel.co.uk

Built in the golden age of rail travel, the magnificent 19th-century hotel next to Liverpool Street station was recently given a makeover by the Conran Group – the design consultancy of style guru Terence Conran. The result is a dramatic marriage of Victorian grandeur (marble staircases, soaring ceilings, ornate plasterwork) with 21st-century design (contemporary colour schemes, modern furniture, high-tech facilities). Exciting works of contemporary art are displayed throughout, some on loan from the nearby Whitechapel Gallery. The Conran aesthetic runs to the bedrooms, which are furnished with his own designs and original pieces by Eames and Arne Jacobson. Black-and-white tiled bathrooms come complete with natural Ren products, and all the requisite high-tech business facilities are available. The well-equipped gym is set in a former Masonic temple.

With his restaurateur's hat on, Conran has also made this a serious dining destination. There are no fewer than five eateries, the best of which is the glamorous Aurora, with a stunning original stained-glass ceiling dome. The modern brasserie Terminus is a less formal place – noisy, vibrant and fun. **Expensive**

Malmaison *French-inspired mini-chain* `10 B1`
Charterhouse Square, EC1 • 020 7012 3700
>> www.malmaison.com

This converted Victorian nurses' residence maintains its reputation for contemporary luxury at a great price. CD players and minibars stocked with French wines come as standard in the chic, spacious rooms. A buzzing brasserie and bar and high-tech gym complete the thoroughly modern package. **Moderate**

Hotels

The Zetter *eclectic loft style* 10 B1

86–8 Clerkenwell Road, EC1 • 020 7324 4444
>> www.thezetter.com

Clerkenwell is an area known for its cool loft apartments, and it now has a loft hotel. Converted from a 19th-century warehouse, the Zetter has five floors set around a central atrium, and rooms featuring huge factory windows and exposed brick. The decor is an eclectic mix: reconditioned 1970s furniture, hand-printed panels, slick modern elements such as state-of-the-art showers, and cosy touches such as hot-water bottles. Old Penguin paperbacks and free copies of *Time Out* provide inspiring bedtime reading. Instead of minibars, vending machines on each floor dispense everything from toothpaste to champagne; just insert your room card and the charge is put on the tab. The top-floor studios have sundecks with views across the city. The hotel's modern Italian restaurant, with tables on St John's Square in summer, is a destination in its own right. **Moderate**

The Rookery *historic hideaway* 10 B1

Peter's Lane, Cowcross Street, EC1 • 020 7336 0931
>> www.rookeryhotel.com

The Clerkenwell sister of Hazlitt's *(see p187)* occupies six Georgian houses and shops (faded butcher's and baker's signs are still visible). Decorated with quirky antiques, it retains many original features, such as flagstone floors in the hall and ceiling beams in some bedrooms, while offering all mod cons. **Expensive**

La Gaffe *unpretentious Hampstead hotel* 1 A4

107–11 Heath Street, NW3 • 020 7435 8965/4941
>> www.lagaffe.co.uk

Set above an Italian restaurant amid Hampstead's winding lanes and quaint cottages, this small, family-run hotel is very reasonably priced. Its style isn't much to speak of – more provincial B&B than smart hotel – but La Gaffe is handy for the local boutiques and, of course, the Heath *(see p178)*. **Cheap**

London Bridge Hotel `10 D5`

8–18 London Bridge Street, SE1 • 020 7855 2200
>> www.londonbridgehotel.com

Close to Borough Market *(see p169)*, this hotel has comfortable, if somewhat corporate-style, accommodation. "Executive" rooms are better, with more contemporary fittings. Guests can enjoy free entry to the adjoining Fitness First health club, and there's a decent Malaysian restaurant in-house. **Moderate**

Four Seasons Canary Wharf

46 Westferry Circus, E14 • 020 7510 1999 • ☺ Canary Wharf
>> www.fourseasons.com

A spectacular riverfront setting and chic modern interiors make this Canary Wharf outpost of the famous luxury chain really special. Guests have use of Holmes Place gym facilities, and round the corner is Nobu's sister restaurant Ubon. The river-view rooms offer a vista of the Thames looking west to the City. **Expensive**

Mercure London `10 B4`
City Bankside *modern Euro-style chain*

77–9 Southwark Street, SE1 • 020 7902 0800
>> www.mercure.com

This spare, modern hotel is geared mainly towards business travellers, but cheap weekend deals and its position near the Tate Modern and South Bank make it attractive to tourists. There's a small gym, and a stylish restaurant with an extensive wine list. **Moderate**

Chains

If you're after budget accommodation, it's worth considering a chain hotel: the rooms may be bland, but there won't be any nasty surprises, and, increasingly, you can stay in some of London's hottest areas. **Holiday Inn** (www.holiday-inn.com) has an affordable Express branch amid the hip bars of Hoxton (275 Old St, EC1). An outpost of cheap chain **Travel Inn** (www.travelinn.co.uk) is housed in the former County Hall – steps away from the London Eye and South Bank complex. For river views, however, you'll have to stay at the pricier **Marriott** (www.marriott.com), which shares the building. More upmarket is the **London Docklands Hilton** (www.hilton.com), which has a pool, river views from some rooms and cheap special offers.

London Street Finder

Almost every listing in this guide includes a boxed page and grid reference to the maps in this section. The few entries that fall outside the area covered by these maps give transport details instead. The main map below shows the division of the Street Finder, along with postcodes.

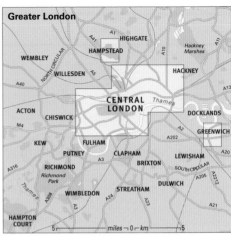

Greater London

Key to Street Finder

Sight/public building	Police station
Underground station	Church
Railway station	Synagogue
Coach station	Mosque
River boat pier	Post office
Tourist information office	Railway line
Hospital with casualty unit	Pedestrian street
	Motorway

Scale of maps 1–16

0 metres   500
0 yards   500

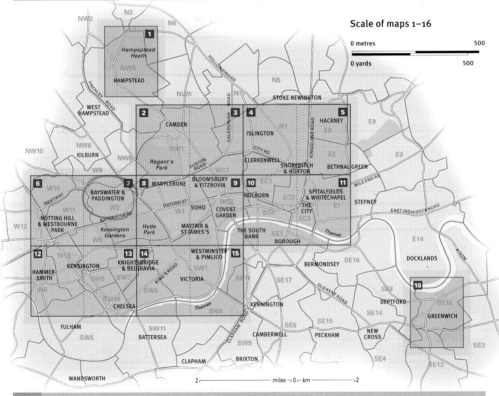

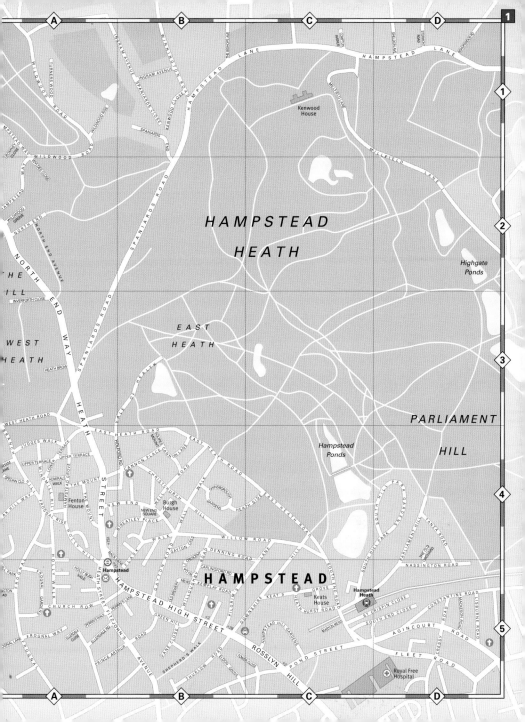

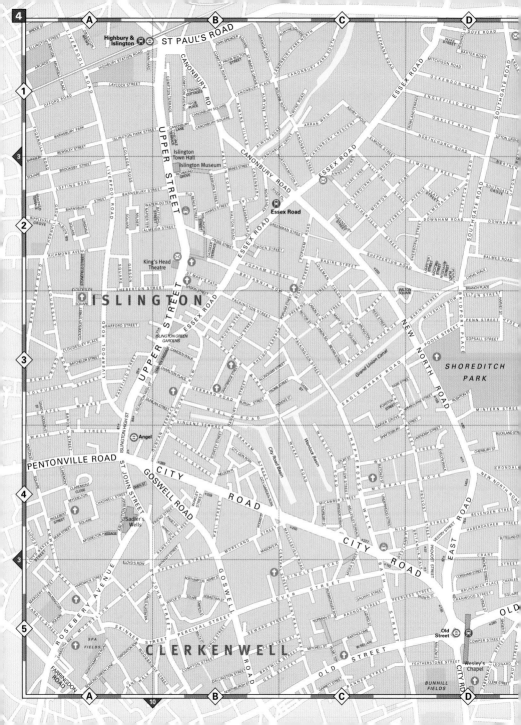

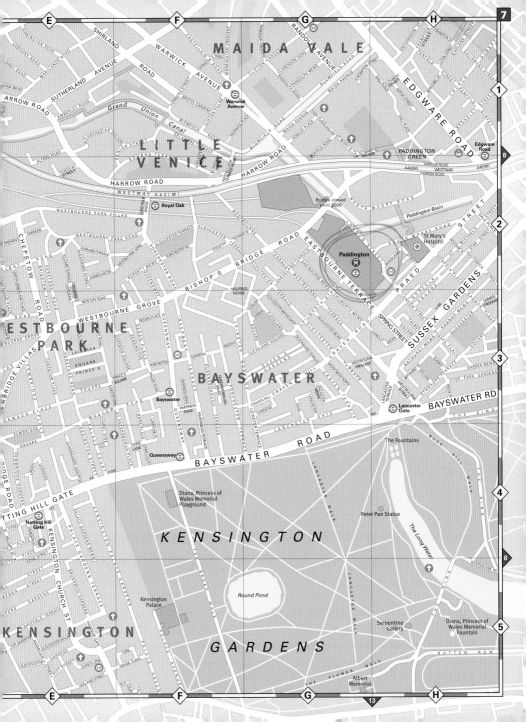

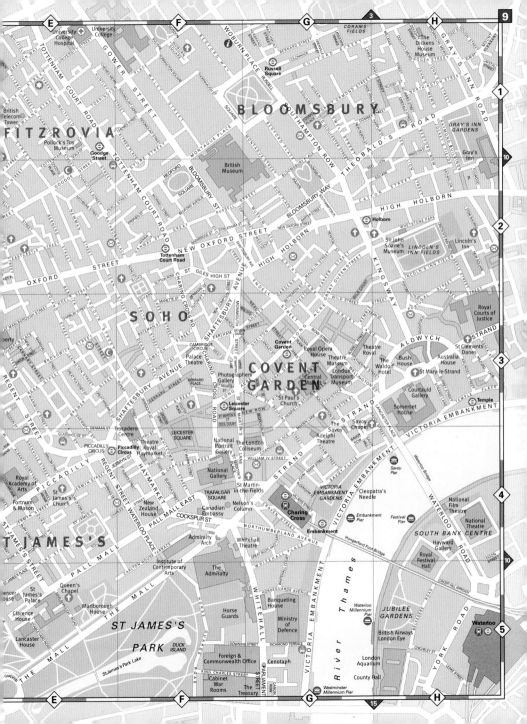

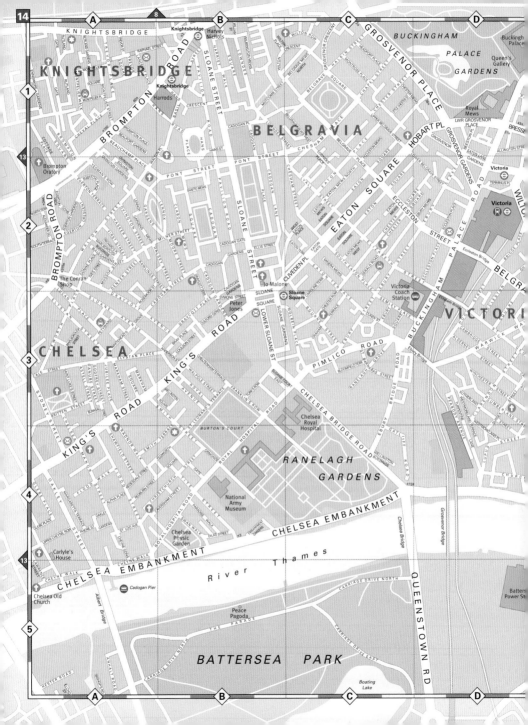

Index by Area

Centre

Restaurants

Covent Garden

Belgo (p47)   ££
50 Earlham Street
(Map 9 F3)
www.belgorestaurants.co.uk
Belgian

Hazuki (p35)   ££
43 Chandos Place (Map 9 G4)
Japanese

The Ivy (p38)   £££
1 West Street (Map 9 F3)
European

J Sheekey (p35)   £££
28–32 St Martin's Court
(Map 9 F3)
British

The National Dining   ££
Rooms (p35)
The National Gallery
(Map 9 F4)
British

Origin (p29)   £££
The Hospital, Endell St, WC2
(Map 9 G2)
Modern European

Paul (p33)   £
20 Bedford Street (Map 9 G3)
Café

Rock & Sole Plaice (p33)   ££
47 Endell Street (Map 9 G3)
British

Rules (p34)   £££
35 Maiden Lane (Map 9 G3)
British

Fitzrovia

Eagle Bar Diner (p31)   £
3–5 Rathbone Place
(Map 9 F2)
North American

Fino (p32)   ££
33 Charlotte Street (Map 9 E2)
Spanish

Hakkasan (p31)   £££
8 Hanway Place (Map 9 F2)
Chinese

Navarro's (p32)   £
67 Charlotte Street (Map 9 E1)
Spanish

Rasa Samudra (p32)   ££
5 Charlotte street (Map 9 E1)
Indian

Sardo (p33)   ££
45 Grafton Way (Map 9 E1)
Italian

Holborn

Matsuri (p33)   £££
71 High Holborn (Map 9 H2)
Japanese

Marylebone

Golden Hind (p38)   £
73 Marylebone La (Map 8 C2)
British

Locanda Locatelli (p38)   £££
8 Seymour Street (Map 8 B3)
Italian

Original Tagines (p40)   ££
7A Dorset Street (Map 8 B2)
African

The Orrery (p39)   £££
55 Marylebone High St
(Map 8 C1)
European

Patogh (p41)   £
8 Crawford Place (Map 8 A2)
Middle Eastern

Phoenix Palace (p40)   £
3–5 Glentworth St (Map 8 B1)
Chinese

The Providores &   £££
Tapa Room (p39)
109 Marylebone High St
(Map 8 C1)
International

Le Relais de Venise (p40)   ££
120 Marylebone La (Map 8 C2)
European

Mayfair & St James's

Al Sultan (p38)   ££
51–2 Hertford St (Map 8 C5)
Middle Eastern

Al Waha (p47)   ££
75 Westbourne Grove (Map 7 E3)
Middle Eastern

Le Caprice (p35)   £££
Arlington Street (Map 9 E4)
European

Kaya (p37)   ££
42 Albemarle Street (Map 8 D4)
Korean

Kiku (p37)   £££
17 Half Moon St (Map 8 D4)
Japanese

Mô/Mômo (p38)   £/£££
23 Heddon Street (Map 9 E3)
North African

Nobu (p38)   £££
19 Old Park Lane (Map 8 C5)
Japanese

Patara (p37)   ££
3 & 7 Maddox St (Map 8 D3)
Thai

Sketch (p38)   £££
9 Conduit Street (Map 8 D3)
European

Tamarind (p37)   £££
20 Queen Street (Map 8 D4)
Indian

The Wolseley (p36)   ££
160 Piccadilly (Map 9 E4)
European

Soho

Andrew Edmunds (p28)   ££
46 Lexington Street (Map 9 E3)
European

Bar Italia (p164)   £
22 Frith Street (Map 9 F3)
Café

Bodean's (p28)   ££
10 Poland Street (Map 9 E3)
North American

Busaba Eathai (see p226)   ££
Thai

Café Emm (p29)   £
17 Frith Street (Map 9 F3)
International

Donzoko (p28)   £
15 Kingly Street (Map 9 E3)
Japanese

ECapital (p29)   £
8 Gerrard Street (Map 9 F3)
Chinese

Itsu (see p225)   ££
Japanese

Lindsay House (p30)   £££
21 Romily Street (Map 9 F3)
British

Mar i Terra (p28)   £
17 Air Street (Map 9 E3)
Spanish

Masala Zone (see p225)   £
Indian

Patisserie Valerie (p30)   £
Old Compton St (Map 9 F3)
Café

Randall & Aubin (p164)   £
14–16 Brewer St (Map 9 E3)
Seafood

Red Fort (p31)   £££
77 Dean Street(Map 9 F3)
Indian

Wagamama (see p225)   £
Japanese

Wong Kei (p29)   £
41–3 Wardour St (Map 9 E3)
Chinese

Westminster & Pimlico

Cinnamon Club (p41)   £££
Old Westminster Library
Great Smith Street
(Map 15 F1)
Indian

Shopping

Bloomsbury

Contemporary Wardrobe (p67)
The Horse Hospital Colonnade
(Map 9 G1)
Fashion

James Smith & Sons (p67)
53 New Oxford St (Map 9 G2)
Shoes & Accessories

Covent Garden

Agnès B (p64)
Floral Street (Map 9 G3)
Fashion

Any Amount of Books (p69)
56 Charing Cross Road
(Map 9 F3)
Books

For the very latest on London go to ▶▶ www.realcity.dk.com

aQuaint (p65)
38 Monmouth St (Map 9 F3)
Fashion

Aram (p64)
110 Drury Lane (Map 9 G3)
Interiors

Blackwell's (p69)
100 Charing Cross Road
(Map 9 F3)
Books

Borders (p69)
Charing Cross Road (Map 9 F3)
Books

Camper (p64)
Floral Street (Map 9 G3)
Fashion

Coco de Mer (p65)
23 Monmouth St (Map 9 F3)
Lingerie

Eatmyhandbagbitch (p68)
37 Drury Lane (Map 9 G3)
Interiors

Forbidden Planet (p67)
179 Shaftesbury Ave (Map 9 F2)
Books

Foyles (p69)
Charing Cross Road (Map 9 F3)
Books

Gay's the Word (p68)
66 Marchmont St (Map 3 G5)
Books

Kiehl's (p65)
29 Monmouth St (Map 9 F3)
Health & Beauty

Kirk Originals (p64)
29 Floral Street (Map 9 G3)
Shoes & Accessories

Koh Samui (p65)
65–7 Monmouth St (Map 9 F3)
Fashion

Magma (p90)
8 Earlham Street (Map 9 F3)
Books

Maharishi (p64)
19a Floral Street (Map 9 G3)
Fashion

Marchpane (p68)
Cecil Court (Map 9 F3)
Books

Neal's Yard Dairy (p66)
17 Shorts Gardens (Map 9 G3)
Food

Nigel Williams (p68)
Cecil Court (Map 9 F3)
Books

Paul Smith (pp64 & 88)
Floral Street (Map 9 G3)
Fashion

PJ Hilton (p68)
Cecil Court (Map 9 F3)
Books

Poste Mistress (p65)
261–3 Monmouth St (Map 9 F3)
Shoes & Accessories

Ray's Jazz (p69)
Foyles Bookshop, Charing
Cross Road (Map 9 F3)
Music

Shipley (p69)
70 Charing Cross Rd (Map 9 F3)
Books

Shipley Media (p69)
80 Charing Cross Rd
(Map 9 F3)
Books

Size? (p66)
17–19 Neal Street (Map 9 G3)
Fashion

Stage Door Prints (p68)
9 Cecil Court (Map 9 F3)
Prints & Posters

Storey's (p68)
3 Cecil Court (Map 9 F3)
Prints & Posters

The Tintin Shop (p64)
34 Floral Street (Map 9 G3)
Prints & Posters

Vertigo (p64)
22 Wellington St (Map 9 G3)
Prints & Posters

The Wild Bunch (p66)
Earlham Street (Map 9 F3)
Florist

Fitzrovia

FCUK (p89)
396 Oxford Street (Map 9 E2)
Fashion

Topshop (p72)
Oxford Circus (Map 9 D2)
Fashion

Marylebone

Calmia (p77)
52–4 Marylebone High St
(Map 8 C1)
Health & Beauty

Carluccio's (p76)
St Christopher's Pl (Map 8 C3)
Food

Daunt Books (p78)
83 Marylebone High St (8 C1)
Books

La Fromagerie (p78)
2–4 Moxton Street (Map 8 C2)
Food

John Lewis (p83)
278–306 Oxford St (Map 8 D3)
www.johnlewis.com
Department Store

Kabiri (p78)
37 Marylebone High Street
(Map 8 C1)
Jewellery

Margaret Howell (p76)
34 Wigmore Street (Map 8 C2)
Fashion

Marimekko (p76)
16–17 St Christopher's Place
(Map 8 C3)
Interiors

Mint (p77)
70 Wigmore Street (Map 8 C2)
Interiors

Mulberry (p76)
11–12 Gees Court (Map 8 C3)
Fashion

Osprey (p76)
St Christopher's Pl (Map 8 C3)
Shoes & Accessories

Paul Rothe (p77)
35 Marylebone Lane
(Map 8 C2)
Food

Selfridges (p75)
400 Oxford Street
(Map 8 C3)
Department Store

Sixty 6 (p77)
66 Marylebone High St
(Map 8 C1)
Fashion

Skandium (p78)
86–7 Marylebone High St
(Map 8 C1)
Interiors

Whistles (p76)
12 St Christopher's Place
(Map 8 C3)
Fashion

Mayfair & St James's

b Store (p71)
6 Conduit Street
(Map 8 D3)
Shoes & Accessories

Browns (p74)
23–7 South Molton Street
(Map 8 D3)
Fashion

Dover Street Market (p73)
17–18 Dover Street
(Map 8 D4)
Fashion

Fenwick (p83)
63 New Bond Street (Map 8 D3)
www.fenwick.co.uk
Department Store

Fortnum & Mason (p83)
181 Piccadilly (Map 9 E4)
www.fortnumandmason.com
Department Store

Georgina Goodman (p73)
12–14 Shepherd St (Map 8 D5)
Shoes & Accessories

Jigsaw (p89)
126 New Bond St (Map 8 D3)
Fashion

Karen Millen (p89)
262–4 Regent St (Map 8 D3)
Fashion

N Peal (p74)
37 & 71 Burlington Arcade
(Map 9 E4)
Fashion

Oki-ni (p72)
25 Savile Row (Map 9 E3)
Fashion

Index by Area

Centre

Shopping continued

Poste (p74)
10 South Molton St (Map 8 D3)
Shoes & Accessories

Prestat (p79)
14 Princes Arcade (Map 9 E4)
Food

REN (p73)
19 Shepherd Market
(Map 8 D4)
Health & Beauty

Stella McCartney (p74)
30 Bruton Street (Map 8 D4)
Fashion

Soho

Agent Provocateur (p71)
6 Broadwick Street (Map 9 E3)
Lingerie

Bond (p72)
Newburgh Street (Map 9 E3)
Fashion

The Dispensary (p72)
Newburgh Street (Map 9 E3)
Fashion

Gerry's (p70)
74 Old Compton St (Map 9 F3)
Wines & Spirits

Jess James (p72)
Newburgh Street (Map 9 E3)
Shoes & Accessories

Kokon To-Zai (p70)
57 Greek Street (Map 9 F3)
Fashion

Liberty (p72)
210–20 Regent St (Map 8 D3)
Department Store

Lina Stores (p71)
18 Brewer Street (Map 9 E3)
Food

Marks & Spencer (p89)
458 Oxford Street (Map 9 E2)
Department Store

Onitsuka Tiger (p72)
Newburgh Street (Map 9 E3)
Fashion

Phonica (p71)
51 Poland Street (Map 9 E3)
Music

Scent Systems (p72)
Newburgh Street (Map 9 E3)
Health & Beauty

The World According To... (p70)
4 Brewer Street (Map 9 E3)
Fashion

Vintage (p70)
39–43 Brewer St (Map 9 E3)
Prints & Posters

Art & Architecture

Bloomsbury

British Museum (pp14 & 104)
Great Russell Street (Map 9 F2)
Museum

Gagosian (p116)
6–24 Britannia St (Map 3 G4)
www.gagosian.com
Art Gallery

Covent Garden

National Gallery (pp13 & 101)
Trafalgar Square (Map 9 F4)
Museum

**National Portrait
Gallery** (p102)
St Martin's Place (Map 9 F4)
Museum

Photographers' Gallery (p101)
5 & 8 Great Newport Street
(Map 9 F3)
Art Gallery

Somerset House (p100)
Strand (Map 9 H3)
Museum

Theatre Museum (p101)
Russell Street (Map 9 G3)

Fitzrovia

RIBA (p103)
66 Portland Place (Map 8 D1)
Modern Architecture

Holborn

Dr Johnson's House (p104)
17 Gough Square
(Map 10 A2)

St Bride's (p106)
Fleet Street (Map 10 A3)
www.stbrides.com

**Sir John Soane's
Museum** (p103)
13 Lincoln's Inn Fields
(Map 9 H2)

Temple Church (p104)
Inner Temple, Fleet St
(Map 10 A3)

Marylebone

Lisson (p116)
52–4 Bell St (Map 8 A1)
Art Gallery

The Wallace Collection (p107)
Manchester Square
(Map 8 C2)
Museum

Mayfair & St James's

Gagosian (p116)
8 Heddon Street (Map 9 E3)
www.gagosian.com
Art Gallery

Royal Academy (RA) (p106)
Piccadilly (Map 9 E4)
Art Gallery

Sadie Coles HQ (p116)
35 Heddon Street (Map 9 E3)
Art Gallery

St James's Piccadilly (p106)
197 Piccadilly (Map 9 E4)

Stephen Friedman (p116)
Old Burlington St (Map 9 E4)
Art Gallery

Westminster & Pimlico

Banqueting House (p105)
Whitehall (Map 9 G5)
Historic Building

Buckingham Palace (p14)
Buckingham Gate (Map 14 D1)
Historic Building

ICA (p102)
The Mall (Map 9 F5)

Queen's Gallery (p14)
Buckingham Palace Road
(Map 14 D1)
Museum

St Margaret's Church (p105)
Sanctuary (Map 15 G1)

Tate Britain (p105)
Millbank (Map 15 G3)
Museum

Westminster Abbey (p12)
Broad Sanctuary (Map 15 F1)

Performance

Bloomsbury

Drill Hall (p125)
16 Chenies Street (Map 9 F1)
Theatre

The Place (p128)
17 Duke's Road (Map 3 F5)
Dance Venue

Scala (p132)
275 Pentonville Rd (Map 3 H4)
Music Venue

Covent Garden

12 Bar Club (p125)
22–3 Denmark St (Map 9 F2)
Music Venue

Donmar Warehouse (p124)
41 Earlham Street (Map 9 F3)
Theatre

ENO @ The Coliseum (p125)
St Martin's Lane (Map 9 G4)
Concert Hall

Royal Opera House (p124)
Bow Street (Map 9 G3)
Concert Hall

Marylebone

Wigmore Hall (p128)
36 Wigmore Street (Map 8 C2)
Concert Hall

Soho

Borderline (p125)
Orange Yard, Manette St (9 F3)
Music Venue

Comedy Store (p127)
1a Oxendon Street (Map 9 F4)
Comedy Club

Curzon Soho (p126)
99 Shaftesbury Ave (Map 9 F3)
Cinema

West

Restaurants *continued*

The River Café (p45) £££
Rainville Road (Map 12 A5)
Italian

Kensington & Earl's Court

Orangery (p176) ££
Kensington Gdns (Map 7 F5)
Café

Knightsbridge & Belgravia

Foliage (p41) £££
Mandarin Oriental,
66 Knightsbridge (Map 8 B5)
European

Hunan (p42) ££
51 Pimlico Road (Map 14 C3)
Chinese

Noura (p42) ££
16 Hobart Place (Map 14 D1)
Middle Eastern

Racine (p43) ££
239 Brompton Rd (Map 14 A2)
French

Zafferano (p43) £££
15 Lowndes Street (Map 14 B1)
Italian

Zuma (p43) £££
5 Raphael Street(Map 14 A1)
Japanese

Notting Hill & Westbourne Park

E&O (p46) ££
14 Blenheim Cres (Map 6 C3)
Oriental

Lisboa Patisserie (p46) £
57 Golborne Road (Map 6 C2)
Café

Lonsdale (p149) ££
44–8 Lonsdale Road
(Map 6 D3)
Gastropub

Rosa's (p166) ££
69 Westbourne Park Road
(Map 7 E2)
European

S&M Café (p46) £
268 Portobello Rd (Map 6 D3)
Café

The Westbourne (p166) ££
101 Westbourne Park Villas
(Map 7 E2)
Gastropub

Shopping

Chelsea & Fulham

Antiquarius (p84)
131–41 King's Rd (Map 14 A4)
Vintage Furniture

The Conran Shop (p82)
81 Fulham Road (Map 14 A2)
Interiors

Designers Guild (p84)
267 & 277 King's Rd (Map 14 A4)
Interiors

Jimmy Choo (p81)
169 Draycott Ave (Map 14 A3)
Shoes & Accessories

Joseph (p81)
77 Fulham Road (Map 13 H3)
Fashion

Kate Kuba (p83)
22 Duke of York Square (14 B3)
Shoes & Accessories

Korres (p83)
124 King's Road (Map 14 A3)
Health & Beauty

Oliver Sweeney (p83)
29 King's Road (Map 14 B3)
Shoes & ccessories

Knightsbridge & Belgravia

Anya Hindmarch (p80)
15–17 Pont Street (Map 14 B2)
Shoes & Accessories

The Chocolate Society (p80)
36 Elizabeth St (Map 14 C2)
Food

Erickson Beamon (p80)
38 Elizabeth St (Map 14 C2)
Shoes & Accessories

Harrods (p83)
87–135 Brompton Rd (Map 14 B1)
www.harrods.com
Department Store

Harvey Nichols (p83)
109–25 Knightsbridge (14 B1)
www.harveynichols.com
Department Store

Jo Malone (p79)
150 Sloane Street (Map 14 B2)
Health & Beauty

Lulu Guinness (p81)
3 Ellis Street (Map 14 B2)
Shoes & Accessories

Maria Grachvogel (p79)
162 Sloane Street (Map 14 B2)
Fashion

Neisha Crosland (p81)
8 Elystan Street (Map 14 A3)
Interiors

Patrick Cox (p79)
129 Sloane Street (Map 14 B2)
Shoes & Accessories

Philip Treacy (p80)
69 Elizabeth St (Map 14 C2)
Shoes & Accessories

Poilane (p80)
46 Elizabeth St (Map 14 C2)
Food

Les Senteurs (p80)
71 Elizabeth Street (Map 14 C2)
Health & Beauty

Tracey Boyd (p80)
42 Elizabeth St (Map 14 C2)
Fashion

Woodhams (p80)
45 Elizabeth St (Map 14 C2)
Florist

Notting Hill & Westbourne Park

202 (p84)
202 Westbourne Gro (Map 7 F3)
Fashion

Bamford & Sons (p88)
79–81 Ledbury Road
(Map 6 D3)
Fashion

Bill Amberg (p85)
10 Chepstow Road (Map 7 E2)
Shoes & Accessories

Blenheim Books (p165)
11 Blenheim Cres (Map 6 C3)
Books

Coco Ribbon (p88)
21 Kensington Park Road
(Map 6 C3)
Fashion

The Cross (p89)
141 Portland Road (Map 6 C4)
Fashion

Duchamp (p86)
75 Ledbury Road (Map 6 D3)
Fashion

Graham & Green (pp89 & 94)
4 & 10 Elgin Crescent
(Map 6 C3)
Interiors

Honest Jon's (p87)
278 Portobello Rd (Map 6 D3)
Music

Intoxica! (p87)
231 Portobello Rd (Map 6 D3)
Music

J&M Davidson (p85)
42 Ledbury Road (Map 6 D3)
Fashion

JW Beeton (p86)
48–50 Ledbury Rd (Map 6 D3)
Fashion

Marilyn Moore (p88)
7 Elgin Crescent (Map 6 C3)
Fashion

Miller Harris (p85)
14 Needham Road
(Map 7 E3)
Health & Beauty

Paul Smith (p88)
120 & 122 Kensington Park
Road (Map 6 D4)
Fashion

Portobello Market (p165)
Map 6 D3
Market

Preen (p87)
Unit 5 Portobello Green
(Map 6 C2)
Fashion

Rellik (p89)
8 Golborne Road (Map 6 C1)
Fashion

Rough Trade (p85)
130 Talbot Road (Map 6 D3)
Music

Simon Finch Art (p86)
61a Ledbury Rd
(Map 6 D3)
Books

Space.NK (p84)
127–31 Westbourne Gr (7 F3)
Health & Beauty

Tonic (p86)
276 Portobello Road
Fashion

Travel Bookshop (p165)
13–15 Blenheim Cres (6 C3)
Books

Willma (p88)
339 Portobello Rd (Map 6 C2)
Shoes & Accessories

Art & Architecture

Kensington

Brompton Cemetery (p111)
Lillie Road (Map 13 E4)

Brompton Oratory (p107)
Brompton Road (Map 14 A2)
Church

**Leighton House
Museum** (p109)
12 Holland Park Rd (Map 12 D1)

Linley Sambourne House (p108)
18 Stafford Terrace
(Map 13 E1)
Historic Building

Natural History Museum (p15)
Exhibition Road
(Map 13 H2)

Science Museum (p15)
Exhibition Road (Map 13 H2)

Serpentine Gallery (p107)
Kensington Gdns (Map 7 H5)
Art Gallery

V&A (p108)
Exhibition Road (Map 13 H2)
Museum

Performance

Chelsea & Fulham

606 Club (p129)
90 Lots Road (Map 13 G5)
Music Venue

Hammersmith

Riverside Studios (p130)
Crisp Road
(Map 12 A4)
Arts Centre

Notting Hill & Westbourne Park

Electric Cinema (p129)
191 Portobello Rd
(Map 6 D3)

Shepherd's Bush

Shepherd's Bush Empire (p129)
Shepherd's Bush Green
(Map 6 A5)
Music Venue

Pubs, Bars & Clubs

Bayswater & Paddington

Cherry Jam (p147)
58 Porchester Road
(Map 7 F2)
Bar

Chelsea & Fulham

Apartment 195 (p148)
195 King's Road (Map 14 A4)
Bar

Hammersmith

The Dove (p160)
19 Upper Mall
(Ⓔ Hammersmith)
Pub

Kensington

Windsor Castle (p150)
114 Campden Hill Rd (Map 7 E5)
Pub

Knightsbridge & Belgravia

Blue Bar (p148) Berkeley Hotel,
Wilton Place (Map 14 B1)
Bar

Nag's Head (p147)
53 Kinnerton St (Map 14 B1)
Pub

Townhouse (p148)
31 Beauchamp Pl (Map 14 A1)
Bar

Notting Hill & Westbourne Park

Golborne Grove (p149)
36 Golborne Road (Map 6 C1)
Bar

Lonsdale (p149)
44–8 Lonsdale Rd (Map 6 D3)
Bar

Notting Hill Arts Club (p150)
21 Notting Hill Gate (Map 7 E4)
Club

Trailer H (p149)
177 Portobello Rd (Map 6 C2)
Bar

Havens: Parks & Gardens

Chelsea & Fulham

Chelsea Physic Garden (p177)
Swan Walk (Map 14 B4)

Kensington

Holland Park (p176)
Map 6 D5

Havens: Spas & Treatments

Bayswater & Paddington

Porchester Spa (p176)
Queensway (Map 7 F3)

Hotels

Bayswater & Paddington

The Colonnade (p191)
2 Warrington Cres (Map 7 F1)

Chelsea & Fulham

Blakes (p191)
33 Roland Gdns (Map 13 G3)

Five Sumner Place (p190)
5 Sumner Place (Map 13 H3)

Kensington

Abbey House (p192)
11 Vicarage Gate (Map 7 E5)

Mayflower (p190)
26–8 Trebovir Rd (Map 13 E3)

Knightsbridge & Belgravia

The Franklin (p190)   £££
28 Egerton Gdns (Map 14 A2)

Topham Belgravia (p189)   ££
28 Ebury Street (Map 14 D2)

Notting Hill & Westbourne Park

Miller's Residence (p192)   ££
111a Westbourne Gr (Map 7 E3)

The Portobello (p192)   ££
22 Stanley Gardens (Map 6 D3)

City & East

Restaurants

The City

Club Gascon (p51)   £££
57 West Smithfield (Map 10 B2)
French

Smiths of Smithfield (p49) £££
Charterhouse St (Map 10 B2)
European

Clerkenwell

The Eagle (p48)   ££
159 Farringdon Rd (Map 10 A1)
Gastropub

Fish Central (p49)   £
149–51 Central St (Map 4 C5)
British

Flâneur Food Hall (p49)   ££
41 Farringdon Rd (Map 10 A1)
European

Moro (p48)   ££
34–6 Exmouth Mkt (Map 4 A5)
Spanish/North African

St John (p50)   £££
26 St John Street (Map 4 B5)
British

The White Swan (p49)   ££
108 Fetter Lane (Map 10 A2)
Gastropub

Hackney

Green Papaya (p52)   £
191 Mare Street (Map 5 H1)
Vietnamese

»» £££ expensive ££ moderate £ cheap (Price ranges: Restaurants, *see p29*, Hotels, *see p187*)

City & East

Restaurants *continued*

Shoreditch & Hoxton

Cantaloupe (p51) ££
35 Charlotte Road (Map 5 E5)
Mediterranean

Fifteen (p38) £££
15 Westland Place (Map 4 C4)
European

**Great Eastern
Dining Room** (p52) ££
54 Great Eastern St (Map 5 E5)
Oriental

The Real Greek (p52) ££
14 Hoxton Market (Map 5 E5)
Greek

Rivington Bar and Grill (p168)
28–30 Rivington St (Map 5 E5)
European

Les Trois Garçons (p51) £££
1 Club Row (Map 5 F5)
French

Viet Hoa (p52) £
70–72 Kingsland Rd (Map 5 E4)
Vietnamese

Spitalfields &
Whitechapel

Arkansas Café (p167) £
Spitalfields Market (Map 11 F1)
North American

Café Spice Namaste (p50) ££
16 Prescot Street (Map 11 F3)
Indian

Shopping

Clerkenwell

Saloon (p90)
23 Arlington Way (Map 4 A4)
Fashion

Shoreditch & Hoxton

ARTWORDS (p168)
65 Rivington Street (Map 5 E5)
www.artwords.co.uk

Columbia Road Market (p167)
Map 5 F4

Hoxton Boutique (p90)
2 Hoxton Street (Map 5 E5)
Fashion

Lara Bohinc 107 (p90)
51 Hoxton Square (Map 5 E5)
Shoes & Accessories

Smallfish Records (p91)
329 Old Street (Map 11 F1)
Music

Spitalfields &
Whitechapel

A Gold (p91)
42 Brushfield St (Map 11 E1)
Food

Artcadia (p91)
108 Commercial St (Map 11 E1)
Prints & Posters

Brick Lane Market (p166)
Map 5 F5

Cheshire Street Market (p92)
Map 11 F1

Labour and Wait (p92)
18 Cheshire Street (Map 5 F5)
Vintage Furniture

Rokit (p92)
101 & 107 Brick Lane (Map 11 F1)
Fashion

Spitalfields Market (p167)
Map 11 F1

Story (p91)
4 Wilkes Street (Map 11 F1)
Interiors

Tatty Devine (p92)
236 Brick Lane (Map 11 F1)
Shoes & Accessories

Art & Architecture

Bethnal Green

The Approach (p116)
Approach Rd (◎ Bethnal Green)

Chisenhale Gallery (p116)
Chisenhale Rd (◎ Bethnal Gr)

Matt's Gallery (p116)
Copperfield Rd (◎ Mile End)

Wilkinson Gallery (p116)
242 Cambridge Heath Road
(◎ Bethnal Green)

The City

Museum of London (p111)
London Wall (Map 5 E4)

**St Bartholomew
the Great** (p109)
West Smithfield (Map 10 B2)

St Mary-le-Bow (p106)
Cheapside (Map 10 C3)

St Paul's Cathedral (p12)
www.stpauls.co.uk (Map 10 B3)

St Stephen Walbrook (p106)
Walbrook (Map 10 D3)

Tower of London (p13)
Tower Hill (Map 11 F4)

Clerkenwell

**Museum of the Order of
St John** (p110)
St John's Gate (Map 10 B1)

Shoreditch & Hoxton

The Agency (p116)
Charlotte Road (Map 5 E5)
Art Gallery

Geffrye Museum (p111)
Kingsland Road (Map 5 E4)

White Cube (p116)
Hoxton Square (Map 5 E5)
Art Gallery

Spitalfields &
Whitechapel

Dennis Severs' House (p110)
18 Folgate Street (Map 11 E1)
Historic Building

19 Princelet Street (p109)
Spitalfields (Map 11 F1)
Historic Building

Whitechapel Gallery (p110)
80 Whitechapel High St (11 F2)

Wapping & Docklands

Wapping Project Space (p111)
Wapping Wall (◎ Wapping)

Museum in Docklands (p112)
West India Quay, www.
museumindocklands.org.uk
(◎ Canary Wharf or DLR to
West India Quay)

Performance

The City

Barbican (p130)
Silk Street (Map 10 C1)
Arts Centre

Hackney

Hackney Empire (p131)
Mare Street (Map 5 H1)
Theatre

Shoreditch & Hoxton

Comedy Café (p131)
66–8 Rivington St
(Map 5 E5)

Spitalfields &
Whitechapel

The Spitz (p130)
Old Spitalfields Market
(Map 11 F1)
Music Venue

Pubs, Bars & Clubs

The City

Black Friar (p150)
174 Queen Victoria Street
(Map 10 B3)
Pub

Vertigo (p151)
Level 42, Tower 42, 25 Old
Broad St (Map 10 D2)
Bar

Clerkenwell

Café Kick (p151)
43 Exmouth Market (Map 4 A5)
Bar

Fabric (p151)
Charterhouse St (Map 10 B1)
Club

Fluid (p152)
40 Charterhouse St (Map 10 B1)
Bar

Jerusalem Tavern (p152)
55 Britton Street (Map 10 B1)
Pub

Turnmills (p152)
63a Clerkenwell Rd (Map 10 B1)
Club

Hackney

Royal Inn on the Park (p159)
Grove Road (⊖ Bethnal Green)
Pub

Shoreditch & Hoxton

333/Mother (p153)
333 Old Street (Map 5 E5)
Club

Bar Kick (p168)
127 Shoreditch High Street
(Map 5 E5)
Bar

The Bricklayer's Arms (p168)
63 Charlotte Road (Map 5 E5)
Pub

Cargo (p152)
83 Rivington Street (Map 5 E5)
Bar/Club

Elbow Room (p168)
97–113 Curtain Rd (Map 5 E5)
Bar

Herbal (p153)
10–14 Kingsland Rd (Map 5 E4)
Club

Hoxton Square Bar & Kitchen
(p153)
2–4 Hoxton Square (Map 5 E5)
Bar

Loungelover (p155)
1 Whitby Street (Map 5 F5)
Bar

Zigfrid (p168)
11 Hoxton Square (Map 5 E5)
Bar

Spitalfields & Whitechapel

93 Feet East (p154)
150 Brick Lane (Map 11 F1)
Club

Golden Hart (p155)
110 Commercial St (Map 11 F1)
Pub

Pride of Spitalfields (p154)
3 Heneage Street (Map 11 F1)
Pub

Vibe Bar (p154)
91–5 Brick Lane (Map 11 F1)
Bar

Wapping & Docklands

The Grapes (p155)
76 Narrow Street (⊖ Wapping)
Pub

Prospect of Whitby (p155)
57 Wapping Wall (Wapping)
Pub

Hotels

The City

Great Eastern (p193)   fff
Liverpool Street (Map 11 E2)

Clerkenwell

Malmaison (p193)   ff
Charterhouse Sq (Map 10 B1)

The Rookery (p194)   fff
Peter's Lane, Cowcross Street
(Map 10 B1)

The Zetter (p194)   ff
86 Clerkenwell Rd (Map 10 B1)

North

Restaurants

Camden

Café Corfu (p54)   ff
7 Pratt Street (Map 3 E2)
Greek

Lock Tavern (p158)   ff
35 Chalk Farm Rd (Map 2 D2)
Gastropub

Mango Room (p55)   ff
10 Kentish Town Rd (Map 2 D1)
Caribbean

El Parador (p54)   f
245 Eversholt St (Map 3 E4)
Spanish

Hampstead

Giraffe (see p225)   ff

Holly Bush (p56)   ff
22 Holly Mount (Map 1 A5)
British

The Wells (p55)   ff
30 Well Walk (Map 1 B4)
Gastropub

Islington

The Drapers Arms (p53)   ff
44 Barnsbury St (Map 4 A2)
Gastropub

Gallipoli (p53)   f
102 Upper Street (Map 4 B2)
Turkish

The House (p53)   ff
63–9 Canonbury Rd (Map 4 B1)
Gastropub

Masala Zone (see p225)   f

Kilburn

Kovolam (p56)   f
12 Willesden Lane (⊖ Kilburn)
Indian

Primrose Hill

The Lansdowne (p55)   ff
90 Gloucester Ave (Map 2 C2)
Gastropub

Manna (p55)   ff
4 Erskine Road (Map 2 B2)
Vegetarian

Odette's (p54)   fff
130 Regent's Park Rd (Map 2 B2)
European

Shopping

Islington

After Noah (p93)
121 Upper Street (Map 4 B2)
Vintage Furniture

Annie's Vintage Clothes (p94)
Camden Passage (Map 4 B3)
Fashion

Aria (p93)
295–6 & 133 Upper Street
(Map 4 B2)
Interiors

Camden Lock Market (p169)
Map 2 D2

Caroline Carrier's (p94)
Pierrepont Arcade
Camden Passage (Map 4 B3)
Interiors

Comfort & Joy (p92)
109 Essex Road (Map 4 B3)
Fashion

Judith Lasalle (p94)
Camden Passage
(Map 4 B3)
Vintage Furniture

Labour of Love (p93)
193 Upper Street (Map 4 B2)
Fashion

Origin (p94)
Camden Passage
(Map 4 B3)
Interiors

Rock Archive (p94)
110 Islington High St
(Map 4 A3)
Prints & Posters

twentytwentyone (p93)
274 Upper Street (Map 4 B2)
Interiors

Primrose Hill

Anna (p94)
126 Regent's Park Rd (Map 2 B2)
Fashion

Graham & Green (p94)
164 Regent's Park Rd (Map 2 B2)
Interiors

Primrose Hill Books (p94)
134 Regent's Park Rd (Map 2 B2)
Books

Rachel Skinner (p94)
13 Princess Road (Map 2 B2)
Shoes & Accessories

Studio Perfumery (p94)
170 Regent's Park Rd
(Map 2 B2)
Health & Beauty

Art & Architecture

Hampstead

Camden Arts Centre (p112)
Arkwright Rd (⊖ Finchley Rd)
Art Gallery

Camden

Fenton House (p113)
Windmill Hill (Map 1 A4)
Historic Building

Freud Museum (p114)
20 Maresfield Gardens
(⊖ Finchley Road)

South Bank

Calder Bookshop (p95)
51 The Cut (Map 10 A5)
Books

Grammex (p95)
25 Lower Marsh
(Map 10 A5)
Music

Odie & Amanda (p95)
Oxo Tower (Map 10 A4)
Fashion

Oxo Tower Wharf (p95)
Barge House St (Map 10 A4)
Interiors/Fashion

Radio Days (p95)
87 Lower Marsh (Map 10 A5)
Fashion

What the Butler Wore (p95)
131 Lower Marsh (Map 10 A5)
Fashion

Art & Architecture

Borough

Design Museum (p116)
28 Shad Thames (Map 11 F5)
Art Gallery

Jerwood Space (p115)
171 Union Street (Map 10 B5)
Art Gallery

Old Operating Theatre (p116)
9a St Thomas's St
(Map 10 D5)
Museum

Southwark Cathedral (p115)
Montague Close
(Map 10 D4)
Church

Tate Modern (p117)
Bankside (Map 10 B4)

Camberwell

South London Gallery (p116)
65 Peckham Rd (☺ Elephant &
Castle, then 171 bus)
Art Gallery

Dulwich

Dulwich Picture Gallery (p118)
Gallery Road
(train to Dulwich)

Eltham

Eltham Palace (p118)
Court Yard (train to Eltham)
Historic Building

Greenwich & Deptford

**National Maritime
Museum** (p119)
Greenwich Park (Map 16 C2)

Queen's House (p119)
Greenwich Park (Map 16 C2)
Historic Building

Nunhead

Nunhead Cemetery (p111)
Linden Grove (train to
Nunhead)

South Bank

Hayward Gallery (p115)
South Bank Centre (Map 9 H4)
Art Gallery

Saatchi Gallery (p108)
County Hall (Map 9 H5)
Art Gallery

Performance

Battersea

**BAC (Battersea
Arts Centre)** (p137)
Lavender Hill
(train to Clapham Junction)

Borough

Shakespeare's Globe (p136)
Bankside (Map 10 C4)
Theatre

Brixton

Ritzy (p137)
Brixton Oval (☺ Brixton)
Cinema

Greenwich & Deptford

Laban (p136)
Creekside (Map 16 A3)
Dance Venue

South Bank

National Theatre (p135)
South Bank
(Map 9 H4)

NFT (p136)
South Bank (Map 9 H4)

Old Vic (p136)
The Cut (Map 10 A5)
Theatre

South Bank Centre (p135)
Belvedere Rd (Map 9 H4)
Concert Halls

Pubs, Bars & Clubs

Borough

Anchor Bankside (p158)
34 Park Street (Map 10 C4)
Pub

Founders Arms (p160)
Bankside (Map 10 B4)
Pub

George Inn (p169)
77 Borough High St (Map 10 D5)
Pub

Globe Tavern (p169)
Bedale Street (Map 10 D4)
Pub

Market Porter (p169)
9 Stoney St (Map 10 C4)
Pub

Brixton

Babalou (p160)
St Matthews Church (☺ Brixton)
Bar

Dogstar (p160)
389 Coldharbour La (☺ Brixton)
Club

Fridge/Fridge Bar (p159)
1 Town Hall Parade (☺ Brixton)
Club

Substation South (p171)
Trinity Road (☺ Brixton)
Club

Clapham

Bread & Roses (p161)
68 Clapham Manor Street
(☺ Clapham North)
Pub

Prince of Wales (p161)
38 Old Town
(☺ Clapham Common)
Pub

Windmill (p159)
Clapham Common
(☺ Clapham South)
Pub

Greenwich & Deptford

Greenwich Union (p161)
56 Royal Hill (Map 16 B3)
Pub

Trafalgar Tavern (p161)
Park Row (Map 16 C1)
Pub

Kennington

Ministry of Sound (p159)
103 Gaunt Street
(☺ Elephant & Castle)
Club

Vauxhall Tavern (p159)
372 Kennington Lane
(Map 15 H4)
Club

Richmond

White Cross (p160)
Water Lane (☺ Richmond)
Pub

Havens: Parks & Gardens

Greenwich & Deptford

Greenwich Park
(p180)Greenwich (Map 16 C3)

Kew

Kew Gardens (p181)
Kew (☺ Kew)

Hotels

Borough

London Bridge Hotel (p195) **££**
8–18 London Bridge Street
(Map 10 D5)

**Mercure London City
Bankside** (p195)   **££**
71–9 Southwark St (Map 10 B4)

Canary Wharf

**Four Seasons
Canary Wharf** (p195)   **£££**
46 Westferry Circus
(☺ Canary Wharf)

Restaurants

Recommended places to eat, including cafés and pubs

Belgian

Belgo (p47)   ££
50 Earlham Street (Map 9 F3)
www.belgorestaurants.co.uk
Centre/Covent Garden

British

Fish! (p169)   ££
Cathedral Street (Map 10 D4)
South/Borough

Fish Central (p49)   £
149–151 Central St (Map 4 C5)
City & East/Clerkenwell

Golden Hind (p38)   £
73 Marylebone Lane
(Map 8 C2)
Centre/Marylebone

Holly Bush (p56)   ££
22 Holly Mount (Map 1 A5)
North/Hampstead

J Sheekey (p35)   £££
28–32 St Martin's Court
(Map 9 F3)
Centre/Covent Garden

Lindsay House (p30)   £££
21 Romilly Street (Map 9 F3)
Centre/Soho

Livebait (p57)   £££
41–5 The Cut (Map 10 A5)
South/South Bank

Masters Super Fish (p57)   £
191 Waterloo Road (Map 10 A5)
South/South Bank

The National Dining   ££
Rooms (p35)
National Gallery
(Map 9 F4)
Centre/Covent Garden

Randall & Aubin (p164)
14–16 Brewer Street
(Map 9 E3)
Centre/Soho

Roast (p58)   £££
Stoney Street, Borough Market
(Map 10 D5)
South/Borough

Rock & Sole Plaice (p33)   ££
47 Endell Street
(Map 9 G3)
Centre/Covent Garden

Rosa's (p166)
69 Westbourne Pk Rd
(Map 7 E2)
*West/Notting Hill &
Westbourne Park*

Rules (p34)   £££
35 Maiden Lane (Map 9 G3)
Centre/Covent Garden

St John (p50)   £££
26 St John Street (Map 4 B5)
City & East/Clerkenwell

Cafés

Arkansas Café (p167)
Spitalfields Market
(Map 11 F1)
City & East/Spitalfields

Bar Italia (p164)   £
22 Frith Street (Map 9 F3)
Centre/Soho

**The Bridge House Canal
Theatre Café** (p177)
Delamere Terrace (Map 7 G1)
West/Bayswater & Paddington

Lisboa Patisserie (p46)   £
57 Golborne Road
(Map 6 C2)
*West/Notting Hill &
Westbourne Park*

Market Coffee House (p167)
Brushfield Street (Map 11 E1)
City & East/Spitalfields

Orangery (p176)   ££
Kensington Gardens
(Map 7 F5)
West/Kensington

Patisserie Valerie (p30)   £
44 Old Compton Street
(Map 9 F3)
Centre/Soho

Paul (p33)   £
20 Bedford Street (Map 9 G3)
Centre/Covent Garden

S&M Café (p46)   £
268 Portobello Road
(Map 6 D3)
*West/Notting Hill &
Westbourne Park*

Caribbean

Mango Room (p55)   ££
10 Kentish Town Rd (Map 2 D1)
North/Camden

Chinese

ECapital (p29)   £
8 Gerrard Street (Map 9 F3)
Centre/Soho

Hakkasan (p31)   £££
8 Hanway Place (Map 9 F2)
Centre/Fitzrovia

Hunan (p42)   ££
51 Pimlico Road (Map 14 C3)
West/Knightsbridge & Belgravia

Magic Wok (p47)   £
61 Queensway (Map 7 F3)
West/Bayswater & Paddington

Phoenix Palace (p40)   £
3–5 Glentworth St (Map 8 B1)
Centre/Marylebone

Wong Kei (p29)
41–3 Wardour Street (Map 9 E3)
Centre/Soho

European

Andrew Edmunds (p28)   ££
46 Lexington Street (Map 9 E3)
Centre/Soho

Blueprint Café (p56)   £££
Shad Thames (Map 11 F5)
South/Borough

Cantina Vinopolis (p169)   ££
1 Bank End (Map 10 C4)
South/Borough

Le Caprice (p35)   £££
Arlington House
Arlington Street (Map 9 E4)
Centre/Mayfair & St James's

Chez Bruce (p59)   £££
2 Bellevue Road
(train to Wandsworth Common)
South/Wandsworth

Fifteen (p38)   £££
15 Westland Place (Map 4 C4)
City & East/Shoreditch & Hoxton

Flâneur Food Hall (p49)   ££
41 Farringdon Road
(Map 10 A1)
City & East/Clerkenwell

Foliage (p41)   £££
Mandarin Oriental Hyde Park
Hotel, 66 Knightsbridge
(Map 8 B5)
West/Knightsbridge & Belgravia

Gordon Ramsay (p38)   £££
68–79 Royal Hospital Road
(Map 14 B4)
West/Chelsea & Fulham

The Ivy (p38)   £££
1 West Street (Map 9 F3)
Centre/Covent Garden

Odette's (p54)   £££
130 Regent's Park Rd (Map 2 B2)
North/Primrose Hill

Origin (p29)   £££
The Hospital, Endell Street
(Map 9 G2)
Centre/Covent Garden

The Orrery (p39)   £££
55 Marylebone Hight St
(Map 8 C1)
Centre/Marylebone

Oxo Tower Restaurant,   £££
Bar & Brasserie (p58)
Top Floor, Oxo Tower Wharf
Barge House Street (Map 10 A4)
South/South Bank

Ransome's Dock (p58)   £££
35–7 Parkgate Road
(train to Clapham Junction)
South/Battersea

Sketch (p38)   £££
9 Conduit Street (Map 8 D3)
Centre/Mayfair & St James's

Smiths of   ££/£££
Smithfield (p49)
67–77 Charterhouse St
(Map 10 B2)
City & East/The City

Tom Aikens (p43)   £££
43 Elystan Street (Map 14 A3)
West/Chelsea & Fulham

The Wolseley (p36)   ££
160 Piccadilly (Map 9 E4)
Centre/Mayfair & St James's

French

Club Gascon (p51)   £££
57 West Smithfield
(Map 10 B2)
City & East/The City

Racine (p43)   ££
239 Brompton Rd (Map 14 A2)
West/Knightsbridge & Belgravia

Le Relais de Venise (p40)   ££
120 Marylebone Lane
(Map 8 C2)
Centre/Marylebone

Le Trois Garçons (p51)   £££
1 Club Row (Map 8 C2)
City & East/Shoreditch

Gastropubs

The Drapers Arms (p49)   ££
44 Barnsbury Street (Map 4 A2)
North/Islington

The Eagle (p48)   ££
159 Farringdon Road
(Map 10 A1)
Centre/Clerkenwell

The House (p53)   ££
63–9 Canonbury Rd (Map 4 B1)
North/Islington

The Lansdowne (p55)   ££
90 Gloucester Avenue
(Map 2 C2)
North/Primrose Hill

Lots Road Pub &   ££
Dining Room (p44)
114 Lots Road (Map 13 G5)
West/Chelsea & Fulham

The Wells (p55)   ££
30 Well Walk (Map 1 B4)
North/Hampstead

The Westbourne (p166)   ££
101 Westbourne Pk Villas
(Map 7 E2)
West/Notting Hill &
Westbourne Park

The White Swan (p49)   ££
108 Fetter Lane
(Map 10 A2)
City & East/Holborn

Greek

Café Corfu (p54)   ££
7 Pratt Street (Map 3 E2)
North/Camden

The Real Greek (p52)   ££
14–15 Hoxton Market
(Map 5 E5)
City & East/
Shoreditch & Hoxton

Indian

Café Spice Namaste (p50)   ££
16 Prescot Street (Map 11 F3)
City & East/Spitalfields &
Whitechapel

Chutney Mary (p44)   £££
535 King's Road (Map 13 G5)
West/Chelsea & Fulham

Cinnamon Club (p41)   £££
Old Westminster Library
Great Smith Street (Map 15 F1)
Centre/Westminster & Pimlico

Kovolam (p56)   £
12 Willesden Lane (⊝ Kilburn)
North/Kilburn

Masala Zone (p47)   £
9 Marshall Street,
020 7287 9966 (Map 9 E3)
Centre/Soho
80 Upper Street
020 7359 3399 (Map 4 B3)
North/Islington

The Painted Heron (p44)   ££
112 Cheyne Walk (Map 13 H5)
West/Chelsea & Fulham

Rasa Samudra (p32)   ££
5 Charlotte street (Map 9 E1)
Centre/Fitzrovia

Red Fort (p31)   £££
77 Dean St (Map 9 F3)
Centre/Soho

Tamarind (p37)   £££
20 Queen Street (Map 8 D4)
Centre/Mayfair & St James's

International

Café Emm (p29)   £
17 Frith Street (Map 9 F3)
Centre/Soho

Giraffe (p47)   ££
46 Rosslyn Hill (Map 1 C5)
www.giraffe.net
North/Hampstead

The Providores &   ££
Tapa Room (p39)
109 Marylebone High St
(Map 8 C1)
Centre/Marylebone

Rivington Bar and Grill (p168)
28–30 Rivington St (Map 5 E5)
City & East/Shoreditch & Hoxton

Italian

Locanda Locatelli (p38)   £££
8 Seymour Street (Map 8 B3)
Centre/Marylebone

The River Café (p45)   £££
Rainville Road (Map 12 A5)
West/Hammersmith

Sardo (p33)   ££
45 Grafton Way (Map 9 E1)
Centre/Fitzrovia

Strada (p47)   ££
8–10 Exmouth Market
(Map 4 A5) www.strada.co.uk
City & East/Clerkenwell

Zafferano (p43)   £££
15 Lowndes Street (Map 14 B1)
West/Knightsbridge & Belgravia

Japanese

Donzoko (p28)   £
15 Kingly Street (Map 9 E3)
Centre/Soho

Hazuki (p35)   ££
43 Chandos Place (Map 9 G4)
Centre/Covent Garden

Itsu (p47)   ££
103 Wardour Street (Map 9 E3)
www.itsu.co.uk
Centre/Soho

Kiku (p37)   £££
17 Half Moon St (Map 8 D4)
Centre/Mayfair & St James's

Matsuri (p33)   £££
71 High Holborn (Map 9 H2)
Centre/Holborn

Nobu (p38)   £££
19 Old Park Lane (Map 8 C5)
Centre/Mayfair & St James's

Tsunami (p59)   £££
5 Voltaire Road
(⊝ Clapham North)
South/Clapham

Wagamama (p47)   £
Lexington Street (Map 9 E3)
www.wagamama.com
Centre/Soho

Yo! Sushi (p47)   £
52 Poland Street (Map 9 E3)
www.yosushi.co.uk
Centre/Soho

Zuma (p42)   £££
5 Raphael Street (Map 14 A1)
West/Knightsbridge & Belgravia

Korean

Kaya (p37)   ££
42 Albemarle Street (Map 8 D4)
Centre/Mayfair & St James's

Malaysian

Champor-Champor (p56)   ££
62 Weston Street (Map 10 D5)
South/Borough

Satay House (p47)   ££
13 Sale Place (Map 7 H2)
West/Bayswater & Paddington

Mediterranean

Cantaloupe (p51)   ££
35 Charlotte Road (Map 5 E5)
City & East/Shoreditch & Hoxton

Middle Eastern

Maroush Gardens (p40)   ££
1–3 Connaught Street (8 A3)
West/Bayswater & Paddington

Noura (p42)   ££
16 Hobart Place (Map 14 D1)
West/Knightsbridge & Belgravia

Patogh (p41)   £
8 Crawford Place (Map 8 A2)
Centre/Marylebone

Al Sultan (p38)   ££
51–2 Hertford St (Map 8 C5)
Centre/Mayfair & St James's

Al Waha (p47)   ££
75 Westbourne Grove (7 E3)
West/Notting Hill &
Westbourne Park

North African

Mô (p38)   £
23 Heddon Street (Map 9 E3)
Centre/Mayfair & St James's

Original Tagines (p40)   ££
7A Dorset Street (Map 8 B2)
Centre/Marylebone

North American

Bodean's (p28)   ££
10 Poland Street (Map 9 E3)
Centre/Soho

>> **£££ expensive   ££ moderate   £ cheap**   (Price ranges: Restaurants, *see p29*, Hotels, *see p187*)

Index by Type

Restaurants

North American
continued

Eagle Bar Diner (p31) £
3–5 Rathbone Pl (Map 9 F2)
Centre/Fitzrovia

**Gourmet Burger
Kitchen** (p47) £
www.gbkinfo.co.uk
North/South/West

Hamburger Union (p47) £
www.hamburgerunion.com
Centre/North

Oriental

E&O (p46) ££
14 Blenheim Cres (Map 6 C3)
*West/Notting Hill &
Westbourne Park*

**Great Eastern
Dining Room** (p52) ££
54–6 Great Eastern St
(Map 5 E5)
City & East/Shoreditch & Hoxton

Spanish

Fino (p32) ££
33 Charlotte Street (Map 9 E2)
Centre/Fitzrovia

Mar i Terra (p28) £
17 Air Street (Map 9 E3)
Centre/Soho

Mesón Don Felipe (p57) £
53 The Cut (Map 10 A5)
South/South Bank

Moro (p48) £££
34–6 Exmouth Mkt (Map 4 A5)
City & East/Clerkenwell

Navarro's (p32) £
67 Charlotte Street (Map 9 E1)
Centre/Fitzrovia

El Parador (p54) £
245 Eversholt St
(Map 3 E4)
North/Camden

Tendido Cero (p44) ££
174 Old Brompton Rd
(Map 13 G3)
West/Chelsea & Fulham

Thai

Busaba Eathai (p47) ££
106–10 Wardour Street,
020 7255 8686 (Map 9 E3)
Centre/Soho

Patara Thai (p37) ££
3 & 7 Maddox St (Map 8 D3)
Centre/Mayfair & St James's

Turkish

Gallipoli (p53) £
102 Upper Street (Map 4 B2)
North/Islington

Tas (p57) ££
33 The Cut (Map 10 A5)
South/South Bank

Vegetarian

The Gate (p45) ££
51 Queen Charlotte St
(Map 12 A3)
West/Hammersmith

Manna (p55) ££
4 Erskine Road (Map 2 B2)
North/Primrose Hill

Vietnamese

Green Papaya (p52) £
191 Mare Street (Map 5 H1)
City & East/Hackney

Viet Hoa (p52) £
70–2 Kingsland Rd
(Map 5 E4)
City & East/Shoreditch & Hoxton

Shopping

Books

Any Amount of Books (p69)
56 Charing Cross Rd
(Map 9 F3)
Centre/Covent Garden

ARTWORDS (p168)
65 Rivington Street (Map 5 E5)
www.artwords.co.uk
City & East/Shoreditch & Hoxton

Blackwell's (p69)
100 Charing Cross Rd
(Map 9 F3)
Centre/Covent Garden

Blenheim Books (p165)
11 Blenheim Crescent
(Map 6 C3)
*West/Notting Hill &
Westbourne Park*

Borders (p69)
Charing Cross Road (Map 9 F3)
Centre/Covent Garden

Calder Bookshop (p95)
51 The Cut (Map 10 A5)
South/South Bank

Daunt Books (p78)
83 Marylebone High Street
(Map 8 C1)
Centre/Marylebone

David Drummond (p68)
Cecil Court (Map 9 F3)
Centre/Covent Garden

Forbidden Planet (p67)
179 Shaftesbury Ave (Map 9 F2)
Centre/Covent Garden

Foyles (p69)
Charing Cross Road (Map 9 F3)
Centre/Covent Garden

Gay's the Word (p68)
66 Marchmont St (Map 3 G5)
Centre/Bloomsbury

Henry Pordes (p69)
58–60 Charing Cross Road
(Map 9 F3)
Centre/Covent Garden

Magma (p90)
117–19 Clerkenwell Road
(Map 10 A1)
City & East/Clerkenwell

Marchpane (p68)
Cecil Court (Map 9 F3)
Centre/Covent Garden

Nigel Williams (p68)
Cecil Court (Map 9 F3)
Centre/Covent Garden

PJ Hilton (p68)
Cecil Court (Map 9 F3)
Centre/Covent Garden

Primrose Hill Books (p94)
134 Regent's Park Rd (Map 2 B2)
North/Primrose Hill

Quinto (p69)
48a Charing Cross Rd (Map 9 F3)
Centre/Covent Garden

Shipley (p69)
70 Charing Cross Rd (Map 9 F3)
Centre/Covent Garden

Shipley Media (p69)
80 Charing Cross Rd (Map 9 F3)
Centre/Covent Garden

Simon Finch Art (p86)
61a Ledbury Road (Map 6 D3)
*West/Notting Hill &
Westbourne Park*

Travel Bookshop (p165)
13–15 Blenheim Cres (Map 6 C3)
*West/Notting Hill &
Westbourne Park*

Department Stores

Fenwick (p83)
63 New Bond Street (Map 8 D3)
www.fenwick.co.uk
Centre/Mayfair & St James's

Fortnum & Mason (p83)
181 Piccadilly (Map 9 E4)
www.fortnumandmason.com
Centre/Mayfair & St James's

Harrods (p83)
87–135 Brompton Road
(Map 14 B1) www.harrods.com
West/Knightsbridge & Belgravia

Harvey Nichols (p83)
109–25 Knightsbridge
(Map 14 B1)
www.harveynichols.com
West/Knightsbridge & Belgravia

John Lewis (p83)
278–306 Oxford St (Map 8 D3)
www.johnlewis.com
Centre/Marylebone

Liberty (p72)
210–20 Regent St (Map 8 D3)
Centre/Soho

Marks & Spencer (p89)
458 Oxford Street (Map 9 E2)
Centre/Soho

Selfridges (p75)
400 Oxford Street (Map 8 C3)
Centre/Marylebone

Fashion

202 (p84)
202 Westbourne Grove
(Map 7 F3) *West/Notting Hill &
Westbourne Park*

Agnès B (p64)
Floral Street (Map 9 G3)
Centre/Covent Garden

All Saints (p66)
5 Earlham Street (Map 9 F3)
Centre/Covent Garden

Anna (p94)
126 Regent's Pk Rd (Map 2 B2)
North/Primrose Hill

Annie's Vintage Clothes (p94)
Camden Passage (Map 4 B3)
North/Islington

aQuaint (p65)
38 Monmouth St (Map 9 F3)
Centre/Covent Garden

Bamford & Sons (p88)
79–81 Ledbury Rd (Map 6 D3)
West/Notting Hill

Bond (p72)
Newburgh Street (Map 9 E3)
Centre/Soho

Browns (p74)
23–7 South Molton St
(Map 8 D3)
Centre/Mayfair & St James's

Bunny London (p95)
Oxo Tower Wharf, Barge House
Street (Map 10 A4)
South/South Bank

Coco Ribbon (p88)
21 Kensington Pk Rd (Map 6 C3)
*West/Notting Hill &
Westbourne Park*

Comfort & Joy (p92)
109 Essex Road (Map 4 B3)
North/Islington

Contemporary Wardrobe (p67)
The Horse Hospital
Colonnade (Map 9 G1)
Centre/Bloomsbury

The Cross (p89)
141 Portland Road (Map 6 C4)
*West/Notting Hill &
Westbourne Park*

Cyberdog (p66)
9 Earlham Street (Map 9 F3)
Centre/Covent Garden

The Dispensary (p72)
Newburgh Street (Map 9 E3)
Centre/Soho

Dover Street Market (p73)
17–18 Dover Street (Map 8 D4)
West/Mayfair & St James's

Duchamp (p86)
75 Ledbury Road (Map 6 D3)
*West/Notting Hill &
Westbourne Park*

FCUK (p89)
396 Oxford Street (Map 9 E2)
Centre/Fitzrovia

Gloria's Super Deluxe (p166)
Dray Walk, Brick La (Map 11 F1)
*City & East/Spitalfields &
Whitechapel*

Hoxton Boutique (p90)
2 Hoxton Street (Map 5 E5)
City & East/Shoreditch & Hoxton

Jigsaw (p89)
126 New Bond St (Map 8 D3)
Centre/Mayfair & St James's

Joseph (p81)
77 Fulham Road (Map 13 H3)
West/Chelsea & Fulham

Junky (p166)
Dray Walk, Brick La (Map 11 F1)
*City & East/Spitalfields &
Whitechapel*

JW Beeton (p86)
48–50 Ledbury Rd (Map 6 D3)
*West/Notting Hill &
Westbourne Park*

Karen Millen (p89)
262–4 Regent Street
(Map 8 D3)
Centre/Mayfair & St James's

Koh Samui (p65)
65–7 Monmouth St (Map 9 F3)
Centre/Covent Garden

Kokon To-Zai (p70)
57 Greek Street (Map 9 F3)
Centre/Soho

Labour of Love (p93)
193 Upper Street (Map 4 B2)
North/Islington

Maharishi (p64)
19a Floral Street (Map 9 G3)
Centre/Covent Garden

Margaret Howell (p76)
34 Wigmore Street (Map 8 C2)
Centre/Marylebone

Maria Grachvogel (p79)
162 Sloane Street (Map 14 B2)
West/Knightsbridge & Belgravia

Marilyn Moore (p88)
7 Elgin Crescent (Map 6 C3)
*West/Notting Hill &
Westbourne Park*

Mulberry (p76)
11–12 Gees Court (Map 8 C3)
Centre/Marylebone

Nicole Farhi (p64)
Floral Street (Map 9 G3)
Centre/Covent Garden

N Peal (p74)
37 & 71 Burlington Arcade
(Map 9 E4)
Centre/Mayfair & St James's

Odie & Amanda (p95)
Oxo Tower (Map 10 A4)
South/South Bank

Oki-ni (p72)
25 Savile Row (Map 9 E3)
Centre/Mayfair & St James's

Paul Smith (pp64 & 88)
Floral Street (Map 9 G3)
Centre/Covent Garden
120 & 122 Kensington Park
Road (Map 6 D4)
*West/Notting Hill &
Westbourne Park*

Preen (p87)
Unit 5 Portobello Green
(Map 6 C2)
*West/Notting Hill &
Westbourne Park*

Public Beware (p166)
Dray Walk, Brick Lane
(Map 11 F1)
*City & East/Spitalfields &
Whitechapel*

Radio Days (p95)
87 Lower Marsh (Map 10 A5)
South/South Bank

Red Hot (p87)
Unit 9 Portobello Green
(Map 6 C2)
*West/Notting Hill &
Westbourne Park*

Rellik (p89)
8 Golborne Road (Map 6 C1)
*West/Notting Hill &
Westbourne Park*

Rokit (p92)
101 & 107 Brick Lane
(Map 11 F1)
*City & East/Spitalfields &
Whitechapel*

Saloon (p90)
23 Arlington Way (Map 4 A4)
City & East/Clerkenwell

Sixty 6 (p77)
66 Marylebone High Street
(Map 8 C1)
Centre/Marylebone

Stella McCartney (p74)
30 Bruton Street
(Map 8 D4)
Centre/Mayfair & St James's

Stüssy (p66)
19 Earlham Street
(Map 9 F3)
Centre/Covent Garden

Suite 20 (p87)
Unit 20 Portobello Green
(Map 6 C2)
*West/Notting Hill &
Westbourne Park*

Ted Baker (p64)
Floral Street (Map 9 G3)
Centre/Covent Garden

Tonic (p86)
Portobello Road (Map 6 C2)
*West/Notting Hill &
Westbourne Park*

Topshop (p72)
Oxford Circus (Map 9 D2)
Centre/Fitzrovia

Tracey Boyd (p80)
42 Elizabeth St (Map 14 C2)
West/Knightsbridge & Belgravia

Urban Outfitters (p66)
42–56 Earlham St (Map 9 F3)
Centre/Covent Garden

What the Butler Wore (p95)
131 Lower Marsh
(Map 10 A5)
South/South Bank

Whistles (p76)
12 St Christopher's Pl (Map 8 C3)
Centre/Marylebone

The World According To... (p70)
4 Brewer Street (Map 9 E3)
Centre/Soho

Shopping

Florists

The Wild Bunch (p66)
Earlham Street (Map 9 F3)
Centre/Covent Garden

Woodhams (p80)
45 Elizabeth Street
(Map 14 C2)
West/Knightsbridge & Belgravia

Food

A Gold (p91)
42 Brushfield St (Map 11 E1)
*City & East/Spitalfields &
Whitechapel*

Camisa (p164)
61 Old Compton St (Map 9 F3)
Centre/Soho

Carluccio's (p76)
St Christopher's Pl (Map 8 C3)
Centre/Marylebone

The Chocolate Society (p80)
36 Elizabeth St (Map 14 C2)
West/Knightsbridge & Belgravia

La Fromagerie (p78)
2–4 Moxton Street (Map 8 C2)
Centre/Marylebone

Gerry's (p70)
74 Old Compton St
(Map 9 F3)
Centre/Soho

Lina Stores (p71)
18 Brewer Street
(Map 9 E3)
Centre/Soho

Neal's Yard Dairy (p66)
17 Shorts Gardens
(Map 9 G3)
Centre/Covent Garden

Paul Rothe (p77)
35 Marylebone Lane (Map 8 C2)
Centre/Marylebone

Poilane (p80)
46 Elizabeth St (Map 14 C2)
West/Knightsbridge & Belgravia

Prestat (p79)
14 Princes Arcade (Map 9 E4)
Centre/Mayfair & St James's

Health & Beauty

Calmia (p77)
52–4 Marylebone High St
(Map 8 C1)
Centre/Marylebone

Jo Malone (p79)
150 Sloane Street (Map 14 B2)
West/Knightsbridge & Belgravia

Kiehl's (p65)
29 Monmouth St (Map 9 F3)
Centre/Covent Garden

Korres (p83)
124 King's Road (Map 14 A3)
West/Chelsea & Fulham

Miller Harris (p85)
14 Needham Road (Map 7 E3)
*West/Notting Hill &
Westbourne Park*

REN (p73)
19 Shepherd Market (Map 8 D4)
Centre/Mayfair & St James's

Scent Systems (p72)
Newburgh Street (Map 9 E3)
Centre/Soho

Les Senteurs (p80)
71 Elizabeth Street (Map 14 C2)
West/Knightsbridge & Belgravia

Space.NK (p84)
127–31 Westbourne Grove
(Map 7 F3)
*West/Notting Hill &
Westbourne Park*

Studio Perfumery (p94)
170 Regent's Park Rd (Map 2 B2)
North/Primrose Hill

Interiors

After Noah (p93)
121 Upper Street (Map 4 B2)
North/Islington

Antiquarius (p84)
131–41 King's Rd (Map 14 A4)
West/Chelsea & Fulham

Aram (p64)
110 Drury Lane (Map 9 G3)
Centre/Covent Garden

Aria (p93)
295–96 & 133 Upper St
(Map 4 B2)
North/Islington

Bedstock (p87)
Unit 26 Portobello Green
(Map 6 C2)
*West/Notting Hill &
Westbourne Park*

Black & Blum (p95)
Oxo Tower Wharf, Barge House
Street (Map 10 A4)
South/South Bank

Bodo Sperlein (p95)
Oxo Tower Wharf, Barge House
Street (Map 10 A4)
South/South Bank

Caroline Carrier's (p94)
Pierrepont Arcade
Camden Passage (Map 4 B3)
North/Islington

The Conran Shop (p82)
Michelin House
81 Fulham Road (Map 14 A2)
West/Chelsea & Fulham

Designers Guild (p84)
267 & 277 King's Road
(Map 14 A4)
West/Chelsea & Fulham

Eatmyhandbagbitch (p68)
Drury Lane (Map 9 G3)
Centre/Covent Garden

Graham & Green (pp89 & 94)
4 & 10 Elgin Cr (Map 6 C3)
West/Notting Hill
164 Regent's Pk Rd (Map 2 B2)
North/Primrose Hill

Judith Lasalle (p94)
Pierrepont Arcade
Camden Passage (Map 4 B3)
North/Islington

Inexterior (p92)
14 Cheshire Street (Map 5 F5)
*City & East/Spitalfields &
Whitechapel*

Labour and Wait (p92)
18 Cheshire Street (Map 5 F5)
*City & East/Spitalfields &
Whitechapel*

Marimekko (p76)
16–17 St Christopher's Pl (8 C3)
Centre/Marylebone

Mar Mar Co (p92)
16 Cheshire Street (Map 5 F5)
*City & East/Spitalfields &
Whitechapel*

Mint (p77)
70 Wigmore Street (Map 8 C2)
Centre/Marylebone

Neisha Crosland (p81)
8 Elystan Street (Map 14 A3)
West/Knightsbridge & Belgravia

Origin (p94)
Camden Passage (Map 4 B3)
North/Islington

Skandium (p78)
86–7 Marylebone High St
(Map 8 C1)
Centre/Marylebone

Story (p91)
4 Wilkes Street (Map 11 F1)
*City & East/Spitalfields &
Whitechapel*

twentytwentyone (p93)
274 Upper Street (Map 4 B2)
North/Islington

Lingerie

Agent Provocateur (p71)
6 Broadwick Street (Map 9 E3)
Centre/Soho

Coco de Mer (p65)
23 Monmouth St
(Map 9 F3)
Centre/Covent Garden

Music

Honest Jon's (p87)
278 Portobello Rd
(Map 6 D3)
*West/Notting Hill &
Westbourne Park*

Intoxica! (p87)
231 Portobello Rd
(Map 6 D3)
*West/Notting Hill &
Westbourne Park*

Phonica (p71)
51 Poland Street (Map 9 E3)
Centre/Soho

Ray's Jazz (p69)
Foyles Bookshop, Charing
Cross Road (Map 9 F3)
Centre/Covent Garden

Rough Trade (p85)
130 Talbot Road (Map 6 D3)
*West/Notting Hill &
Westbourne Park*

Smallfish Records (p91)
329 Old Street (Map 11 F1)
City & East

Vinyl Junkies (p164)
Berwick St (Map 9 E3)
Centre/Soho

Prints & Posters

Artcadia (p91)
108 Commercial St
(Map 11 F1)
*City & East/Spitalfields &
Whitechapel*

Rock Archive (p94)
110 Islington High St (Map 4 A3)
North/Islington

Stage Door Prints (p68)
9 Cecil Court (Map 9 F3)
Centre/Covent Garden

Storey's (p68)
3 Cecil Court (Map 9 F3)
Centre/Covent Garden

The Tintin Shop (p64)
34 Floral Street (Map 9 G3)
Centre/Covent Garden

Vertigo (p64)
22 Wellington St (Map 9 G3)
Centre/Covent Garden

Vintage (p70)
39–43 Brewer St (Map 9 E3)
Centre/Soho

Shoes & Accessories

Anya Hindmarch (p80)
15–17 Pont Street (Map 14 B2)
West/Knightsbridge & Belgravia

Bill Amberg (p85)
10 Chepstow Road (Map 7 E2)
*West/Notting Hill &
Westbourne Park*

b Store (p71)
6 Conduit Street (Map 8 D3)
Centre/Mayfair & St James

Camper (p64)
Floral Street (Map 9 G3)
Centre/Covent Garden

Erickson Beamon (p80)
38 Elizabeth Street
(Map 14 C2)
*West/Knightsbridge &
Belgravia*

Georgina Goodman (p73)
12–14 Shepherd St (Map 8 D5)
Centre/Mayfair & St James's

James Smith & Sons (p67)
53 New Oxford St (Map 9 G2)
Centre/Bloomsbury

Jess James (p72)
Newburgh Street (Map 9 E3)
Centre/Soho

Jimmy Choo (p81)
169 Draycott Avenue
(Map 14 A3)
West/Chelsea & Fulham

J&M Davidson (p85)
42 Ledbury Road (Map 6 D3)
*West/Notting Hill &
Westbourne Park*

Kabiri (p78)
37 Marylebone High Street
(Map 8 C1)
Centre/Marylebone

Kate Kuba (p83)
22 Duke of York Square,
King's Road (Map 14 B3)
West/Chelsea & Fulham

Kirk Originals (p64)
29 Floral Street (Map 9 G3)
Centre/Covent Garden

Lara Bohinc 107 (p90)
51 Hoxton Square (Map 5 E5)
Ctiy & East/Shoreditch & Hoxton

Lulu Guinness (p81)
3 Ellis Street (Map 14 B2)
West/Knightsbridge & Belgravia

Oliver Sweeney (p83)
29 King's Road (Map 14 B3)
West/Chelsea & Fulham

Onitsuka Tiger (p72)
Newburgh Street (Map 9 E3)
Centre/Soho

Osprey (p76)
St Christopher's Pl (Map 8 C3)
Centre/Marylebone

Patrick Cox (p79)
129 Sloane Street (Map 14 B2)
West/Knightsbridge & Belgravia

Philip Treacy (p80)
69 Elizabeth St (Map 14 C2)
*West/Knightsbridge &
Belgravia*

Poste (p74)
10 S Molton St (Map 8 D3)
Centre/Mayfair & St James's

Poste Mistress (p65)
261–3 Monmouth Street
(Map 9 F3)
Centre/Covent Garden

Rachel Skinner (p94)
13 Princess Road (Map 2 B2)
North/Primrose Hill

Size? (p66)
17–19 Neal Street (Map 9 G3)
Centre/Covent Garden

Tatty Devine (p92)
236 Brick Lane (Map 11 F1)
*City & East/Spitalfields &
Whitechapel*

Art &
Architecture

Art Galleries

The Agency (pp116 & 168)
Charlotte Road (Map 5 E5)
City & East/Shoreditch & Hoxton

The Approach (p116)
Approach Road
(Ⓤ Bethnal Green)
City & East/Bethnal Green

Camden Arts Centre (p112)
Arkwright Road (Hampstead)
North/Hampstead

Chisenhale (p116)
Chisenhale Road
(Ⓤ Bethnal Green)
City & East/Bethnal Green

Gagosian (p116)
www.gagosian.com
6–24 Britannia Street
(Map 3 G4)
Centre/Bloomsbury
8 Heddon Street
(Map 9 E3)
Centre/Mayfair & St James's

Hayward Gallery (p115)
South Bank Centre (Map 9 H4)
South/South Bank

ICA (p102)
The Mall (Map 9 F5)
Centre/Westminster & Pimlico

Jerwood Space (p115)
171 Union Street (Map 10 B5)
South/Borough

Lisson (p116)
52–4 Bell Street
(Map 8 A1)
Centre/Marylebone

Matt's Gallery (p116)
42–4 Copperfield Road
(Ⓤ Mile End)
City & East/Bethnal Green

Photographers' Gallery (p101)
5 & 8 Great Newport Street
(Map 9 F3)
Centre/Covent Garden

Saatchi Gallery (p108)
The Duke of York's HQ,
Sloane Square
(Map 14 B3)
West/Chelsea

Sadie Coles HQ (p116)
35 Heddon Street (Map 9 E3)
Centre/Mayfair & St James's

Serpentine Gallery (p107)
Kensington Gardens
(Map 7 H5)
West/Kensington

South London Gallery (p116)
65 Peckham Rd (Ⓤ Elephant &
Castle, then 171 bus)
South/Camberwell

Stephen Friedman (p116)
Old Burlington Street
(Map 9 E4)
Centre/Mayfair & St James's

Wapping Project Space (p111)
Wapping Wall (Ⓤ Wapping)
*City & East/Wapping &
Docklands*

Whitechapel Gallery (p110)
80 Whitechapel High Street
(Map 11 F2)
*City & East/Spitalfields &
Whitechapel*

White Cube (pp116 & 168)
Hoxton Square
(Map 5 E5)
City & East/Shoreditch & Hoxton

Wilkinson Gallery (p116)
242 Cambridge Heath Road
(Ⓤ Bethnal Green)
City & East/Bethnal Green

Art & Architecture

Cemeteries

Abney Park Cemetery (p179)
Stoke Newington Church St
(train to Stoke Newington or
73 bus)
North/Stoke Newington

Brompton Cemetery (p111)
Lillie Road (Map 13 E4)
West/Kensington

Bunhill Fields (p175)
City Road (Map 10 D1)
City & East/City

Highgate Cemetery (p111)
Swain's Lane (ⓔ Highgate)
www.highgate-cemetery.org
North/Highgate

Kensal Green Cemetery (p111)
(ⓔ Kensal Green)
www.kensalgreen.co.uk
North/Kensal Green

Nunhead Cemetery (p111)
Linden Grove
(train to Nunhead)
South/Nunhead

Churches

Brompton Oratory (p107)
Brompton Road (Map 14 A2)
West/Kensington

**St Bartholomew
the Great** (p109)
West Smithfield (Map 10 B2)
City & East/The City

St Bride's (p106)
Fleet Street (Map 10 A3)
www.stbrides.com
Centre/Holborn

St James's Piccadilly (p106)
197 Piccadilly (Map 9 E4)
Centre/Mayfair & St James's

St Margaret's Church (p105)
Sanctuary (Map 15 G1)
Centre/Westminster & Pimlico

St Mary-le-Bow (p106)
Cheapside (Map 10 C3)
www.stmarylebow.co.uk
City & East/The City

St Olave's (p175)
Heart Street (Map 11 E3)
City & East/The City

St Paul's Cathedral (p100)
www.stpauls.co.uk (Map 10 B3)
City & East/The City

St Stephen Walbrook (p106)
Walbrook (Map 10 D3)
City & East/The City

Southwark Cathedral (p115)
Montague Close (Map 10 D4)
South/Borough

Temple Church (pp104 & 174)
Off Fleet Street (Map 10 A3)
Centre/Holborn

Westminster Abbey (p12)
Broad Sanctuary (Map 15 F1)
Centre/Westminster & Pimlico

Historic Buildings

Banqueting House (p105)
Whitehall (Map 9 G5)
Centre/Westminster & Pimlico

Buckingham Palace (p14)
Buckingham Gate (Map 14 D1)
Centre/Westminster & Pimlico

Dennis Severs' House (p110)
18 Folgate Street (Map 11 E1)
*City & East/Spitalfields &
Whitechapel*

Eltham Palace (p118)
Court Yard (train to Eltham)

Fenton House (p113)
Windmill Hill (Map 1 A4)
North/Hampstead

Houses of Parliament (p12)
Old Palace Yard (Map 15 G1)
Centre/Westminster & Pimlico

Linley Sambourne House (p108)
18 Stafford Terrace
(Map 13 E1)
West/Kensington

19 Princelet Street (p109)
Spitalfields (Map 11 F1)
*City & East/Spitalfields &
Whitechapel*

Queen's House (p119)
Greenwich Park (Map 16 C2)
South/Greenwich & Deptford

Tower of London (p13)
Tower Hill (Map 11 F4)
City & East/The City

Modern Architecture

Barbican *(See Combined Arts)*

Docklands (p112)
Isle of Dogs (ⓔ Canary Wharf)
City & East/Canary Wharf

Laban Centre *(See Dance)*

London Eye (p13)
Jubilee Gardens (Map 9 H5)
South/South Bank

Lord's (p112)
Wellington Road
(ⓔ St John's Wood)
North/St John's Wood

National Theatre *(See Theatres)*

RIBA (p103)
66 Portland Place (Map 8 D1)
Centre/Fitzrovia

2 Willow Road (p113)
Hampstead (Map 1 c4)
North/Hampstead

Museums

British Museum (pp14 & 104)
Great Russell Street (Map 9 F2)
Centre/Bloomsbury

Design Museum (p116)
28 Shad Thames (Map 11 F5)
South/Borough

Dr Johnson's House (p104)
17 Gough Square (Map 10 A2)
Centre/Holborn

Dulwich Picture Gallery (p118)
Gallery Road (train to Dulwich)
South/Dulwich

Estorick Collection (p112)
39 Canonbury Square
(Map 4 B1)
North/Islington

Freud Museum (p114)
20 Maresfield Gardens
(ⓔ Finchley Road)
North/Hampstead

Geffrye Museum (p111)
Kingsland Road (Map 5 E4)
City & East/Shoreditch & Hoxton

Keats House (p114)
Keats Grove (Map 1 C5)
North/Hampstead

Kenwood House (p114)
Hampstead Heath (Map 1 C1)
North/Hampstead

Leighton House Museum (p109)
12 Holland Pk Rd (Map 12 D1)
West/Kensington

Museum in Docklands (p112)
West India Quay, www.museum
indocklands.org.uk
(ⓔ Canary Wharf)
*City & East/Wapping &
Docklands*

Museum of London (p111)
London Wall (Map 5 E4)
City & East/City

**Museum of the Order of
St John** (p110)
St John's Gate (Map 10 B1)
City & East/Clerkenwell

National Gallery (pp13 & 101)
Trafalgar Square (Map 9 F4)
Centre/Covent Garden

**National Maritime
Museum** (p119)
Greenwich Park (Map 16 C2)
South/Greenwich

National Portrait Gallery (p102)
St Martin's Place (Map 9 F4)
Centre/Covent Garden

Natural History Museum (p15)
Exhibition Road (Map 13 H2)
West/Kensington

Old Operating Theatre (p116)
9a St Thomas's St (Map 10 D5)
South/Borough

Queens Gallery (p14)
Buckingham Pal Rd (Map 14 D1)
Centre/Westminster & Pimlico

Royal Academy (p106)
Piccadilly (Map 9 E4)
Centre/Mayfair & St James's

Science Museum (p15)
Exhibition Road (Map 13 H2)
West/Kensington

Sir John Soane's Museum (p103)
13 Lincoln's Inn Fields (Map 9 H2)
Centre/Holborn

Somerset House (p100)
Strand (Map 9 H3)
Centre/Covent Garden

Tate Britain (p105)
Millbank (Map 15 G3)
Centre/Westminster & Pimlico

Tate Modern (pp15 & 117)
Bankside (Map 10 B4)
South/Borough

Theatre Museum (p101)
Russell Street (Map 9 G3)
Centre/Covent Garden

V&A (p108)
Exhibition Road
(Map 13 H2)
West/Kensington

The Wallace Collection (p107)
Manchester Square
(Map 8 C2)
Centre/Marylebone

Performance

Cinemas

Curzon Soho (p126)
99 Shaftesbury Ave
(Map 9 F3)
Centre/Soho

Electric Cinema (p129)
191 Portobello Rd (Map 6 D3)
West/Notting Hill

Everyman (p134)
5 Holly Bush Vale (Map 1 A5)
North/Hampstead

NFT (p136)
South Bank (Map 9 H4)
South/South Bank

Prince Charles Cinema (p127)
7 Leicester Place (Map 9 F3)
Centre/Soho

Ritzy (p137)
Brixton Oval (Ⓔ Brixton)
South/Brixton

Combined Arts

BAC (p137)
Lavender Hill (train to
Clapham Jctn)
South/Clapham

Barbican (p130)
Silk Street (Map 10 C1)
City & East/The City

Drill Hall (p125)
16 Chenies Street (Map 9 F1)
Centre/Holborn

Riverside Studios (p130)
Crisp Road (Map 12 A4)
West/Hammersmith

Tricycle (p135)
269 Kilburn High Rd (Ⓔ Kilburn)
North/Kilburn

Comedy

Comedy Café (p131)
66–8 Rivington St (Map 5 E5)
City & East/Shoreditch & Hoxton

Comedy Store (p127)
1a Oxendon Street (Map 9 F4)
Centre/Soho

Jongleurs (p134)
Middle Yard
Chalk Farm Road (Map 2 D2)
North/Camden

Dance

Laban (p136)
Creekside (Map 16 A3)
South/Greenwich & Deptford

The Place (p128)
17 Duke's Road (Map 3 F5)
Centre/Bloomsbury

Sadler's Wells (p132)
Rosebery Avenue (Map 4 A4)
North/Islington

Music Venues

Borderline (p125)
Orange Yard,
Manette Street (Map 9 F3)
Centre/Soho

ENO @ The Coliseum (p125)
St Martin's Lane (Map 9 G4)
Centre/Covent Garden

Jazz Café (p133)
5 Parkway (Map 2 D3)
North/Camden

Koko (p133)
1A Camden Road (Map 2 D2)
North/Camden

Mean Fiddler (p126)
168 Charing Cross Road
(Map 9 F3)
Centre/Soho

Ronnie Scott's (p127)
47 Frith Street (Map 9 F3)
Centre/Soho

Royal Opera House (p124)
Bow Street (Map 9 G3)
Centre/Covent Garden

St John's (p128)
Smith Square (Map 15 G2)
Centre/Westminster

Scala (p132)
275 Pentonville Rd (Map 3 H4)
Centre/Bloomsbury

Shepherd's Bush Empire (p129)
Shepherd's Bush Green
(Map 6 A5)
West/Shepherd's Bush

606 Club (p129)
90 Lots Road (Map 13 G5)
West/Chelsea & Fulham

South Bank Centre (p135)
Belvedere Rd/South Bank
(Map 9 H4)
South/South Bank

The Spitz (p130)
Spitalfields Market (Map 11 F1)
City & East/Spitalfields

12 Bar Club (p125)
22–3 Denmark St (Map 9 F2)
Centre/Convent Garden

Union Chapel (p133)
Compton Avenue (Map 4 B1)
North/Islington

Wigmore Hall (p128)
36 Wigmore Street (Map 8 C2)
Centre/Marylebone

Theatres

Almeida (p132)
Almeida Street (Map 4 B2)
North/Islington

Donmar Warehouse (p124)
41 Earlham Street (Map 9 F3)
Centre/Covent Garden

Hackney Empire (p131)
Mare Street (Map 5 H1)
City & East/Hackney

Hampstead Theatre (p134)
Eton Avenue (Ⓔ Swiss Cottage)
North/Swiss Cottage

King's Head Theatre Bar (p132)
115 Upper Street (Map 4 B2)
North/Islington

National Theatre (p135)
South Bank (Map 9 H4)
South/South Bank

Old Vic (p136)
The Cut (Map 10 A5)
South/South Bank

Shakespeare's Globe (p14)
Bankside (Map 10 C4)
South/Borough

Soho Theatre (p126)
21 Dean Street (Map 9 F3)
Centre/Soho

Pubs, Bars & Clubs

Pubs

Anchor Bankside (p158)
34 Park Street (Map 10 C4)
South/Borough

Albion (p159)
10 Thornhill Road (Map 4 A2)
North/Islington

Black Friar (p150)
174 Queen Vic St (Map 10 B3)
City & East/The City

Bread & Roses (p161)
68 Clapham Manor Street
(Ⓔ Clapham North)
South/Clapham

The Bricklayer's Arms (p168)
63 Charlotte Road (Map 5 E5)
City & East/Shoreditch

Blue Anchor (p160)
13 Lwr Mall (Ⓔ Hammersmith)
West/Hammersmith

Coach & Horses (p150)
29 Greek Street (Map 9 F3)
Centre/Soho

Crown (p157)
116 Cloudesley Rd (Map 4 A3)
North/Islington

Pool (p168)
104–8 Curtain Road (Map 5 E5)
City & East/Shoreditch

The Social (p146)
5 Little Portland St (Map 8 D2)
Centre/Fitzrovia

Townhouse (p148)
31 Beauchamp Pl (Map 14 A1)
West/Knightsbridge & Belgravia

Trailer H (p149)
177 Portobello Rd (Map 6 C2)
*West/Notting Hill &
Westbourne Park*

Vertigo (p151)
Level 42, Tower 42,
25 Old Broad St (Map 10 D2)
City & East/The City

Vibe Bar (p154)
Old Truman Brewery,
91–5 Brick Lane (Map 11 F1)
*City & East/Spitalfields &
Whitechapel*

Zeta Bar (p146)
Mayfair Hilton Hotel,
35 Hertford Street (Map 8 C5)
Centre/Mayfair & St James's

Zigfrid (p168)
11 Hoxton Square (Map 5 E5)
City & East/Shoreditch

Clubs

333 (p153)
333 Old Street (Map 5 E5)
City & East/Shoreditch & Hoxton

93 Feet East (p154)
150 Brick Lane (Map 11 F1)
*City & East/Spitalfields &
Whitechapel*

Cargo (p152)
83 Rivington Street (Map 5 E5)
City & East/Shoreditch & Hoxton

The End (p147)
18 West Central St (Map 9 G2)
Centre/Covent Garden

Fabric (p151)
77a Charterhouse St (Map 10 B1)
City & East/Clerkenwell

Fridge/Fridge Bar (p159)
1 Town Hall Parade (ⓔ Brixton)
South/Brixton

Heaven (p142)
Under the Arches,
Villiers Street (Map 9 G4)
Centre/Covent Garden

Herbal (p153)
10–14 Kingsland Rd (Map 5 E4)
City & East/Shoreditch & Hoxton

Madame Jo-Jos (p144)
8–10 Brewer Street (Map 9 E3)
Centre/Soho

Ministry of Sound (p159)
103 Gaunt Street
(ⓔ Elephant & Castle)
South/Kennington

Notting Hill Arts Club (p150)
21 Notting Hill Gate (Map 7 E4)
*West/Notting Hill &
Westbourne Park*

Substation South (p171)
Trinity Road (ⓔ Brixton)
South/Brixton

Turnmills (p152)
63a Clerkenwell Rd (Map 10 B1)
City & East/Clerkenwell

Vauxhall Tavern (p159)
372 Kennington Lane
(Map 15 H4)
South/Kennington

Hotels

Expensive

Blakes (p191)
33 Roland Gdns (Map 13 G3)
West/Chelsea & Fulham

Charlotte Street Hotel (p187)
15 Charlotte Street (Map 9 E2)
Centre/Fitzrovia

Claridge's (p189)
Brook St (Map 8 D3)
www.savoygroup.com
Centre/Mayfair & St James's

Covent Garden Hotel (p186)
10 Monmouth St (Map 9 F3)
Centre/Covent Garden

Dorchester (p189)
Park Lane (Map 8 C4)
www.dorchesterhotel.com
Centre/Mayfair & St James's

Dorset Square (p189)
39 Dorset Square (Map 8 B1)
Centre/Marylebone

**Four Seasons
Canary Wharf** (p195)
46 Westferry Circus
(ⓔ Canary Wharf)
City & East/Canary Wharf

Great Eastern (p193)
Liverpool Street (Map 11 E2)
City & East/The City

Hazlitt's (p187)
6 Frith Street (Map 9 F3)
Centre/Soho

The Metropolitan (p188)
Old Park Lane (Map 8 C5)
Centre/Mayfair & St James's

One Aldwych (p186)
1 Aldwych (Map 9 H3)
Centre/Covent Garden

Ritz (p189)
150 Piccadilly (Map 8 D4)
www.theritzlondon.com
Centre/Mayfair & St James's

The Rookery (p194)
Peter's Lane, Cowcross Street
(Map 10 B1)
City & East/Clerkenwell

The Savoy (p189)
Strand (Map 9 G4)
www.savoygroup.com
Centre/Covent Garden

Moderate

City Inn Westminster (p190)
30 John Islip St (Map 15 F3)
Centre/Westminster & Pimlico

The Colonnade (p191)
2 Warrington Crescent
(Map 7 F1)
West/Bayswater & Paddington

Durrants (p188)
George Street (Map 8 B2)
Centre/Marylebone

Five Sumner Place (p190)
5 Sumner Place (Map 13 H3)
West/Chelsea & Fulham

The Franklin (p190)
28 Egerton Gdns (Map 14 A2)
West/Knightsbridge & Belgravia

London Bridge Hotel (p195)
8–18 London Bridge St
(Map 10 D5)
South/Borough

Malmaison (p193)
Charterhouse Sq (Map 10 B1)
City & East/Clerkenwell

**Mercure London City
Bankside** (p195)
71–9 Southwark St (Map 10 B4)
South/Borough

Miller's Residence (p192)
111a Westbourne Grove
(Map 7 E3)
*West/Notting Hill &
Westbourne Park*

The Portobello (p192)
22 Stanley Gardens (Map 6 D3)
*West/Notting Hill &
Westbourne Park*

Topham Belgravia (p189)
28 Ebury Street (Map 14 D2)
*West/Knightsbridge &
Belgravia*

The Zetter (p194)
86–8 Clerkenwell Road
(Map 10 B1)
City & East/Clerkenwell

Cheap

Abbey House (p192)
11 Vicarage Gate (Map 7 E5)
West/Kensington

Crescent Hotel (p187)
49–50 Cartwright
Gardens (Map 3 F5)
Centre/Bloomsbury

Dover Hotel (p189)
42–4 Belgrave Rd (Map 15 E3)
Centre/Westminster & Pimlico

La Gaffe (p194)
107–11 Heath Street (Map 1 A4)
North/Hampstead

Generator (p187)
Compton Place (Map 3 G5)
Centre/Bloomsbury

Mayflower (p184)
26–8 Trebovir Rd (Map 13 E3)
West/Kensington

General Index

General Index

General Index

Produced by Blue Island Publishing
www.blueisland.co.uk
Editorial Director Rosalyn Thiro
Art Director Stephen Bere
Commissioning Editor Michael Ellis
Editor Jane Simmonds
Proofreader Val Phoenix

Published by DK
Publishing Managers Jane Ewart and Scarlett O'Hara
Senior Editor Christine Stroyan
Senior Designers Paul Jackson and Marisa Renzullo
Website Editor Gouri Banerji
Cartographic Editor Casper Morris
Senior Cartographer Uma Bhattacharya
DTP Designers Jason Little and Natasha Lu
Production Coordinator Louise Minihane
Fact Checker Kamin Mohammadi

PHOTOGRAPHY PERMISSIONS

The publishers would like to thank all the churches, museums, hotels, restaurants, bars, clubs, shops, galleries and other sights for their assistance and kind permission to photograph at their establishments.

Placement Key: t = top; tc = top centre; tca = top centre above; tcb = top centre below; tl = top left; tr = top right; cl = centre left; cla = centre left above; clb = centre left below; cr = centre right; cra = centre right above; crb = centre right below; bl = bottom left; br = bottom right.

Works of art have been reproduced with the permission of the following copyright holders: Jerwood Space: © Trevor Appleson *Uniforms* 115cr.

The publishers would like to thank the following companies and picture libraries for permission to reproduce their photographs:

ALAMY IMAGES: Jon Arnold Images/Doug Pearson 1.
ASTOR BAR AND GRILL: 143clb.

BABALOU: 160tl.
STEPHEN BERE: 56tr, 99tl, 104tl, 175cl.
BERKELEY HOTEL: 148tr.
BLAKES: 191tl/tr/cl.
LARA BOHINC: 90cra.

CARGO: 152bl.
CHARLOTTE STREET HOTEL: 187cra.
CHEZ BRUCE: 59bl.
CORBIS: Gail Marie Orenstein 17tr; Reuters/Peter Macdiarmid 17tc; John Slater 12bl.

DENNIS SEVERS HOUSE: Deidi von Schaewen 110cra; M. Stacey Shaffer 110tr.
DK IMAGES: Stephen Bere 11tr, 13tl/cra/br, 14cl, 15tl/tr, 17tl, 19tc, 58bl, 67bl, 88tl, 92tl/cl, 94tl/cla/cra, 98cr, 99tc, 100tl, 101bl, 125clb, 152cra, 167tr/cra; Tim Draper 13tr, 15cla, 98tl; Mike Ellis 19tl, 95br, 181tl; Paul Harris and Anne Heslope 15crb; Lindsey Stock 12cr, 13clb; Rough Guides/Victor Borg 12tl, 13tc, 14tr, 14br, 15tc.
DORSET SQUARE: 189tr.
DRILL HALL: Richard Scandrett 125cr.
DULWICH PICTURE GALLERY: 99cla, 118tl.

MICHAEL ELLIS: 19tr, 113tl.
THE END: 147clb.
EVERYMAN CINEMA: 134br.

FABRIC: Tom Stapley 140bl, 151bl.
FIRM DALE HOTELS: 185bl, 186br, 187cra.
FOUR SEASONS CANARY WHARF: 195br.
FREUD MUSEUM: 114tr.

THE GATE: 45bl.
GREAT EASTERN HOTEL: 184bl, 193tl/tr.

HACKNEY EMPIRE: 131tr.
HAYWARD GALLERY: 115bl.

KABIRI JEWELLERY: 78clb.

Acknowledgments

KOKO: 133cl.
KORRES NATURAL PRODUCTS: 83br.

LOBBY BAR: 142tr.
LOUNGELOVER: 155cra.

MASH: 146cra.
THE METROPOLITAN: 185tl, 188t.
MINISTRY OF SOUND: 159cra.
MOTHER/333: 153bl.
MUSEUM OF LONDON: 111tr.

THE NATIONAL DINING ROOMS, NATIONAL GALLERY: 35crb.
NATIONAL MARITIME MUSEUM, LONDON: 99bl, 119t/cl/cr.
NATIONAL TRUST: 113cr/bl.

ONE ALDWYCH: 184cr, 186tl/tr.
ORIGIN: 29cla.

REDFERNS MUSIC PICTURE LIBRARY: Nicky J. Sims 123tl, 127tl.
LA RELAIS DE VENISE: 40clb.
ROAST: 26tl, 58cr.
ROYAL ACADAMY OF ARTS, LONDON: 106clb.
ROYAL BOROUGH OF KENSINGTON AND CHELSEA: 109tr, 108br.
RULES: Gary Alexandra 34bl/clb/br.

SAATTCHI GALLERY LONDON: 108cl.
SARDO: 33tr.
SCALA: 132cla.
SCIENCE MUSEUM: 15bl, 98bl.
SELFRIDGES: 75tc/tr/cr.

SERPENTINE GALLERY, LONDON: 107cl.
SHAKESPEARE'S GLOBE: photo of the John Tramper production of *Edward II* 136clb.
SIR JOHN SOANE'S MUSEUM: 99crb/tr, 103 tr/crb.
SOMERSET HOUSE PRESS OFFICE: 100tr.
SOUTH LONDON GALLERY: photo Marcus Leith – all works courtesy Tomio Koyama Gallery, Tokyo; Feature Inc, New York/ and Stephen Friedman Gallery, London 166br.
SPACE.NK: 84crb.

TATE BRITAIN: 105bl/clb.
TOM AIKENS: 43bl.

WALTHAMSTOW STADIUM: 131bl.
WHITECHAPEL GALLERY: exhibition: Gerhard Richter *Atlas* 110br.
THE WHITE SWAN: 49bl.

ZEFA VISUAL MEDIA: Masterfile/Lloyd Sutton: 6–7.
THE ZETTER RESTAURANT & ROOMS: 185cla/tr, 194tl/tca/tcb.

Full Page Picture Captions: Malmaison: 2; Oxo Tower Restaurant, Bar & Brasserie: 8–9; Tsunami: 24–5; Skandium: 60–61; Eltham Palace: 96–7; Riverside Studios: 120–21; Fluid: 138–9; Columbia Road: 162–3; Holland Park: 172–3; The Portobello: 182–3; London Eye: 196.

Jacket Images
Front and Spine: ALAMY IMAGES: Jon Arnold Images/ Doug Pearson.
Back: DK IMAGES: all.

Special Editions of DK Travel Guides

DK Travel Guides can be purchased in bulk quantities at discounted prices for use in promotions or as premiums. a We are also able to offer special editions and personalized jackets, corporate imprints, and excerpts from all of our books, tailored specifically to meet your own needs.

To find out more, please contact:
(in the United States) SpecialSales@dk.com
(in the UK) Sarah.Burgess@dk.com
(in Canada) DK Special Sales at general@tourmaline.ca
(in Australia) business.development@pearson.com.au